Sport, Leisure and Physical Education
Trends and Developments
Volume 3

Racism and Xenophobia
in European Football

Sport, Leisure and Physical Education
Trends and Developments
Volume 3

Udo Merkel/Walter Tokarski (eds.)

Racism and Xenophobia

in European Football

Meyer & Meyer Verlag

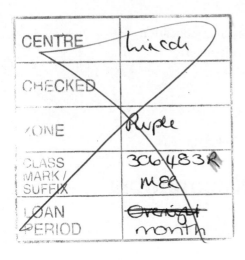
Die Deutsche Bibliothek – CIP-Einheitsaufnahme

Racism and xenophobia in European football
Udo Merkel/Walter Tokarski (Hrsg.).
– Aachen: Meyer und Meyer, 1996
(Sport, leisure and physical education ; Vol. 3)
ISBN 3-89124-343-X
NE: Merkel, Udo [Hrsg.]; GT

© 1996 by Meyer & Meyer Verlag, Aachen
Cover design: Walter J. Neumann, N & N Design-Studio, Aachen
Cover exposure: frw, Reiner Wahlen, Aachen
Printed by Druckerei Hahnengress, Aachen
Printed in Germany
ISBN 3-89124-343-X

CONTENTS

FOREWORD

Klaus Hänsch
The President of the European Parliament

It is with great pleasure that I welcome this book and its contribution to a better understanding of the nature and causes of racism and xenophobia in European football. The project is an excellent illustration of the advantages to be gained from bringing together experts from different countries to consider the same topic in comparative perspective. Such a process is essential to bringing the Union closer to its citizens and enabling us to confront the common problems of the European society.

For myself I am very conscious of the ability of football to act as an important form of integration between citizens. It offers a potent source of collective memories, which transcend the differences between citizens across frontiers. What German of my generation (or indeed what Englishman or woman!) can forget the 1966 World Cup Final and the contested third goal of Geoff Hurst? We continue to argue about it but in a healthy manner which reflects an ongoing commitment to the game.

The years since 1966 have seen extraordinary changes in the shape of European football. In nearly all countries teams have been enriched by the arrival of foreign players, bringing their own special skills and traditions. But at the same time, we have witnessed the growth of the uglier side of football discussed in this book. This combination is one that reminds us of the need for those who favour closer integration to be constantly on our guard against nationalist reflexes that express themselves in the rejection of other cultures.

The European Parliament has made the fight against such attitudes an important part of its work. Ten years ago it convinced the Commission and the Member States to sign a joint declaration against racism and xenophobia. It was a major step forward, establishing a benchmark against which to measure progress. But the problems identified then have not yet disappeared. The freedom of movement across Europe has added a new dimension to the issue as we seek to decide what balance should be struck between controlling hooliganism and protecting the rights of individuals to move across Europe.

Yet the fight against racism must continue. We in the Parliament are delighted that 1997 has been declared European Year against Racism but we surely need more permanent forms of action. The latest intergovernmental conference on the future of the Union should actively consider the idea of including a non-discrimination clause in the Treaty. This would be the surest way of showing that the Union is committed to a set of values which go beyond the economic sphere and extend to the everyday life of its citizens, on and off the football pitch.

March, 1996   vii

ACKNOWLEDGEMENTS

We are grateful to a number of people for their comments, encouragement, advice and support. The idea of *Racism and Xenophobia in European Football* grew out of a one year exploratory research project entitled " The Impact of Euro-Racism on Human Mobility: as reflected in and resisted through Sport and Leisure" funded by the European Union to whom we would herewith express our appreciation and gratitude. Our objective was to conduct an exploratory, comparative study with a multi-disciplinary approach in order to identify the various forms of racism, xenophobia and anti-Semitism in European sport, particularly in soccer, one of the most popular games in Europe, and to look into the specific ways different countries try to combat these problems. We believe that *Racism and Xenophobia in European Football* makes an important contribution not only to the existing sports literature but also to the area of race relations in general.

Meyer & Meyer are to be thanked for their encouragement of this project. We are indebted to the Scarman Centre for the Study of Public Order at the University of Leicester for permission to reprint Jon Garland's and Mike Rowe's project report. The research and production of these chapters would not have been possible without the funding of the European Union which was meticulously administered by Kurt Sombert at the German Sports University in Cologne. Scott Fleming and Alan Tomlinson have provided critical and constructive advice on many chapters of this book, whilst Mike Cole developed to become our 'conceptual conscience' during the course of the project. We also want to thank all the participants of our regular meetings and workshops, particularly John Benyon and Christian Bromberger, for their contributions, discussions and constructive criticisms, as well as all those, in particular Stefanie Knerr and Sara Al-Askari, who provided us with a lot of practical help. Above all we should like to thank Myrene McFee for her meticulous preparation of the final manuscript.

If we have omitted anyone who made a major contribution to the preparation of the book may we offer our apologies. We would also like to offer our thanks to the large number of people who helped in more minor ways through provision of information and practical support. Needless to say, none of those mentioned bears any responsibility for the contents of this book. The analysis and views expressed in the individual chapters remain the responsibility of the authors.

Udo Merkel

Walter Tokarski

ABOUT THE AUTHORS

Diethelm Blecking teaches at a Comprehensive School in Hattingen and lectures at the German Sport University in Cologne. He studied Physical Education, History, Philosophy and Pedagogy and has published on the Polish Solidarity Movement, the history of workers' sport and the issue of migration and sport. His forthcoming publication is *Sport and Ethnic Minorities in Germany* (1996).

Mike Cole is Senior Lecturer in the School of Education at the University of Brighton, England. He has published extensively in the field of antiracism and the promotion of equality in general. He is the editor of *The European Union and Migrant Labour* (1996).

Scott Fleming is Senior Lecturer in Social Science at the Cardiff Institute of Higher Education in Wales, Faculty of Education and Sport. His academic and research interests are in the area of ethnicity and sport, with particular reference to South Asian groups. Most recently he has published *Home and Away: Sport and South Asian Male Youth* (1995).

Gyöngyi Szabó Földesi is Professor for the Sociology of Sport in the Department of Sociology at the Hungarian University of Physical Education, Budapest, Hungary. Her academic and research interests are the sociological analysis of sport. Most recently (1995) she has published a book on football fan behaviour in Hungary (*Helyzetkép a lelátóról*).

Jon Garland is researcher and tutor at the Scarman Centre for the Study of Public Order at the University of Leicester, England. His academic and research interests are in the areas of Information Technology and crime prevention, racism, xenophobia and sport as well as media coverage of race relations. He is co-author of *African Caribbean People in Leicestershire: Community Experiences and Opinions* and is on the editorial board of *Politics Review*.

Roman Horak is researcher at the Institute for Cultural Studies, Vienna, Austria. He also lectures at the universities of Vienna and Graz. His academic and research interests are in the areas of Popular Culture, Cultural Studies and Youth, Sport and Leisure. Most recently he has published (with Matthias Marschik) *Vom Erlebnis zur Wahrnehmung — Der Wiener Fußball und seine Zuschauer 1945-1990* (1995).

Jean Marc Mariottini is researcher at the University of the Provence, Aix-en-Provence, France. His academic and research interests are in the areas of anthropology, ethnology and sport, with particular reference to football fandom. Recently (1993) he has published **"'Allez l'O.M., forza Juve'": The passion for**

football in Marseille and Turin' (with Christian Bromberger), in S. Redhead, *The Passion and the Fashion — Football Fandom in the New Europe* (1993).

Matthias Marschik is researcher at the Institute for Applied Psychology, Vienna, Austria. His academic and research interest is the Viennese working-class football in the inter-war period. Most recently he has published *Dem Volk gilt's während wir zu spielen scheinen* (1995).

Udo Merkel is Senior Lecturer in the Chelsea School at the University of Brighton, England. His academic and research interests are the Sociology of Sport and Leisure, Comparative (European) Studies and Football. Most recently he has published **'Jugend in Großbritannien — Die Sorgenkinder der britischen Gesellschaft'**, in J. Baur, *Jugend, Sport und Jugendlichkeit* (1996).

Michael Rowe is researcher at the Scarman Centre for the Study of Public Order at the University of Leicester, England. His academic and research interests are race, disorder and national identity as well as the media. He is co-author of *African Caribbean People in Leicestershire: First and Second Interim Reports* and is on the editorial board of *Politics Review*.

Kurt Sombert is Research Officer in the Centre for European Sport and Leisure Studies at the German Sports University, Cologne, Germany. His academic and research interests are the role of modern Information Technologies for the development of sport and leisure. Most recently he has conducted a major investigation into *Leisure Development in Europe* (1995).

Walter Tokarski is Professor and Head of Department for Leisure Science, and Head of Department of the Centre for European Sport and Leisure Studies at the German Sports University, Cologne, Germany. His academic and research interests are in the structures and development of leisure systems in Europe. Recently he edited *Der Sport im zusammenwachsenden Europa* (1993).

Alan Tomlinson is Professor and Reader in the Chelsea School Research Centre, University of Brighton, England. His academic and research interests are in the application of a critical sociology and social history of consumption to the study of sport and leisure cultures. He is co-editor (with John Sugden) of *Hosts and Champions: Soccer Cultures, National Identities and the USA World Cup* (1994).

Bart Vanreusel is Professor in the Department for Physical Education and Sports Science at the Catholic University of Leuven, Belgium. His academic and research interest is in the sociology of human movement and sport. Most recently he has edited the volume *Sport and Contested Boundaries*, the proceedings of the Sport Sociology sessions at the World Congress of Sociology in Bielefeld, 1994.

x

I

CONCEPTUAL AND HISTORICAL
CONSIDERATIONS

INTRODUCTION: RACISM AND XENOPHOBIA IN EUROPEAN FOOTBALL — THE PROJECT

Udo Merkel

Most European nations have undergone and continue to undergo major economic, social, ideological and socio-demographic changes —the latter the result of increasing levels of mobility across national boundaries. Unfortunately, Europe has also experienced and continues to experience waves of racism, xenophobia and anti-Semitism which have reached alarming levels in the first half of the 1990s. Although many governments tend to ignore or play down these developments, the Council of the European Union has acknowledged that racism and xenophobia are facts of daily life which threaten the ongoing process of European integration. During its June 1994 meeting in Corfu (Greece), the Council initiated a Consultative Commission on Racism and Xenophobia, charged with the task of developing recommendations for the cooperation of governments and other national organisations in their fight against racism and xenophobia in Europe. A final report covering a wide range of relevant issues was submitted in April 1995. This report recognises the magnitude and seriousness of the problem, and even recommends an amendment of the Maastricht Treaty to provide the Community — on a supra-national level, despite the principle of subsidarity — with the competence and powers to enforce measures to fight discrimination on grounds of 'race', religious or ethnic or national origins. The report argues that an explicit change of the Maastricht Treaty would be the clearest expression of the European Union's intention to combat, and not merely protest against, the rising tide of racism and xenophobia.

Despite this very clear stance — and although 1997 has been declared the European "Year against Racism" — neo-Nazi, fascist and other extreme right-wing groups and political parties are on the increase partly within, partly outside the established political systems all over Europe. Among the most successful extreme right-wing parties are the *Freiheitliche Partei Österreich* in Austria, the *Vlaams Blok* in Belgium, the *Front National* in France, *Die Republikaner* in Germany and the *Movimento Sociale Italiano* in Italy. In many European countries, the successes of these parties have meant that respectable well-established parties, particularly the Conservative parties, have adapted some of the themes, rhetoric and programme of the Far Right in an attempt to woo back their voters. Gradually over the last 10 years, social and economic problems such as unemployment, poor housing, deprivation and crime have been increasingly portrayed in a close relationship to the immigration and presence of minority ethnic groups, as well as to the growing numbers of asylum seekers and refugees.

The increasing number of violent attacks with racist and xenophobic motives is particularly aimed at migrants and their descendants, and at asylum-seekers and refugees. In addition, minority ethnic groups which have lived in Europe for many generations have also been the targets both of violence and of the threat of it. Although the victims are individuals there is no doubt that they were targeted as members of minority groups in the population — on the basis of their religion, skin colour and ethnic, cultural or national origins.

It is in this context that racism, xenophobia and anti-Semitism also frequently occur in the area of sport and leisure. The last fifteen years have seen a notable increase of interest in the study of social problems related to sport and leisure. Racism and xenophobia in sport constitute such a problem, as did football hooliganism particularly in the 1980s. It is the former this book focuses upon.

The research — objectives and methodology

The research for this volume was made possible by funding from the European Union. The initial research proposal, submitted to the European Union (EU) in 1994, was entitled: *"The Impact of Euro-Racism on Human Mobility — as reflected in and resisted through Sport and Leisure"*.

Two fundamental questions were to be investigated: firstly, the various forms of racism and xenophobia which occur in the world of sport and leisure. Due to sport's complexity three different areas had to be distinguished: elite sport, recreational sport and Physical Education in schools. Secondly, the project aimed to investigate how sport is used to combat these problems and how it has been utilised in some European countries to advance the process of integration of 'foreigners' from within and outside the European Union and of minority ethnic groups. The project objectives were to:

(i) investigate the various forms of racism and xenophobia in sport whilst recognising the set of social, political and economic conditions which have caused the growth of racism and xenophobia in Europe;

(ii) examine the variety of means by which race relations in the world of sport are transmitted and the ways in which such images are understood by audiences and constituencies within sport and leisure cultures;

(iii) consider the forms and effects of anti-racist campaigns, such as the initiatives of sport organisations and individual sport stars;

(iv) study some of the programmes, strategies and concepts through which it is intended to achieve the integration of foreigners and minority ethnic groups.

In doing so the project attempted both to identify and explain some of the most significant causes of the growing racism and xenophobia in the world of sport and leisure and to critically assess a number of different strategies and models aiming for an increase of the integrating effects of sport. Further, it was our intention to present the findings in a such a way that they can be utilised to:

(i) supply information relevant to the question of European integration, enabling us to look more closely at future developments of societies in a comparative perspective. They can also be used as a base for subsequent programmes initiated and supported by either individual states or the European Union and they will generally be made available for other users providing guidance for international and national sports policy making;

(ii) contribute to wider debates about human migration and social relationships; to debates about those factors promoting the integration and solidarity of geographically mobile individuals and groups in Europe; and to debates about imaginative, sensitive and constructive policies to tackle racism and xenophobia;

(iii) benefit professionals working in education, culture, politics, leisure, and inform the policy-formation process in these fields;

(iv) form the basis to improve and recommend different concepts and strategies for the integration of minorities with the help of sport;

(v) assist decision making processes in the area of politics, economics, culture. They will also be of great relevance to the growing field of sport- and leisure studies as well as for the social sciences promoting a better understanding of sport's social functions in a European context.

Whilst exploring these questions, experts from various social-scientific branches cooperated, and relevant approaches were drawn from the fields of Anthropology, Cultural Studies, Education, History, Politics, Sociology, Sport- and Leisure Studies utilising both quantitative and qualitative methods. These included:

(i)   analysis and assessment of the relevant academic literature dealing with racism and xenophobia;

(ii)   quantitative and qualitative study of racist incidents and racial discrimination in the world of sport with particular reference to their history, development, causes and underlying ideologies;

(iii) critical evaluation of anti-racist campaigns and other initiatives aiming to combat racism and xenophobia in sport;

(iv)   critical evaluation of the ways in which sport is employed by different agencies, such as the state, local authorities, voluntary sports organisations as a means promoting the integration of individuals and groups.

The analysis intended to integrate conceptual, historical and contemporary aspects and to look at selected aspects of the sporting world. When we designed the project we agreed that exploratory research into such unexplored European territory required both a multidisciplinary and comparative approach. Therefore each team conducted and carried out similar sets of tasks with different foci so that the results can partly be juxtaposed and compared. The team in Cologne, Germany, was responsible for the overall planning and evaluation of the project. However, since each team has an outstanding reputation within an individual discipline they coordinated and advised on all matters relating to this discipline. In addition, each team concentrated on particular in-depth studies of certain aspects within their own discipline which is clearly reflected in the emphases of the following chapters.

The research teams derive from the following countries and institutions:

Austria: Institute for Cultural Studies, Vienna

Belgium: Catholic University of Leuven

England: University of Brighton and University of Leicester

France: University of the Provence, Aix-en-Provence

Germany: The German Sports University, Cologne

Hungary: The Hungarian University of Physical Education, Budapest

Some findings

The patterns of racism, xenophobia and anti-Semitism in sport and leisure are far from uniform across the European countries. Recent years have seen a significant increase in racist, xenophobic and anti-Semitic abuse and violence in all countries we investigated. The most significant increase can certainly be noted in Germany, although, as in many other countries, the violence tends to come in waves.

There are also differences among many of the countries we have dealt with in terms of the attention given to this violence. Whilst some nations and states ignore it and even deny its existence or play it down, the media have certainly defined it as newsworthy; some states have developed anti-discriminatory legislation, whilst others take hardly any notice.The same applies to the world of sport. Some sport associations have initiated systematic and structured campaigns, whilst others prefer and rely on merely token gestures.

The scale and intensity of racist violence differs as well. A comparative analysis of statistical data is almost impossible since these figures are usually based on different labelling practices and definitions. Equally important in this context is that the number of reported violent incidents with a racist background constitutes only the visible tip of the iceberg, whilst the majority are not registered.

In addition to the differences in terms of types and patterns of racist violence, target groups also differ from country to country. Migrants and their descendants from Turkey and other Mediterranean countries as well as refugees and asylum seekers have been most frequently attacked in Germany; in German football it is predominantly black players, many of them coming from Africa. People of Moroccan origin constitute the main target in Belgium, whilst in some countries it is the migrants from former colonies, such as Afro-Caribbeans and Asians in England and people of Algerian origin in France. In former communist countries, such as Hungary, the victims of racist and xenophobic violence are generally Romanys, whilst in Austria both anti-Semitic tendencies and racist attitudes towards migrants from the former Yugoslavia can be observed.

There are also various ways in which both the victims of racism and xenophobia and the violence itself is labelled. Mike Cole provides a critical overview of this issue in the following chapter, clearly identifying the importance of an adequate terminology and nomenclature. In the process of this research it has become very clear that most European languages have not developed terms which adequately reflect the status and position of the migrants concerned. The terms used are very often discriminatory, occasionally even explicitly or implicitly racist and most of them distort reality. Consequently, in this book several labels are used according to the various definitions of the contributors and according to the most acceptable standard practice of the countries in focus. However, some of these terms contain, in both the native language and the English translation, undesirable connotations, so we have used inverted commas to identify and highlight the problematic nature of these labels (as very often there was no acceptable alternative). Equally heterogeneous is the set of labels which refer to the different kinds of racism(s) and xenophobia. Commonly used labels are "racist violence", "hostility against foreigners", "anti-immigrant violence", "right-wing extremist violence" — which point out both the (potential) victims and the motives of the perpetrators. Again, we have deliberately chosen not to use one term or label, in order to provide the reader with a sense of 'nativeness'. Consequently, there will be a variety of terms used reflecting the linguistic reality of the country in focus. The meaning of these labels is usually defined by the author(s) of the appropriate chapter.

Although there has been a considerable amount of academic research dealing with racism and extreme right-wing organisations in general, there has been surprisingly little research carried out with respect to racism, xenophobia and anti-Semitism in European sport (the Anglo-American literature provides a notable exception), not to speak of any comparative analyses. There are a number of reasons for this lack of research. Certainly, a major obstacle and equally a major contradiction is the firm belief and regularly repeated claim that sport in general is an area in which integration of minorities and outsiders is successfully achieved — a myth which is crucial for the justification of the large amounts of continuous public funding for sport. However, it was this deficit of research and the obvious gap between reality and wishful thinking that convinced the editors of this book to initiate the research network and to publish some of the findings in this volume, which we believe provides valuable information which may be of interest and use to a variety of individuals, groups, organisations and institutions.

The structure of this volume

In this book experts from across Europe reflect upon the nature of racism and xenophobia in European football, the measures taken by some agencies and institutions to combat this problem and the issue of integration through sport and leisure. Since these were the key areas of our research we asked all authors to cover these three areas as far as possible. The majority of writers are not just researchers but also committed sportspeople and football supporters.

The following two chapters of the first section look broadly at the historical context and theoretical concepts. **Mike Cole** offers a critical assessment of key concepts, linking them with important aspects of nomenclature. **Diethelm Blecking** deals with the historical relationship between sport and the integration of minorities, providing a detailed evaluation of some popular myths. His focus is on the Ruhr area, a heavy industrial part of Germany, where the population increased dramatically around the turn of this century due to the extensive migration of people from an area which is now Poland. He clearly outlines the ambiguous meaning of sport for both the integration and segregation of these groups.

The second section comprises seven essays, each presenting selected aspects of the research undertaken in a particular country. **Roman Horak** and **Mathias Marschik** start off with a critical appraisal of the Austrian situation, particularly focusing on professional football in Vienna, and compare the findings of their research with those of a similar project. **Bart Vanreusel** looks at the Belgian situation and offers a critical examination of the more structural forms of racism, the arbitrary construction and deconstruction of national identities for individuals by the media, and of the various attempts to combat racism and xenophobia through sport and leisure.

The next two essays focus on the English situation. **Scott Fleming** and **Alan Tomlinson** provide a general overview contextualising and conceptualising the development and current shape of racism and xenophobia in English football, with particular reference to the Cantona incident and the politics of both British and world football. **Jon Garland** and **Mike Rowe** summarise the findings of their empirical research which focused on a critical appraisal of the wide range of measures taken by various bodies and institutions in the UK to fight racism in football, focusing in particular on the nationwide "Let's Kick Racism Out Of Football" campaign, and other local initiatives.

Jean Marc Mariottini provides a summary of his ethnographic research into the football culture of Marseille, drawing particular attention to the role and the status of 'foreigners' in amateur football and emphasising the need to be cautious with the use of terms such as 'racism' and 'xenophobia'.

Udo Merkel, **Kurt Sombert** and **Walter Tokarski** describe the regular display of racist, xenophobic and nationalist attitudes in German football grounds against the background of the generally growing popularity of extreme right-wing ideologies and parties. As one key issue to explain this development the relationship between football and "Germanness" is explored. In addition, they provide a critical appraisal of those initiatives and campaigns which have sought to tackle these problems.

In the final chapter **Gyöngyi Szabó Földesi** provides an insight into the Eastern European experience. She outlines the major results of her research into the world of football spectators in Hungary and explores the frequency, targets, nature of and responses to racist and xenophobic behaviour of Hungarian football fans.

What all the following chapters clearly show is that the problem of racism, xenophobia and anti-Semitism in sport, particularly in football, is not confined to state borders, even if certain quantitative and qualitative characteristics, the general socio-historical background or the demographic structures of the countries vary. Despite these differences, policies in this area should be based on comparative analyses, and coordinated, in order to be effective. Particularly, comparative studies will inform those involved in policy decision making processes about the kinds of problems encountered in other countries, the conditions under which they have arisen, and about the types and effectiveness of policies developed to combat these problems.

This book does not claim to provide answers to all the questions raised. But there is no doubt that these are vital questions, and that all the contributors have provided a basis from which some answers might be found, so making some contribution to the project and progress of European integration.

'RACE', RACISM AND NOMENCLATURE: A CONCEPTUAL ANALYSIS

Mike Cole

Synopsis

In this Chapter, I begin by offering a reformulated definition of the concepts of 'race' and racism. I then turn to a consideration of the related issue of nomenclature, in Britain, Austria, Belgium, France, Germany and Hungary. Arguing that political and academic discussion of nomenclature is more advanced in Britain than in these other countries, I suggest that there is an urgent need for a serious debate about this issue amongst antiracist political activists and academics in these countries.

Introduction

Resistance to racism takes many forms. It can entail, for example, action on the streets, work in and by political parties, trade unions, educational establishments and other organisations, and the actions of parliaments. For the combating of racism to be fully effective, however, it is important to understand exactly what is meant by the concept of racism.

This chapter represents first, then, an attempt to move beyond restricted and unhelpful standard dictionary definitions (e.g. 'a belief in the superiority of a particular race', The Concise Oxford Dictionary Eighth Edition 1990) and to formulate a definition which informs and aids antiracist struggle.

There is a dialectical relationship between the way we treat people and how we refer to them — a non-positive nomenclature reinforces non-positive thoughts and actions and vice versa. This is the case whether the issues under consideration are social class, gender, disability and special needs, sexuality or, as in our case here, 'race' (for an extended analysis of all of these issues, see Cole, 1996a). The Radical Right's attempt to dismiss all debates on forms of address as 'political correctness' should not go unchallenged. As we shall see in

11

this chapter, the issue of nomenclature is closely related to racism. If we insist on calling someone 'coloured' or 'foreign', for example, when they wish to be referred to as 'black' or 'Austrian' or whatever, then we are acting in a racist way. After a consideration of 'race' and racism, I deal secondly, therefore, with the issue of nomenclature, first in a general sense, and then on a country by country basis.

'Race' and racism

'Race' as a concept is problematic. Robert Miles has argued cogently against the notion that there exist distinct 'races' (1982: pp. 9-16). After a review of the literature, and following Bodmer, he gives three reasons for this. First, the extent of genetic variation within any population is usually greater than the average difference between populations. Second, while the frequency of occurrence of possible forms taken by genes does vary from one so-called 'race' to another, any particular genetic combination can be found in almost any 'race'. Third, owing to interbreeding and large-scale migrations, the distinctions between 'races', identified as dominant gene frequencies, are often blurred (Miles, 1982: p. 16).

If 'race' has no genetic validity, it still has use as an analytic concept (in comparing and contrasting 'race' with other equality issues, for example). In addition, it does, of course, also exist as *'a social construct'* in discourse. It is therefore still necessary to use the term. When this is the case, for the reasons outlined above, I would argue that it should be put in inverted commas.

The (false) belief that there exist distinct 'races' is the genesis of the concept of racism[1]. Racism, Miles has argued, is a process whereby social relations between people are structured by biological and / or cultural characteristics in such a way as to define and construct differentiated social groups. These groups, Miles continues, are perceived as having a 'natural' unchanging origin and status, as being inherently different and as possessing negatively evaluated characteristics and / or as inducing negative consequences for other collectivities (1989: p. 75 and p. 79).

I have two comments to make on this definition. First, I believe that it is important to distinguish cultural from biological racism (c.f. Cope and Poynting, 1989; Modood, 1992[2] and 1994; Cole 1996a and 1996b). In certain instances, biological racism may be more obviously predominant than cultural racism (e.g. the nineteenth century notion of 'scientific racism', which classified black Africans, for example, as a distinct stock or species). In others, cultural racism may be pre-eminent (e.g. situations where people are thought 'odd' or 'peculiar', and therefore threatening, because of their customs or because of their religion). In yet other instances, the racisms may be equally significant; in other instances still, it may be difficult or impossible to decide which form of racism is predominant.

Second, while the perception of certain groups as having negative characteristics obviously encompasses certain forms of racism, I believe, following Smina Akhtar (personal correspondence), that it precludes other forms — namely those forms of racism related to seemingly positively evaluated characteristics. I will give two examples:

(i) 'Negatively evaluated characteristics' includes such instances of racist discourse as 'black children are not as clever as white children', but excludes seemingly positive statements such as 'black children are good at sports' (Akhtar's examples). This latter statement can lead to short-term individual and / or group enhancement (an unmerited place, perhaps, in the school football team for the individual, or enhanced status for the group as a whole in an environment where prowess at sport is highly regarded). However, it is potentially racist and likely to have racist consequences. This is because, like most stereotypes, it is distorted and misleading and typically appears as part of a discourse which works to justify black children's exclusion from academic activities.

(ii) Nazi propaganda portrayed Jewish people as alien and morally subhuman and, therefore, a threat to the Aryan 'race' (an obviously negative perception, which was part of a process that led eventually to the holocaust). However, Jews were also characterised as a clever 'race' and (at least implicitly) one which was superior in terms of ability (a perception, which, on the surface, could seem positive). Thus, along with perceived threats of German 'racial degeneration' were fears that, through having superordinate skills of organisation, the ability to dominate and act collectively as one entity, the Jews were able to control the world. This 'clever', 'super-able' stereotype, open at face value to positive interpretation, led to allegations that Jewish people were part of a conspiracy to take over the world — a notion which was also in part responsible for the holocaust. This provides a particularly stark reason for the need to consider 'seemingly positively evaluated characteristics' in any definition of racism.

Racism is thus reformulated as entailing a process whereby social relations between people are structured by the significance of human biological

and / or cultural characteristics in such a way as define and construct differentiated social groups. Such groups are assumed to have a natural, unchanging
origin and status. They are seen as being inherently different and as causing
negative consequences for other groups and / or as possessing certain evaluated
characteristics. Since these evaluated characteristics are stereotypes, they are
likely to be distorted and misleading. If they are at first seemingly positive
rather than negative, they are likely to be ultimately negative (cf. Cole, 1996b).

Nomenclature[3]

Sociology has two major problems with respect to 'racial'/ethnic categori-
sation: the white / non-white classification[4] which flows from the structure and
processes of racist societies on the one hand, and the claims to ethnic and
cultural conceptions of self-definition through which people struggle to
construct positive social identities on the other. The need to understand and to
describe the ideological processes which serve to mask racism, together with
the focused political resistance which it generates, entail a dilemma — a
dilemma which is shared by political writers and activists. There is the need to
make explicit the racist divide within societies by the use of an all-embracing
term or terms *and* the necessity to cope with multiple, unstable, shifting and
contested social identities. All this presents enormous practical problems with
respect to nomenclature.

    In the rest of this chapter I will address myself to issues of nomenclature
in Britain, Austria, Belgium, France, Germany and Hungary. In so doing, I will
take cognisance of Floya Anthias's reminder that "[t]here are no 'accurate'
definitions of [an ethnic] group", and that "the notion of where and how the
boundary [between groups] is constructed is diverse, contextual and relational",
with the boundaries often changing "over time, and in response to concrete
economic, political or ideological conditions" (1992: p. 423).

    The issue of nomenclature is and has been the subject of serious debate
in Britain. This is not the case with the other countries analysed in this volume.
Most of the terms used are, as we shall see, self-evidently negative. For
example, common terms used in these countries translate as 'foreigner(s)' or
'immigrant(s)', irrespective of whether the person or persons referred to were
born in the respective countries of habitation. This is most unfortunate and
indicates the need for urgent and serious debate amongst antiracist political
activists and academics in the countries of concern in this volume, as well as in
the countries of Europe in general. In such debate, the voices of the members of
the minority ethnic communities themselves should predominate[5].

Britain

Historically, the nomenclature used in Britain — at least with respect to black and Asian[6] people — was 'coloured'. This is now considered offensive by most people. More recently, 'black' became the orthodoxy. For some writers and activists this nomenclature is still used to refer not only to black and Asian people, but to *all* who are oppressed on 'racial' grounds. In this sense, it is thus political rather than phenotypical in intention.

For others, 'black' has exclusionary undertones because of its association with Africa and with the countries of the Caribbean. From discussions with minority ethnic women and men, from my own life experiences, and from reading and listening to the arguments, it now seems to me that the adoption of the nomenclature 'Asian, black and other minority ethnic' is a preferable formulation both to 'black' and to — what seems to have become the British sociological orthodoxy — 'black and ethnic minority'[7].

I will deal in turn with my reasons for not favouring 'black' and 'black and ethnic minority'. As far as the former is concerned, racism, as argued above, has cultural as well as biological dimensions and 'black' is not an adequate term for those people of, for example, Jewish or Irish origin who are on the receiving end of racism. This is less the case with people of Asian origin, since there is a history of identification with this term. However, I believe that 'Asian, black and other minority ethnic' (followed by 'communities' for example) is less likely to cause offence to those of Asian origin who prefer to be described as 'black' than is the use of 'black' to raise objections from those who incline towards the self-description,'Asian'.

Second, my reasons for rejecting 'black and ethnic minority' are as follows:

i.   The omission of the word 'other' between 'and' and 'ethnic' implies that only 'ethnic minorities' (people of Cypriot and Irish origin, for example) are minority constituencies, whereas black people (however perceived) are not. This is, of course, not accurate.

ii. The everyday usage of the nomenclature 'ethnic minority' has meant that majority groups are not perceived to have ethnicity, which, of course, is not true (Leicester 1989: p. 17). (The sequencing of 'minority' before 'ethnic' does not carry this implication, since the placing of 'minority' *first* facilitates the conceptualisation of a *majority* ethnic group too.)

iii. For those people of Asian origin who have not adopted black self-identification, the fact is masked that, in Britain, Asian people form the majority of 'non-white' minority women and men. For these reasons, I would advocate that, *at the present moment in Britain,* 'Asian, black and other minority ethnic' (followed by, for example, 'communities') be used whenever there is a need for an all-embracing nomenclature.

Austria

In the 1960s and 1970s, the nomenclature *Gastarbeiter* (guest worker) was common, and was used to describe cheap labour from the former Yugoslavia, and later Turkey. The key term in Austria now is *Ausländer,* which translates directly as 'foreigner'. In everyday discourse, it refers to members of minority ethnic groups, e.g. persons whose origins are Turkey or the former Yugoslavia, irrespective of country of birth. *Ausländer,* a term not generally associated with those people from western countries, is used even by the political left, with the intention, of course, to give it positive images (see the discussion on Germany below). *Ausländerquote,* the number of migrants gaining a permit to stay in Austria, is a highly politically contentious issue.

More recent and more racist terms include *Wirtschaftsflüchtling* (economic refugees) — a cynical term used to distinguish such migrants from *Asylant* (asylum seekers and those who have successfully sought asylum) and coined with the overall intention of curbing the numbers of such migrants, and *Balkanisierung. Balkanisierung* refers to people from south-east Europe, with implications that their culture (uncivilised, Islamic, etc.) is threatening 'Austrian culture'. It is used by the Extreme Right and, more recently, by the tabloid press.

As in Germany, the concept of 'racism', being associated with the Nazi era, is taboo, and other terms are used. In the case of Austria, it is *Ausländerfeindlichkeit* ('hostility towards foreigners' or xenophobia). This is unfortunate, since it tends to underplay the degree and extent of racism actually existing in Austria and Germany[8].

Belgium

As far as Belgium is concerned, it is, of course, necessary to consider nomenclature in both the Flemish and French languages. As in Austria and Germany (see below), Flemish speaking Belgians used to use the term *gastarbeiders*. Starting off neutral, *gastarbeiders* soon acquired a deprecating connotation in everyday language and is now little used. *Vreemdelingen* (foreigners) has replaced *gastarbeiders* to refer to those without Belgian nationality. *Vreemdelingen* is the legislative term and also has negative connotations in everyday language.

The most common term is *migranten* (migrants) which applies to first, second and third generations. Never used to describe highly qualified professional migrants who came to work in international institutions, this nomenclature in everyday language is restricted to working class communities whose origins lie in eastern Europe and North Africa.

Even more disturbing, however, is the cultural term *allochtonen*, used in official documents and in academia. Derived from the Ancient Greek, *allos* (other), in Modern Greek, *alokotos* ('queer' or 'odd'), it is contrasted with the term used for 'indigenous Belgians', *autochtonen* (in Ancient Greek, *autos* means self). *Allochtonen* applies to first, second and third generation members of minority ethnic communities and includes those who have Belgian nationality.

In overtly racist discourse, *marokkanen* (Moroccan) is used to refer to the minority ethnic communities in general. The term has strong negative connotations and is commonly used in racist 'jokes'.

In the French-speaking areas, *étrangers* (foreigners) is the most common nomenclature and, like *vreemdelingen,* is the only official legislative term. Often heard is the non-official term *immigrés* (immigrants). There is no French equivalent to *migranten* (migrants). As in Flemish areas, *allochtones* is increasingly being used in official French discourse.

France

Étranger is, not surprisingly, used in France too. As an official term, distinctions are made between EU and non EU 'foreigners'. In popular discourse, *étranger* has a twofold meaning. On the one hand, it can refer in a neutral or praising tone to those 'foreigners' who are viewed as culturally similar to 'the French', and therefore not a problem, or to those seen as culturally different (colour of skin, cultural patterns and behaviour), but well-off and therefore also not posing a problem. On the other hand, there are black and Maghrebian (North African) *étrangers*, *'les étrangers dehors'* (outside foreigners), who *are* seen as a threat.

Words derived from the French for 'immigrant' are used in academic and popular discourse. With respect to the former, terms such as *'population immigrée'* or *'les migrants'* tend to be used. In popular parlance, *'les immigrés'* refers, echoing the social class connotations of the Belgian nomenclature, *migranten*, to poor workers or unemployed people, conspicuous by skin colour, mode of dress, religion, food or language. It refers especially to people of Maghrebian origin, whether or not they have French citizenship. *Maghrébin* is a more euphemistic nomenclature, often aiming to sound non-racist.

More deprecatory in everyday usage is the word *Arabe,* especially if there is a strong stress on the second syllable. For even more racist effect, this is accompanied by '*sale*', as in *sales Arabes* (dirty Arabs).

In the 1980s, the children or grandchildren of Maghrebian migrants with French citizenship coined the term *Beur* (*Arabe* with the syllables inverted) to refer to themselves. Today, however, *Beur* is used, sometimes in a derogatory sense, to refer to Maghrebian teenagers.

Clearly, then, in France, people of Maghrebian origin are at the receiving end of racism. This is also the case with black people of African origin — even though, following world-wide practice, the term *noirs* or the English word *black* tends to be used, rather than the derogatory nomenclature *nègres*.

Germany

As in Austria, the term *Gastarbeiter* began to be used in the 1960s to describe workers imported as cheap labour. At the end of the 1960s, economic problems, the rise of a fascist party (the National Democratic Party), and open racism meant that the negative nomenclature *Fremdarbeiter* ('foreign worker'), a term used in the mid 1950s, re-emerged. In order to resist this development, politicians, particularly from the Social Democratic Party, invented what they saw as more positive terms, e.g. *ausländische Mitbürger* ('foreign fellow-citizens'). At the same time, in popular discourse, *die Türken* ('the Turks') almost became a synonym for all minority ethnic groups, to such an extent that for a while *Türkenfeindlichkeit* ('hostility towards Turks') even began to replace *Ausländerfeindlichkeit* ('xenophobia') as a generic term.

Although there are a large number of terms used to refer to people perceived as 'non-Germans', *Asylbewerber* ('asylum seekers'), *Armutsflüchtling* ('poverty refugee'), *Kriegsflüchtling* ('war refugee'), *Bürgerkriegsflüchtling* ('civil war refugee'), the term *Ausländer* ('foreigner') is the most common. In everyday discourse, *Ausländer* tends to refer to all those whose origins lie outside Germany, irrespective of how many generations have lived in Germany and of whether or not German citizenship is held. In particular, *Ausländer* refers to those whose countries of origin are around the Mediterranean, such as Turkey, the former Yugoslavia, Italy, Spain and Greece.

The extent to which the generic term *Ausländer* remains problematic is evidenced by rather pathetic attempts by antiracists to rescue the word's neutrality by slogans like "*Alle Menschen sind Ausländer — fast überall*" ("All people are foreigners — almost everywhere") and "*Wir Deutschen sind Ausländer in 178 Ländern dieser Welt*" ("We Germans are foreigners in 178 countries of the world").

Even the academic treatment of Germany's minority ethnic communities very often reflects a distorted understanding of reality. Terms such as *Arbeitsmigranten* ('work migrants') (still) stress the migration process, and thus notions of temporary rather than permanent residence.

In public discourse, unsuccessful attempts have been made to differentiate between '*Ausländer*' according to length of stay by adding *erster, zweiter,* or *dritter Generation* (first, second or third generation) to *Ausländer/ Gastarbeiter.*

Hungary

Before the overthrow of 'communism', traditional minority ethnic groups living in Hungary were referred to according to ethnic and National origin, *cigányok* ('the Gypsies'), *zsidék* ('the Jews'), *szlovákok* ('the Slovakians'), *horvátok* ('the Croations'), *németek* ('the Germans'). Racism directed at 'Gypsies' and Jews has been rampant for many years. With respect to the former, there is even differentiation within the 'Gypsy' communities, with Hungarian 'Gypsies' considered to be superior to Romanian and Wallachian 'Gypsies'. In an attempt to deter escalating racism, in the last couple of years the term *Romany*, a term preferred by members of those communities, has been used officially.

Prior to 1989, international migration to Hungary did not exist, with rare exceptions (e.g. Greek political refugees fleeing from the right-wing government in the late 1940s, from Chile in 1973/4, and foreign students who were invited to study in Hungary, based on governmental agreements, with the aim of supporting developing countries in the name of internationalism). The rather neutral word *külföldi, idegen* ('foreigner') was synonymous with *idegen, külföldi* ('alien') and referred only to people from other countries.

Since the late 1980s, with increasing migration into Hungary, a number of new terms have arisen, '*politikai menekült*' ('political refugee'), '*gazdasági menekült*' ('economic refugee'), '*háborús menekült*' ('war refugee'), *bevándorló* (immigrant), *vándorló* (migrant), *vándegmunkás* ('guest worker'). Surveys (e.g. Závecz, 1992) indicate that these terms have become pejorative in recent years, especially '*gazdasági menekült*' ('economic refugee'), in particular when it is used in reference to minority ethnic groups from remote countries.

Since the advent of the free movement of peoples, post-1989, *vendég-munkás* ('guest worker') and *külföldi, idegen* ('foreigner') are forms of nomenclature becoming increasingly associated with negative connotations.

The aim of this chapter has been to provide a *conceptual* overview of the complex issues of 'race', racism and nomenclature in selected European countries. It is hoped that the analysis will be of use to readers in understanding racism in the very *concrete* world of European football, which is the subject of the rest of this book, and, as such, that it makes some contribution to the broader Europe-wide struggle against racism.

Acknowledgements

I would like to thank Christian Bromberger, Gyöngyi Szabó Földesi, Helen Haji-Alexandrou, Dave Hill, Roman Horak, Mark Mazower, Udo Merkel and Bart Vanreusel for their help in the compilation of this chapter. Responsibility for any inadequacies remains mine.

Notes

[1] The following analysis draws heavily on Cole, 1996a and 1996b.

[2] I should point out here that I would distance myself from Modood's overall project in this book, which entails the wholesale rejection of historical materialism, the privileging of functionalist analysis, and the promotion of a liberal concept of 'ethnic pluralism' (for an analysis, see Cole, 1993a: p. 23)

[3] The following general conceptual analysis and arguments *pertaining to Britain* draw heavily on Cole 1993b.

[4] I would not advocate 'white/non-white' as acceptable nomenclature, because it implies negativity to people in the latter category, and because it does not necessarily encompass those who experience certain forms of cultural racism.

[5] As a white person, I realise that I am laying myself open to perhaps justified criticism in seeming to set the agenda. However, Britain notwithstanding, I do not make specific suggestions for usage. I make suggestions for Britain, in the light of a long-standing debate, informed by *Asian, black and other minority ethnic* individuals and communities in Britain. I now return to my reasons for using this particular nomenclature.

[6] In the context of Britain, 'Asian' refers to people of South Asian origin. This is in itself problematic, since it has exclusionary implications for Asians whose origins are not from the south of the Asian continent.

7   The latest indication that this is the case comes in a note sent out to members
     by the General Secretary of the British Sociological Association dated
     12 February 1995. The note, which gives details of a forthcoming Annual
     General Meeting, asks for nominations for the 'Black and Ethnic Minority
     Women's Sub Committee'.

8   The term xenophobia is derived from the Ancient Greek, *xenos*, meaning
     'strange', 'foreign' or 'stranger' and *phobeio* (the Greek word from which
     phobia is derived) which means 'I fear' (in earlier times it meant also 'I am put
     to flight') (Lewin, 1968: p. 81). Xenophobia is a somewhat vague psychological
     notion, and, unlike the concept of *racism*, it does not tell us much; either about
     the nature of such a disposition, or indeed about its underlying causes. For these
     reasons, it has only a very limited analytical value and has virtually fallen from
     the vocabulary of contemporary debate on 'race', racism and ethnicity in the
     English speaking world (Cashmore 1994).

References

Anthias, F. (1992) 'Connecting "race" and ethnic phenomena', *Sociology,* Vol. 26,
    No. 3: pp. 421-438.

Cashmore, E. (1994) *Dictionary of Race and Ethnic Relations.* London: Routledge.

Cole, M. (1989) (ed) *The Social Contexts of Schooling.* Lewes: The Falmer Press.

Cole, M. (1993a) 'Widening the cricket test', *The Times Higher Education
    Supplement,* Vol. 26, March: p. 23.

Cole, M. (1993b) '"Black and ethnic minority" or "Asian, black and other minority
    ethnic": A further note on nomenclature', *Sociology,* Vol. 27, No. 4: pp. 671-
    673.

Cole, M. (1996a forthcoming) 'Equality and primary education: What are the
    conceptual issues?', in M. Cole, D. Hill and S. Shan (eds) *Promoting Equality
    in Primary Schools.* London: Cassell.

Cole, M. (1996b) '"Race" and racism', in M. Payne (ed) *The Dictionary of Cultural
    and Critical Theory.* Oxford: Blackwell Publishers, pp. 449-453.

Cope, B. and Poynting, S. (1989) 'Class, gender and ethnicity as influences on
    Australian Schooling: An overview', in M. Cole (ed) *The Social Contexts of
    Schooling.* Lewes: The Falmer Press, pp. 217-237.

Leicester, M. (1989) *Multicultural Education: From Theory to Practice.* Windsor:
    Nfer-Nelson.

Lewin, B. D. (1968) 'Phobias', in D. L. Sills (ed) *International Encyclopedia of the
    Social Sciences.* The United States of America: The Macmillan Company &
    The Free Press, pp. 81-85.

Miles, R. (1982) *Racism and Migrant Labour*. London: Routledge and Kegan Paul.

Miles, R. (1989) *Racism*. London: Routledge.

Modood, T. (1992) *Not Easy Being British: Colour, Culture and Citizenship*. London: Runnymede Trust and Trentham Books.

Modood, T. (1994) 'Political blackness and British Asians', *Sociology*, Vol. 28, No. 4: pp. 858-876.

Závecz, T. (1992) 'Csökkenö rokonszenv' (Decreasing sympathy), in E. Sik (ed) *Menekulök, vándorlók, szerencsét próbálók*. Budapest: MTA Politikai Tudományok Intézete, pp. 49-58.

SPORT AND THE INTEGRATION
OF MINORITIES:
A HISTORICAL CASE STUDY*

Diethelm Blecking

Introduction

The focus of this chapter is on issues related to the integration of minorities in and through sport in historical perspective and, more specifically, the role and importance of sport in the integration of minorities in the Ruhr area, a heavily industrialised region in Germany. It is impossible to cover all the issues involved, so this paper aims simply to draw attention to those areas of sports research that are as yet uncharted, to clearly mark the blind alleys, and to provide an adequate description of the familiar terrain.

Any attempt to explore the historical background in greater detail could only be done with due reference to the standard works on social history and its published results. But — judging by the following three statements made by people 'in the field' — it is clear that, as far as the problem of migrants and sport is concerned, insufficient research has been carried out. In 1989 the then German Home Secretary, Wolfgang Schäuble, stated that: "Sports clubs for mineworkers from Poland [...] helped the workers integrate into society" (Schäuble, 1989: p. 9). No doubt a ghost writer is responsible for these words, but that does not change the fact that such an assertion contradicts the findings of historical research. The same applies to the words penned by sports sociologist, Klaus Heinemann, who claimed apodictically: "Guest workers have only been around since the second half of this century..." (quoted in Bammel and Becker, 1985: p. 5). If that were true, the file on this issue could be closed for good. But the clear league winner is the spokesman of the German Football Association who, in a radio programme, asserted: "In recent years foreigners have become fully integrated into organised club football. We don't think there are any particular problems for foreigners in organised football" (Biermann, 1993: p. 7). But there certainly are problems (see Weber-Klüver, 1994), and we can see from these

---

* Translated by Andrew Marson   23

quotes that research in this field should feature more prominently on the agenda of sports research.

The emergence of minorities as a problem in Germany and Europe in the 19th century

The integration of minorities into society in and through sport began in the 19th century with the emergence of the gymnastics and sports movements in Europe (see Eichberg, 1979; Krüger, 1993). These movements were the legitimate children of a wider process that can be referred to as *modernisation*.[1] The term modernisation is used to describe a process of change at the end of the 18th century that affected not only the social but also the economic structures of the European states, and was characterised by the demise of feudalism, finally killed off by the French Revolution in 1789 and the onset of the Industrial Revolution in England in the 1780/90s.[2]

Concurrent with, and clearly also functionally related to, the modernisation of social conditions and the resultant improvements in communication[3] (greater literacy, new forms of transport, the mass media, clubs and societies, telegraphy, etc.), the phenomenon of nationalism emerged in Europe (Alter, 1985). It appeared in one of two guises: either rebellious, liberal, Risorgimento* nationalism in the nationalist movements of small population groups with the status of "ethnic groups lacking full citizenship" (Hroch, 1968: p. 16) living in multinational empires such as the Danube Monarchy; or radical, subordinated, integral nationalism in the case of the "belated nations" (Plessner, 1985) Germany (1871) and Italy (1861).

The birth of the German Empire during the wars of unification against Denmark (1864), Austria (1866) and France (1870/71)[4] gave rise to a minorities problem, in which the Risorgimento nationalism of the minorities and the inherent nationalism of the Empire became ever more irreconcilably opposed. Meanwhile, with the industrialisation of the Empire and the growth of an economic divide between east and west, a steady flow of migrants began from the agricultural eastern provinces, where a large number of Poles resided, to the industrial centres, especially the Ruhr area. There, from the 1880s onwards, a Polish minority began to take root.

With the growth of "new" minorities in the industrial centres and the national mobilisation of "old" minorities, for example the southern Slavs and the Czechs in the Habsburg Empire, the scene was set for the gymnastics and sports

---

*   "Rebirth". Its historical role model is the Italian nationalism of the 19th Century (Alter, 1985: p. 33).

clubs, whose room for manoeuvre was limited by the fact that the nation state was "The general system of reference for social orientations" (Lepsius, 1966: p. 38). Consequently, clubs often adopted political and cultural objectives of a nationalist persuasion, the goal of integration being to imbue their members with the nationalist idea. In the case of the *Deutsche Turnerschaft* (German Gymnastics Association) this meant excluding "Enemies of the Empire", whether ethnic minorities or workers who were members of the Social Democratic movement. As for the minorities, such as the Polish minority in the Ruhr area, there was a desire to build up an "externally closed and internally integrated sub-culture" (Nipperdey, 1990: p. 278). "They did not want to be a minority, rather a counter-nation" (Nipperdey, 1990: p. 268).

Thus, with a nationality conflict in full swing, gymnastics and sport seemed on the surface more a vehicle for the segregation of minority and majority than a means for integration. However, if one looks more closely at what was happening in the Ruhr area, in particular at the dynamics of developments there, one sees that this point of view is simplistic; there are clearly deficiencies and gaps in the research that would have to be investigated before any final conclusion could be reached. But it is evident, even at this stage, that the German example cannot be taken in isolation. Against the background of developments in the Ruhr area we can make a comparison with other multinational, organised communities in Europe. Vienna and Trieste would seem to be obvious cases in point. Preliminary analyses, similar to that for the Ruhr area, have already been carried out for both these cities (Cattaruzza, 1989; Glettler, 1970).

Minorities in the German Empire

The German Kaiserreich was — though this fact is often suppressed — a "multi-ethnic, that is a multi-lingual construction" (Sauer, 1973: p. 408); in short: "it was not a nation state, nor could it, in the strict sense of the term, ever be one" (Klessmann, 1984: pp. 127-138). One in every eleven inhabitants of Prussia was Polish-speaking (some 3,326 million), in addition to which in the east there were 72,500 Kashubs, 248,000 Masurians and 101,500 Lithuanians (Klessmann, 1984: p. 129). With the annexation of Alsace-Lorraine, a nationalities problem arose in the west, the size of which was initially underestimated. True enough, the majority of the inhabitants of Alsace-Lorraine spoke German but, in this "Poland of the West", as Marx ironically referred to the French *départements* annexed in 1871 (Wehler, 1978: p.28), the German language did not go hand in hand with affinity to the German state. As far as the inhabitants of Alsace-Lorraine were concerned, their affinity was to France, and even the German-speakers defended "French language and culture as a valuable asset" (Wehler, 1978: p. 57).

In the north, the acquisition of North Schleswig after victory over the Danes in 1864 had led to the emergence of a Danish minority in the German Empire. The Danish minority set up the "Electoral Organisation for North Schleswig" and fought for annexation to Denmark (Klessmann, 1984: p. 132).

Another essentially unresolved problem was that of the 600,000 German Jews, who had attained such a high level of assimilation that the remaining social barriers preventing entry to universities and the army were all the more painfully evident. Under pressure of anti-Semitism laden with ideas of racial biology, parts of the Jewish population, in a kind of "national renaissance", constituted a new and self-aware minority in the Zionist movement (Zmarzlik, 1981: pp. 249-270).

At the end of the 19th century, a similar renaissance of national ideas was experienced by the Sorbs in Lausatia who, since 1896, as a part of increased efforts to Germanise the population in the east, had been subjected to closer state scrutiny (Oschlies, 1991).

The Polish-German conflict became a model for opposition to a state administration that backed ethnic homogenisation of the nation state, i.e. Germanisation. Since the end of the 1880s, hundreds of thousands of migrants had left the eastern areas of the Empire to work and settle in the Ruhr area. The majority (approximately 350,000) were Poles. On the eve of the First World War, approximately ten percent of the inhabitants of the Ruhr area were Poles or Masurians (Klessmann, 1984: p. 137). Besides the Poles, there were other small minority groups of Italians, Dutch and Slovenians. The Ruhr area formed a multi-cultural core to the Empire even prior to 1914.

In virtually all the regions described here, where minorities struggled against the homogenisation policy of the Prussian-German administration, gymnastics and sports organisations grew up on the fringes of the ethnic and cultural conflict zones. Although the Polish organisations and the Jewish Gymnastics Association (König, 1989: pp. 9-28) have been quite adequately researched, research on Alsace-Lorraine, the Danes and the Sorbs is rather patchy.

It is possible, on the basis of the integration of the Polish minority in the Ruhr area and the role of sport in this process, to develop research questions that illuminate the links between sport and integration in general.

Polish sport in the Ruhr area, from subculture to integration (1899-1939)

The emergence of the Polish minority

The Polish minority in the Ruhr area grew as a result of large-scale internal migration before the First World War that brought over two million people from the eastern provinces to the industrial centres of the Empire: i.e. Berlin, central Germany and the industrial areas of Rhineland-Westphalia (Klessmann, 1978: p. 38).

There were a number of social, economic and political factors initiating this migration process. Firstly, overpopulation in the agricultural areas in the east; secondly, the uneven geographical distribution of German industrialisation, centred on a number of individual centres dominating German industry; and thirdly, the statutory legality of free movement in the large economic zone that the German Empire had turned into since 1871 (Wehler, 1973: p. 437).

Though the motives of the 'guest workers' who flooded from the agricultural peripheries of Europe to the booming industrial economy of the Federal Republic from the mid 1950s onwards were similar to those of the migrants of the Kaiserreich, the latter were usually German citizens with all the rights that the Empire's-constitution guaranteed its citizens.[5]

By 1914, the number of young Poles who had found work in the coal mines of the Ruhr area had grown to a colony of 300,000–350,000. But their fellow citizens considered them to be foreigners:

> The Ruhr area Poles were socially (at least the vast majority) labourers, 'racially' (this obscure biological feature was important at the time) Slavs, linguistically and ethnically Poles, and denominationally Catholics. (Klessmann, 1978: p. 16)

The national awareness of these Polish immigrants, who came mostly from the sub-rural strata of society, was only rudimentary. But under the pressure of acculturation and the at times violent Germanisation strategy of the German administration, a sense of group identity developed — one that soon became laden with Polish nationalist sentiments, and led to the founding of a distinct system of Polish clubs. This eventually culminated in the establishment of a separate Polish community (*Spoleczenstwo*) and corresponding infrastructure with its own bank, its own press and a Polish union.

Polish sports clubs in the Ruhr area

Starting in 1899, with the self-organisation of the Polish minority in the Ruhr area, the first Polish gymnastics societies were founded. Shortly before the outbreak of World War I, these organisations, named *Sokol* ("Falcon"), had almost 6,000 Polish members in 152 clubs (Blecking, 1990a: p. 165). Their importance to the integration process of Polish mineworkers was analysed by Blecking:

> From the outset, the Polish gymnastics clubs gave their activity the strategic objective of recreating a sovereign Polish state, and were [...]

from the very beginning, a part of the Polish nationalist movement. The nationalities conflict, that had sowed the seeds of the gymnastics clubs, also dictated the place of these clubs in the Polish subculture. So to ask what role these clubs played in the integration of the Ruhr area Poles is to miss the point. In fact the clubs helped further to differentiate the "activities" of the "Polish Community" (Bernhard, 1907) in the Ruhr area and to promote the internal integration of the Polish subculture. In day-to-day life, and especially in any dealings the minority had with the institutions (schools, authorities, companies), it was brought face to face with a dominant Prussian/German society that pursued a policy of Germanisation (i.e. the Prussian way to integrate foreigners), and found itself on the defensive [...].

By placing their activity on an ideological pedestal and by aligning it to a strategic objective, these Polish gymnasts created an "internally binding" and "externally repelling" function in their ethnic socialisation, this finding expression in a rigid self-definition of the group and leading to a clear delineation vis-à-vis the other ethnic group. The exclusion of Germans from Sokol celebrations, the membership ban on Sokol members in German clubs, and pressure on members who were married to Germans were all tools used in the process of collective self-definition and led to heightened pressure on the small community of Polish gymnasts.

The elitist self-perception of the Sokol gymnasts, who saw themselves as the avant-garde of the Polish movement in the Ruhr area (and thus also of cessionist nationalism) collided with the integrationist nationalism that was concealed behind the Germanisation concept of the Prussian-German Poland policy. [...]

[The Sokol organisation] was an integral component of the national Polish subculture in the Ruhr area which, in turn, revealed itself to be a considerable obstacle in the path of assimilation of the Ruhr Poles. Before World War I, mixed ethnic marriages, an important indicator of the assimilation processes, were rare. The ethnic community of the Ruhr Poles gave Polish mineworkers a discernibly Polish social environment from cradle to grave. (Blecking, 1991: p. 168ff)

We can no longer deduce from historical sources how many Poles were actually members of the German gymnastics or sports clubs. This question must remain unanswered.

Access to cliques, clubs and institutions of the 'host society' — a feature that in American migration sociology is referred to as "structural assimilation" (Gordon, 1964: p. 81) and is a key sequence in the integration processes — was not promoted, at least not by the mono-ethnic gymnastics societies; even "marital assimilation" was heavily opposed.

Pluralistic integration or assimilative integration?

This historical stocktaking shows that simply to concentrate on the question of the role played by sport in integration is to lose sight of the more interesting social changes taking place between minorities and majority. In the clash between minorities and majority, something new is usually generated. Integration is a process that initiates changes on both sides.

The migration sociologist Heckmann, with his concept of the "ethnic colony" has stressed the positive aspects of mono-ethnic sports societies, arguing that they provide the migrants with emotional and mental stability in a culturally familiar environment. However, at the heart of his integration concept is the notion of *pluralistic integration*, whereby migrants retain parts of their original culture. This is in contrast to the more frequently applied model of *assimilative integration*, which calls for the adoption of the majority culture and the relinquishing of the culture of origin (Heckmann, 1985: pp. 21-33).

And yet, the Polish sports clubs in the Ruhr area also revealed the Janus face of the ethnic colony. Pressurised by a conflict of nationality, illiberal traits came to the fore. The repressive Germanisation strategy of the state created blinkered nationalist thinking in the subordinated group.

Football as medium for integration?

The history of the Polish minority in the Ruhr area and their sports clubs was not brought to an end by World War I. The democratic character of the Weimar Republic provided Polish sport with better conditions. But new migratory movements soon followed, gradually removing the basis for further development.

In the interwar years, as a result of emigration to the newly established Polish state and to the Belgian and French coal fields, the number of Poles in the Ruhr area dropped to about 150,000 (Klessmann, 1978: p. 165). At the same time, the Polish sports clubs, whose very existence was threatened by this emigration, set up football divisions to encourage young people to continue their involvement in Polish sport. The attempt backfired. Although football was not played by larger numbers of workers until after World War I[6], its introduction soon resulted in the young members wanting to play with German clubs. This sounded the death knell of the Polish sports movement in the Ruhr area, which in 1927 was rechristened: "Association of Gymnastics and Sports Clubs in Westphalia" (Blecking, 1991: p. 171). For the migrants and their children left behind in the Empire, integration was the only remaining option. Before the First World War they had had the alternative of fighting for an independent Polish state. Thus, sport presented the migrants with an "opportunity to promote their own assimilation…" (Blecking, 1990a: p. 198). The ethnic enclave gradually dissolved. However, the final point was not the successful social integration, but the German army's invasion of Poland on 1st September 1939. It was a matter of only days before all Polish organisations were banned.

The collected results of historical research suggest that the role of sport is ambivalent: it acts as a medium both for integration and segregation. So it is essential that sports researchers, in their attempts to get to grips with this problem, determine both the precise sociological and historical nature of the society in which integration occurs, and also the definition of the concept — which, as mentioned, can be understood in a variety of ways. To date, no accurate empirical analysis of the role played by football in the dissolution of the ethnic colony has been carried out. A few studies, for example the one on *Schalke 04* (Gehrmann, 1979: pp. 117-130), show that the real stars of Ruhr area football are players of Masurian descent such as Szepan and Kuzorra. One must be careful, however, not to confuse the protestant and loyally Prussian Masurians, speakers of an old Polish dialect, with the Ruhr area Poles. Even Gehrmann´s well-known study (Gehrmann, 1988) does not tackle the important question of whether, and if so how, football contributed to the integration of the Poles[7]. The study could have linked this older example of integration to developments post World War II.

Post-World War II: sport as a means of social control or integration?

Sport for foreigners in a country of immigration

Germany has become a country of immigration[8]; this is confirmed time and again by leading migration experts. Motivated by concern about the lack of an immigration policy, these experts have drafted the "Manifesto of the 60", which describes what the fundamental features of a policy of this sort would be. With regard to the family, young people and education they call for an intercultural upbringing that avoids a one-sided alignment to the German school model, and that sees integration not as a one-way street to German culture but "pluralistically" as a parallel process of change affecting both minorities and majority, far removed from ethnocentric thinking (Boos-Nünning, 1994: pp. 43-48). This concept attributes an important role to the "ethnic colony" in upbringing.

However, neither research nor the integration concepts of the sport organisations or the Conference of Sports Ministers have yet recognised their conceptual implications. It is true that since the mid 1960s sports organisations have been firmly committed to the integration of foreigners. But in 1981, the Deutscher Sportbund (German Sports Association) adopted a policy statement on "Sport for foreign fellow citizens". The Conference of Sports Ministers of the Länder followed suit in 1983 with a decision on "The integration of foreign fellow citizens through sport" (Roman-Schüssler and Schwarz, 1985: p. 65). However, both resolutions are aimed at foreign members of German sports clubs, and take into account neither the historical experiences outlined above nor the German reality, which is once again witnessing the growth of ethnic clubs. The Conference of Sports Ministers has explicitly recognised this fact, stating in the resolution:

> In those exceptional cases where separate Turkish sports groups and clubs exist, they should be able to participate in the sporting activities of the respective German association in accordance with its statutes. (Roman-Schüssler and Schwarz, 1985: p. 65)

According to this definition, individual membership is the rule and the ethnic club the exception. Not only does this fail to take account of historical experience, but it is biased towards a model of integration that facilitates social control.

Until now, sports research has to a great degree endorsed these normative handicaps, and has thus missed its goal of explaining the real interactive links in intercultural contact.[9]

Turkish sport in Berlin

Preliminary studies on Turkish sport in Berlin show, in fact, that the ethnic clubs are very popular. A study carried out in 1985 for the Foreigners' Representative of the Berlin Council reveals that between 1979 and 1983, the number of "separate Turkish sports organisations rose from 1,263 to 3,123" (Roman-Schlüssler and Schwarz, 1985: p. 10). So in 1983, 43.5% of the members of sports clubs preferred the ethnic club (Ibid.). In the five years preceding the end of the study, the trend was significantly in favour of the ethnic clubs (Roman-Schlüssler and Schwarz, 1985: p. 19). A study published two years later came to the conclusion that the trend persists, and concludes that:

> This thesis that ethnic sports clubs are gradually dying out [...] is inaccurate, or at any rate about as likely as the disbanding of Turkish mosque societies, travel agents, take-aways, folk dancing groups, etc. This Turkish infrastructure is necessary to help the migrants cope with day-to-day life in the FRG which, after all, is often marked by unemployment and discrimination. (Schwarz, 1987: pp. 27-38)

The similarities to the Polish minority in the Ruhr area are striking. In fact, in 1983 in Berlin a Turkish sports association was set up as an umbrella organisation for the sports clubs; but under pressure from the Berlin Council had to be closed down in 1984 (Schwarz, 1987: p. 37). Football, it would appear, plays a special role in the Turkish subculture: Schwarz (1987: p. 10) counts over 1,000 clubs in Western Europe! In Berlin there is now even a women's football team, *BSC Agrispor* — although, admittedly, the only one of its kind in Europe (Gaserow and Floss, 1994: pp. 50-57).

One of the desiderata of research is to extend the studies on Berlin to other centres of Turkish workers' migration in Germany (e.g. the Ruhr area) and to the growing subcultures of the Berlin migrants (Gaserow, 1995: p. 6). In the annex to this potential study, the fixation on integration could be abandoned in favour of a more open sociological approach, entailing an empirical assessment and exploration of various problems (such as the clubs' role for the Turkish minority, women's sport, interaction problems in competitions: referees, opponents, physical cultures of Turkish and German sportspersons, generation problems, etc.). For an in-depth study that goes beyond organisational issues into cultural studies, Bourdieu's method (Bröskamp, 1993: pp. 174-207) is available *inter alia*, or Norbert Elias's "established-outsider" approach.[10]

The re-emergence of ethnic segregation in sport

After the reunification of the two German states in 1989/90[11], political debate fell back on the nationalist thought patterns of the 19th century (Habermas, 1993: p. ZB3). Xenophobic attacks have made the climate between the minorities and German society more tense. Against this background, the first trends towards ethnification, i.e. the deliberate ethnic segregation by the minority groups, have also been noted in sport[12]. In addition to the separate Turkish organisations, resident Poles are making attempts to set up organisations along the old Sokol lines. Even the Sorbs in Lausatia are recalling their old Sokol tradition and are seeking closer contacts with other minorities in Europe (Blecking, 1992: p. 34). The monitoring and analysis of these as yet unquantified ethnification trends would no doubt be of interest to sports researchers sensitive to the issues of sport and migrants.

Conclusion

In this analysis of the historical aspects of sport and migration in Germany, certain important areas have had to be neglected, areas that have only recently become socially relevant. For example, since 1989 a project has been running in Germany on the integration of ethnic Germans (*Aussiedler*) through sport, financed by the German Home Office, and organised by the German Sports Association. The problems are similar to those faced by the minority ethnic groups. These returning 'Germans' from Eastern Europe (Rumania, Poland, Russia) are just as foreign in Germany as immigrants from Anatolia (Blecking, 1990: pp. 12-13), the only difference being their legal status. The interesting thing about this project is the systematic way in which it has been set about, and the attempt to fix a theoretical foundation, borrowing from Elias's Established-Outsider-Configuration (Deutscher Sportbund, 1992). Doing this has meant recognising and researching the re-immigrants' social and psychological starting point, their origins, and the attitude of the majority towards them. Nevertheless, the overall aim is still individual membership of German clubs, and even this project excludes other groups such as asylum seekers. Asylum seekers, it would appear, are not currently of any interest to researchers on organised sport: no-one has yet carried out an empirical study on this group. The scope of research on integration in and through sport should be extended to cover these perspectives.

Notes

[1] See Cachay, 1988, on differentiation of the sports system in the modernisation process.

[2] The historian Hans-Ulrich Wehler talks of a "double revolution" at the beginning of the "modern age": "Since the end of the 18th century, the English industrial revolution and the French political revolution have gone hand in hand to create a "double revolution", that, with unparalleled dynamism, has reshaped firstly the European world and then the globe as a whole." (Wehler, 1995: Vol. 3, p. 3).

3   See Tenfelde, 1976: pp. 1-60, for an introduction on the link between modernisation and improved communications.

4   See Dann, 1993: pp. 137-198, on the creation of the German nation state.

5   For a detailed comparison of the history of labour migration and 'guest workers' see Stefanski, 1988: pp. 68-87.

6   The myth of the workers' sport, football, is demolished by Eisenberg, 1994: pp. 181-210.

7   In an as yet unpublished speech, Gehrmann has recently brought up the question of the contribution made by football to the identity of the region (Gehrmann *Football in the Ruhr: on the importance of a popular form of sport in a region's quest for identity*, forthcoming).

8   "Since the end of the Second World War about fifteen million exiles, refugees and ethnic Germans have come to post-war western Germany and the FRG. [...] After the building of the Berlin Wall, which stemmed the flood of people leaving the DDR, the number of foreign workers coming to take part in the rapid and unstoppable economic growth of the FRG soared into millions. [...] In this period, about fourteen million foreigners immigrated to the FRG. Of these, about eleven million returned home. The current size of the foreign population in Germany is about 4.6 million. [...] If one includes the foreign minorities, then about one third of the resident population of the Federal Republic has migrated back home since World War II" (Bade, 1990: p. 6).

9   For a critique of sports research in this context see Bröskampp, 1994: pp. 21-62.

10 A first rate study on the Polish minority in the Ruhr that uses the "established-outsider-figuration" is: Oenning, 1991.

11 In the GDR, the public was generally unaware of the presence of ethnic minorities, who in any case were few in number. Excluding the Sorbs, who had a special status, about 166,000 foreigners lived in the second German state in 1989. The biggest group (53,000) were the Vietnamese. See Krüger-Potratz, 1991.

12 In fact not only in sport. The most significant trends are found in Turkish youth culture. See 'Agitpop aus dem Ghetto', *Der Spiegel*, 1995: pp. 132-134.

References and Bibliography

Alter, P. (1985) *Nationalismus.* Frankfurt: Suhrkamp.

Bade, K. J. (1990) 'Einführung: Wege in die Bundesrepublik', in K. J. Bade (ed) *Neue Heimat im Westen: Vertriebene, Flüchtlinge, Aussiedler.* Münster: Westfälischer Heimatbund, pp. 5-11.

Bammel, H. and Becker, H. (eds) (1985) Sport und ausländische Mitbürger, Fachtagung der Friedrich-Ebert-Stiftung vom 9.-11. November 1984, Bonn: Deutscher Sportbund.

Bernhard, L. (1907) *Das polnische Gemeinwesen im preußischen Staat, Die Polenfrage.* Leipzig: Duncker and Humblot.

Biermann, C. (1993) *Sonntag ist unser Tag, Völkerverbindender Sport? Türkische Fußballer in Deutschland,* Manuskript der Sendung des WDR vom 21.9.1993.

Blecking, D. (1990) 'Aus Erfahrung lernen — Migration und Sport aus historischer Perspektive', in Kultusministerium NW (eds) *Sport mit Aussiedlern, Dokumentation der Jahre 1977-1989.* Frechen: Verlagsgesellschaft Ritterbach, pp. 12-13.

Blecking, D. (1990) *Die Geschichte der nationalpolnischen Turnorganisation "Sokol" im Deutschen Reich 1884-1939, 2nd Edition.* Münster: Lit-Verlag.

Blecking, D. (1991) 'Ethnische Vergemeinschaftung im Sport — das Beispiel der Ruhrpolen', in D. Blecking, *Die slawische Sokolbewegung, Beiträge zur Geschichte von Sport und Nationalismus in Osteuropa.* Dortmund: Forschungsstelle Ostmitteleuropa Universität Dortmund, pp. 164-174.

Blecking, D. (1992) '"Auf Du sorbischer Falke"! Zum Sport im Osten Deutschlands', *Olympisches Feuer,* Vol. 42, No. 3: p. 34.

Blecking, D. (1993) 'Sport and ethnic minorities in Germany', in L. Laine (ed), *On the fringes of sport.* St. Augustin: Academia, pp.149-155.

Boos-Nünning, U. (1994) 'Familie, Jugend, Bildungsarbeit', in K. J. Bade (ed), *Das Manifest der 60: Deutschland und die Einwanderung.* München: C. H. Beck, pp. 43-48.

Bröskamp, B. (1993) 'Ethnische Grenzen des Geschmacks. Perspektiven einer praxeologischen Migrationsforschung', in G. Gebauer and C. Wulf (eds) *Praxis und Ästhetik, Neue Perspektiven im Denken Pierre Bourdieus.* Frankfurt: Suhrkamp, pp. 174-207.

Bröskamp, B. (1994) *Körperliche Fremdheit, Zum Problem der interkulturellen Begegnung im Sport.* St. Augustin: Academia.

Cachay, K. (1988) *Sport und Gesellschaft. Zur Ausdifferenzierung einer Funktion und ihrer Folgen.* Schorndorf: Hofmann.

Cattaruzza, M. (1989) 'Sloveni e italiani a Trieste, La formazione dell' identita nazionale', *Clio*, No. 251: pp. 27-58.

Dann, O. (1993) *Nation und Nationalismus in Deutschland 1770-1990*. München: C. H. Beck.

Der Spiegel (1995) 'Agitpop aus dem Ghetto', No. 17: pp. 132-134.

Deutscher Sportbund (1981) *Sport der ausländischen Mitbürger, Eine Grundsatzerklärung des Deutschen Sportbundes*. Frankfurt: Deutscher Sportbund .

Deutscher Sportbund (1992) *Sport mit Aussiedlern, Zwischenbilanz*. Frankfurt: Deutscher Sportbund .

Eichberg, H. (1979) *Der Weg des Sports in die industrielle Zivilisation* (2nd Edition). Baden-Baden: Nomos.

Eichberg, H. (1989) 'Folkelig gymnastik — über den dänischen Sonderweg in der Körperkultur', in K.-J. Gutsche, and H. J. Medau (eds) *Gymnastik, — ein Beitrag zur Bewegungskultur unserer Gesellschaft*. Schorndorf: Hofmann, pp. 52-95.

Eisenberg, C. (1994) 'Fußball in Deutschland, Ein Gesellschaftsspiel für bürgerliche Mittelschichten', *Geschichte und Gesellschaft* 20: pp. 181-210.

Gaserow, V. (1995) 'Einheit nicht nur zu zweit, Türken, Polen, Russen... Menschen aus 180 Nationen: Berlin ist längst eine multikulturelle Metropole, auch wenn es die Politik nicht wahrhaben will', *Die Zeit*, No. 33: p. 6.

Gaserow, V. and Floss, H. (1994) 'Kicken ohne Kopftuch und Koran', *Zeitmagazin*, No. 46: pp. 50-57.

Gebauer, G. and Wulf, C. (eds) (1993) *Praxis und Ästhetik, Neue Perspektiven im Denken Pierre Bourdieus*. Frankfurt: Suhrkamp.

Gehrmann, S. (1979) 'Der F.C. Schalke 04', in W. Hopf (ed) *Fußball; Soziologie und Sozialgeschichte einer populären Sportart*. Bensheim: päd-extra, pp. 117-130

Gehrmann, S. (forthcoming) *Fußball im Ruhrgebiet— Zur Bedeutung einer populären Sportart für die Identitätsfindung einer Region*.

Gehrmann, S. (1988) *Fußball-Vereine-Politik, Zur Sportgeschichte des Reviers 1900-1940*. Essen: Bouvier.

Glettler, M. (1970) *Sokol und Arbeiterturnvereine der Wiener Tschechen, Zur Entwicklungsgeschichte der nationalen Bewegung in beiden Organisationen*. München and Wien: Oldenbourg.

Godin, S. (1991) *La gymnastique a Haguenau au temps du Reichsland (1871-1914), Luttes ideologiques et enjeux politiques*. M.A. thesis, Straßburg.

Gordon, M. M. (1964) *Assimilation in American life: The role of race, religion and national origin*. New York: Oxford University Press.

Habermas, J. (1993) 'Das deutsche Sonderbewußtsein regeneriert sich von Stunde zu Stunde', *Frankfurter Rundschau*, 12.6, p. ZB3.

Heckmann, F. (1985) 'Sport und die gesellschaftliche Integration von Minderheiten', in H. Bammel and H. Becker (eds) *Sport und ausländische Mitbürger, Fachtagung der Friedrich-Ebert-Stiftung vom 9.-11. November 1984*. Bonn: Deutscher Sportbund, pp. 21-33.

Hroch, M. (1968) *Die Vorkämpfer der nationalen Bewegung bei den kleinen Völkern Europas. Eine vergleichende Analyse zur gesellschaftlichen Schichtung der patriotischen Gruppen*. Prag.

König, H.-J. (1989) 'Die Anfänge der jüdischen Turn- und Sportbewegung', *Stadion*, No. 15, pp. 9-28.

Klessmann, C. (1984) 'Nationalitäten im deutschen Nationalstaat', in D. Lange-wiesche (ed) *Ploetz, Das deutsche Kaiserreich 1867 and 71 bis 1918*. Freiburg and Würzburg: Ploetz, pp. 127-138.

Klessmann, C. (1978) *Polnische Bergarbeiter im Ruhrgebiet, Soziale Integration und nationale Subkultur einer Minderheit in der deutschen Industriegesellschaft*. Göttingen: Vandenhoeck and Ruprecht.

Krüger, M. (1993) *Einführung in die Geschichte der Leibeserziehung und des Sports, Teil 2: Leibeserziehung im 19. Jahrhundert, Turnen fürs Vaterland*. Schorndorf: Hofmann.

Krüger-Potratz, M. (1991) *Anderssein gab es nicht, Ausländer und Minderheiten in der DDR*. Münster and New York: Waxmann.

Lepsius, R. M. (1966) *Extremer Nationalismus. Strukturbedingungen vor der nationalsozialistischen Machtergreifung*. Stuttgart: Kohlhammer.

Nipperdey, T. (1990) *Deutsche Geschichte 1866-1918. Bd. I, Arbeitswelt und Bürgergeist*. München: C. H. Beck.

Oenning, R. K. (1991) *"Du da mitti polnischen Farben...."*, *Sozialisationserfahrungen von Polen im Ruhrgebiet 1918 bis 1939*. Münster and New York: Waxmann.

Oschlies, W. (1991) *Die Sorben — Slawisches Volk im Osten Deutschlands* (2nd Edition). Bonn-Bad Godesberg: Friedrich-Ebert-Stiftung.

Plessner, H. (1985) 'Die verspätete Nation, über die politische Verführbarkeit bürgerlichen Geistes', in H. Plessner *Gesammelte Schriften* (4th Edition). Frankfurt: Suhrkamp, pp. 7-223.

Pooley, J. C. (1972) 'Ethnic soccer clubs in Milwaukee: A study in assimilation', in M. M. Hart (ed) *Sport in the Socio-Cultural Process*. Dubuque: Wm. C. Brown Co., pp. 328-344.

Roman-Schüssler, D. and Schwarz, T. (1985) *Türkische Sportler in Berlin zwischen Integration und Segregation.* Berlin: Ausländerbeauftragter der Stadt Berlin.

Sauer, W. (1973) 'Das Problem des deutschen Nationalstaates', in H.-U. Wehler (ed) *Moderne Deutsche Sozialgeschichte* (4th Edition). Köln: Kiepenheuer and Witsch, pp. 407-436.

Schäuble, W. Die gesellschaftspolitische Bedeutung des Sports, Speech on the occasion of the 21st Richterwoche des Bundessozialgerichts on 17 October 1989 in Kassel. Unpublished manuscript.

Schwarz, T. (1987) 'Eigenorganisierter Ausländersport am Beispiel türkischer Sportvereine in Berlin (West)', *Forum, Zeitschrift für Ausländerfragen und Kultur*, Vol. 10, No. 1: pp. 27-38.

Stefanski, V. M. (1988) 'Zum Vergleich der historischen und der aktuellen Arbeitsmigration: "Ruhrpolen" um die Jahrhundertwende-"Gastarbeiter" heute', *Tagungsprotokolle der Evg. Akademie Iserlohn*, pp. 68-87.

Tenfelde, K. (1976) 'Arbeiterschaft, Arbeitsmarkt und Kommunikationsstrukturen im Ruhrgebiet in den 50er Jahren des 19. Jahrhunderts', *Archiv für Sozialgeschichte*, Bd.XVI: pp. 1-60.

Weber-Klüver, K. (1993) '"Neger raus" gegen "Zeugen Yeboahs", Fußball und Rassismus in Deutschland', *Fußball und Rassismus*. Göttingen: Die Werkstatt, pp. 25-68.

Wehler, H.-U. (1973) 'Die Polen im Ruhrgebiet bis 1918', in H.-U. Wehler (ed) *Moderne Deutsche Sozialgeschichte* (4th Edition). Köln: Kiepenheuer and Witsch, pp. 437-455.

Wehler, H.-U. (1978) 'Das "Reichsland" Elsaß-Lothringen von 1870 -1918', in H.-U. Wehler (ed) *Krisenherde des Kaiserreichs 1871 -1918* (2nd Edition). Göttingen: Vandenhoeck and Ruprecht, pp. 23-69.

Wehler, H.-U. (1995) *Deutsche Gesellschaftsgeschichte, 3.Bd., Von der "Deutschen Doppelrevolution" bis zum Beginn des Ersten Weltkriegs.* München: C. H. Beck.

Wicaz, A. (1990) *Serbski Sokol (Der sorbische Sokol)*. Bautzen and Budysin: Ludowe nakladnistwo Domowina.

Zmarzlik, H.-G. (1981) 'Antisemitismus im Deutschen Kaiserreich 1871-1918', in B. Martin and E. Schulin (eds) *Die Juden als Minderheit in der Geschichte.* München: dtv, pp. 249-270.

II

CASE STUDIES ON FOOTBALL, RACISM AND XENOPHOBIA IN SIX EUROPEAN COUNTRIES

FOOTBALL, RACISM AND XENOPHOBIA IN AUSTRIA: "IF YOU LET THEM, THEY BEHAVE LIKE THE MAFIA"

Roman Horak and Matthias Marschik

Introduction

The notion of using sport, and particularly football, as a vehicle for integration is, of course, nothing new — ever since the 1960s its advantages have repeatedly been cited. It is also often noted that integration goes hand in hand with a second footballing phenomenon — the opportunity for upward social mobility.

But playing football 'together' is not an integrative measure in its own right, and neither lessens the need for governments to send the right political signals nor replaces general mechanisms of social integration. However, it may possibly serve as a model at the individual level, despite — or perhaps precisely because of — the fact that only a restricted group can participate. This is a group with a shared interest, namely football, and a common aim, that of winning. The following arguments appear to suggest that football offers a positive model for the integration of minorities:

- Football possesses a high integrative capacity because the rules on which it is based are the same, or virtually the same, all over the world.

- As football is highly popular almost everywhere, it rapidly creates a climate of understanding, friendship and fellow feeling.

- Football can be played in a largely non-verbal context, and thus enables language barriers to be easily overcome (Abel, 1984).

- As in all team sports, the participants are united by a common idea and aim. Since success depends on teamwork, all the players are of equal status. The maintenance of social and cultural barriers harms the entire team and

41

diminishes the chances of success. A new player must immediately be slotted in the team, and is thus instantly in direct contact with his teammates.

- Football promotes team spirit not just during the game itself, but through the shared experiences of victory and defeat.

- Players are judged less according to their social and cultural origins and status than in terms of their performance and contribution to that of the team as a whole.

- Football is an activity pursued by relatively small groups, and is thus conducive to the making of individual contacts before, during and after the game and training sessions.

- A good manager plays an integrative role, provides leadership, and can resolve conflicts.

- Football attracts relatively large attendances. It can have an impact beyond the team, by changing spectators' attitudes and, through the mass media, influencing others with an interest in the game.

- Finally, particularly for young players belonging to the main immigrant communities, football can be a help in obtaining a residence permit and, at a later stage, citizenship.

The ten points mentioned above may exemplify and support the integration-approach too optimistically, since quite opposite characteristics could be enumerated: for example that football as a spectator sport evokes nationalism, enforces racism, jingoism and violence — especially if one looks at the presentation in the media, particularly the tabloids (Blain, Boyle and O'Donnell, 1993). We leave it to the imagination of the reader to find his or her 'other ten arguments' stressing the dark sides of football in relation to the issues at stake here.

This chapter, however, will focus on the question of whether there is such a thing as integration of minority ethnic groups in Austrian football, and will refer to the findings of an empirical study we undertook in the early 1990s (Horak and Marschik, 1995). We then will confront this presentation through a discussion of arguments elaborated in a recently published essay on racism and football (also based on empirical data) by the sociologist Günter Lesny (1995).

Racism in Austrian society: a few introductory remarks on its past and present

It cannot be denied that there is a strong tradition of racism and xenophobia to be detected in Austrian society. This can partly be explained by the historical weakness of the liberal bourgeoisie since the end of the last century. With the emergence of mass society and a modern party system at the turn of the century, a populist Christian Conservative Party (as opposed to the Social Democrats, and — more explicitly — various German nationalist parties) did not hestitate to refer to the ever present anti-Semitic prejudices in its party policies.

Anti-Semitism as one strand of racism in the Second Republic[1] seemed to have more or less disappeared — the ideology of the postwar years being basically one of democratic consensus and ecomomic reconstruction, though on several occasions it became obvious that it was still present after the holocaust. However, new forms of racism found their target in the representatives of the immigrant groups, when in the 1960s and particularly in the 1970s cheap labour from Yugoslavia (and later Turkey) was introduced to the country's economy.

But it was not until the mid-1980s that the Freedom Party (*Freiheitliche Partei*), which was then taken over and turned into an overtly racist movement by its new leader Jörg Haider, began to increase its electorate to almost 25%, thus changing the political climate in Austria. Xenophobia and racism became more visible and ruthless, though it can be doubted if they have increased. The collapse of the Soviet Union and the Eastern bloc and, particularly, the desintegration of the former Yugoslavia followed by the civil war in Bosnia, with thousands of refugees coming to Austria, has further worsened the situation. On the one hand, we find racist violence as it was expressed through the series of letterbombs in late 1993 and the killing of four Roma[2] in the province of Burgenland in 1995; on the other, a dramatic change in the country's immigration policies. Both can be explained only against the background of the emergence of this 'New Right'.

Since the end of the 1980s the Austrian government — through its Social Democratic Minister of Interior Affairs — has introduced a range of restrictive and discriminatory measures relating to its policy towards migrants, the overall thrust of which has been to obstruct the new arrivals of migrants or to create obstacles for those 'foreigners' who already have settled in Austria. These defensive policies were introduced step by step to restrict the large inflow of East Europeans, due to liberalized border controls in the Eastern bloc.

In a first phase, visa requirements were imposed in 1989 on Bulgarians, and a year later for Turkish and Rumanian citizens. At the same time the Austrian military began patroling the Austrian-Hungarian border to reduce the number of illegal immigrants. These non-legislative measures were soon to be followed by a large-scale reform of the laws regarding asylum seekers and 'foreigners', in general.

The new asylum law of 1991 has created new grounds for the refusal of asylum requests, such as introducing the notion of "safe third country" (according to this criterion, applications for asylum are regarded as manifestly unfounded if the asylum seeker has not travelled directly into Austria but via one or more transit countries), making access to asylum procedures extremely difficult.

An aggravation of the situation for 'foreigners' who had already settled in Austria and who entered the country without a visa or with a touristvisa, was the result of the *"Aliens Act" (Fremdengesetz)* of 1 January 1993. These people were forced to leave the country and apply for a visa outside Austrian borders as they were now considered to be residing illegally. Another violation of the right of liberty of migrants is the extension (from 2 to 6 months) of the maximum period that 'foreigners', pending consideration of their claim, may be detained.

The aim of the *"law concerning the stay of foreigners" (Aufenthaltsgesetz)* of 1 July, 1993 aimed to regulate the "stay of, and create a basis for the restriction of an uncontrollable inflow of foreigners". In order to establish residence in Austria, migrants are now in need of a special permit (*Aufenthaltsgenehmigung*) for which s/he must apply outside Austrian borders, which enables the responsible authorities to select and control the country of origins of incoming migrants. An annual quota of the maximum number of permits to be granted is fixed by the Austrian government. The purpose of this quota is to ensure that the development of the labour market and the security and safety of the Austrian population is not in jeopardy, and to take into account the capacity of the avaible accommodation, and the number of 'foreigners' and asylum seekers already living in Austria. In this process the government is entitled to select and favour special groups of migrants, according to educational standards, age and knowledge or experience in certain economic sectors. This provision not only leads to the creation of an image of an 'ideal immigrant', but aggravates the phenomenon known as 'brain-drain', where highly skilled workers emigrate very much to the disadvantage of the economic development of their home country.

Another policy which reveals that this law has been conceived solely for the purpose of satisfying the needs of the Austrian society is the following provision: in case of the shortage of employees (for example in the catering trade during the summer months), surplus workers can be employed for a period of six months, only to then be dismissed again.

These measures, the denial of a work permit if certain criteria are not fullfilled and the employment of migrants for limited periods, led and leads to an increase in both illegal immigration and illegal employment.

A provision which aggravates not only the position of incoming 'foreigners', but those who have already settled in Austria, is the regulation whereby a 'foreigner' has no right to remain if s/he is without accommodation of a "certain local standard", which according to the Austrian law means that s/he must occupy at least $10m^2$ living space. The fact that this law is not based on integration but on exclusion of immigrants is furthermore reflected in the limited duration periods of the residence permits. Only after five years does the 'foreigner' have an unlimited right to residence, whilst until the end of this period s/he is obliged to apply for an extension every six months. Obviously, his or her stay is therefore in constant jeopardy, with the risk every six months of being expelled. This seriously undermines all efforts for integration.

After this short overview, one comes to the sad conclusion that Austria has, like other European countries, adopted a 'fortress mentality', trying to limit the number of immigrants by restrictive measures, and has not developed adequate responses to the global phenomenon of immigration and integration of migrants.

Football, racism and the hope for integration

Football in Austria: a short introduction

All over Europe supraregional leagues were established after the First World War, but not in Austria. During the monarchy, between the two World Wars and until the late 1940s Viennese champions were automatically considered champions of Austria. Vienna's hegemonic aspirations were not primarily directed towards the provinces but rather towards Prague and Budapest. Even the various football players, who played football as emigrants all over Europe and the USA in the 1920s and 1930s, were in high demand as the representatives of the "Vienna School of Football".

In the season of 1949/1950 a nationwide Austrian championship was created, but the Austrian championships remained a Viennese league with provincial participation until the mid-1960s. The Austrian football identity remained a purely Viennese matter. In 1964/65 a club from the provinces won the Austrian championship for the first time. It was the end of Viennese hegemony, as it was to be seen paradigmatically in the changes in Viennese football culture. What disappeared in the 1960s was the social base of the (sub)-urban Viennese football culture, and economic changes brought about another consequence: the clubs asked higher sums for their Austrian players, which in turn led to an increased number of 'foreign' players working for Austrian clubs.

From the 1930s to the 1960s, Austrian football was characterised by a strong hegemony of Viennese clubs and, within it, by the confrontations of the two major Viennese clubs Austria and Rapid, which stood for the Jewish liberal urban element on the one hand and the suburban proletarian element on the other. So it was obvious that only a Viennese identity could develop in football. From the late 1960s to the late 1980s the situation was characterised by a competition between Viennese and provincial clubs to dominate Austrian football (Horak, 1994).

During those 25 years Austria's football culture was characterised by a three-sided battle between Rapid, Austria and the respective leader of the provincial teams. This was fought not only on the football field, but also among the spectators regarding support of the clubs of the respective towns. To the traditional conflict between Rapid and Austria, another one was added on the levels of anti-metropolitan and anti-provincial attitudes. This confrontation took place primarily among the spectators and supporters. Although these confrontations alone did not lead to an Austrian identity in football, it did create an awareness of Austria since football was now regarded as a nationwide phenomenon.

From the beginning of the 1990s it has been clear that there was another change to be seen in Austria's football culture. It seems as if the 1990s are to be characterised by a confrontation of Austrian against foreign clubs. The — meanwhile well-established — Austrian national identity will increasingly be seen in the European context in the next few years. Whether, in addition to that, a European identity of football develops, remains to be seen. But in this respect it is interesting to see that one identity does not replace, but rather complements another one. So the rivalry between the two major Viennese clubs still exists, just like the rivalry between Vienna and the provinces. Identity construction in football is becoming more and more complex and thus the world of football fans is becoming more complex, even in Austria.

'Foreigners' in Football: between integration and xenophobia

The June 1992 microcensus found 316,969 'foreigners' resident in Vienna. Of this total, 129,757 were from former Yugoslavia and 51,697 from Turkey. Some 28,167 'foreign' inhabitants of Vienna are aged between 10 and 19 years, and they account for a considerable proportion of the 'foreign' footballers playing in Austria in the first teams, and particularly in the youth teams. The degree of acceptance encountered by this group of young people, who live in two worlds — that of "their origins and those of their families" and that of "training, leisure and peers" in the host country (Hausser, 1987: p. 507) — should be a particularly good indicator for measuring the potential integrative power of football, despite the racist attitudes among spectators that have attracted so much comment (Horak, 1991). Williams (1991: p. 147) speaks of a "quasi-institutional racism" in (professional) football, which is however increasingly being countered by anti-racist initiatives on the part of fans.

As early as 1900, a number of 'foreign' players were already active in Viennese football, and not long afterwards the first Viennese players went abroad (Schwind, 1994: pp. 24). These international transfers multiplied in the 1920s, when many other European countries followed Austria in introducing professionalism. Particularly in the 1930s, many Austrians played abroad, notably in France and Switzerland, but also in Czechoslovakia, Poland and Malta (Lafranchi, 1991). Mostly, these were footballers who were not good enough for the top teams. They could hardly earn enough from the game to survive, and mass unemployment meant that they had even worse prospects in their mainstream occupations. They could make a living by playing abroad — a clear parallel to today's football nomads.

There was a renewed wave of emigration after the 1954 World Cup, in which Austria came third. Almost 20 Austrian players left the country. As in pre-war days, their destinations were France and Switzerland. From 1956 onwards there were also some 'foreign' players in Austria, and in the early 1960s their numbers in the First Division leapt. Since then, they have remained roughly stable (Langisch, 1979; Marschik, 1994). What changed was the influx of migrant workers, who have gained an increasingly strong foothold in the lower divisions, while their children now play for the youth squads (Popp, 1987). At present, there are 26 clubs in the Austrian League (First and Second Divisions), with a total of 84 'foreign' players on their books. Twelve of these 26 clubs employ more than the three 'foreigners' permitted as players and substitutes, while only four clubs have less than three 'foreigners', and only one has none at all.

To form a picture of the reality of integration in football, we surveyed a total of 80 players, managers and officials of Viennese football clubs at all levels, from the Premier League down to the bottom divisions. Both 'native' and 'foreign' players were interviewed. This distinction is by no means obvious, but corresponds to the actual situation in the clubs, and to the players' own perceptions. All those not naming German as their mother tongue were classed as 'foreign' players; this group thus comprises not only 'foreigners' but also Austrian citizens for whom German is a second language (even if Austrian born). Consequently the term 'native' refers to all those whose first language is German. The use of the terms 'native' and 'foreign' in the following discussion is intended as no more than a reflection of the status quo.

A first, significant result of the study was that naturalization made no difference to the fact that the person concerned was viewed by both sides as a 'foreigner'. In fact, players faced the same integration problems whether or not they succeeded in obtaining Austrian citizenship, and naturalization had scant effect on their situation. Some 40 percent of the 'foreign' players in the sample were of Turkish origin, and an equal number came from former Yugoslavia. Half were already Austrian citizens. The managers and officials were all native Austrians.

Even on initial inspection, the data yields surprising results. With one exception, all respondents — 'Austrians', 'foreigners' and managers — rated the atmosphere in their teams as good. Relationships between 'native' and 'foreign' players were also characterised as good, and two-thirds of the sample described them as not being in need of improvement. In the responses to the question about possible discrimination by managers, there was virtual unanimity that, at least in the players' own teams, this did not exist. Only one 'foreign' player felt himself to be discriminated against as a result of his nationality. By contrast, the majority of the 'foreign' players found their 'native' teammates and managers helpful, both in dealing with practical problems (accommodation, employment and citizenship) and in terms of everyday tolerance (e.g. of language difficulties).

Communication difficulties owing to language barriers were among the few problems mentioned as hindrances to the 'multicultural' community of the football club. Here, the responses of 'native' players conformed to those of 'foreign' counterparts; the 'foreigners' said that they were given help with language problems. However, it is noteworthy that the 'foreigners' all judged the verbal interaction to be sufficient while the 'locals' were considerably more critical, taking the view that, if not on the pitch then beyond it, the communication problems did constitute a significant obstacle to relationships.

In many cases, encounters with the 'foreign' players were limited to football — to training and competitive matches. Some three-quarters of the 'native' players had either no dealings with other players beyond the sport itself, or had such contacts only with other Austrians — this being partly attributed to a perceived lack of interest on the part of the 'foreign' players. However, the Austrians' assessment did not entirely match the responses of the 'foreigners', only some 20 percent of whom wished to keep their private life separate from those of teammates. Over 60 percent of the 'foreigners' would have preferred more social contacts, but were either unable to put this across or felt themselves to be discriminated against by the 'natives'. Only one 'foreigner' in ten had a 'native' teammate as a friend.

The majority of the 'natives', for their part, believed that the 'foreigners' preferred to keep their distance. Yet a number of 'native' players had already noticed that there was something amiss with their relationships with the 'foreigners', and saw themselves as partly responsible. This was sometimes because they felt that 'foreigners' did not go out of their way to break the ice, or were unable to express their wish for closer companionship. About one player in ten said that he had been approached by 'foreign' players about mutual leisure activities but had not known how to react.

The results of the interviews with footballers thus yield conflicting conclusions which nevertheless, at least at first sight, appear to indicate that sport is a workable basis for integration processes. This must, however, be revised in the light of statements made prior to and after the interviews, which clearly showed that the responses in the interview situation were largely distorted in the direction of social acceptability and bore little relation to reality. The findings must thus be modified to take account of these discrepancies, and of first-hand impressions gained when visiting the clubs.

In Austria as elsewhere, 'foreigners' are evidently a highly explosive and emotionally charged topic, which scarcely allows of a detached perspective. Both sides — the 'native' and 'foreign' players — felt themselves to be exposed to social pressures in the shape of the interview situation and the interviewer. These pressures often left their mark in responses intended to conform with what were believed to be the (politically) correct answers.

The same manager who spoke of his club as "one big family" during the interview said afterwards that he had "knocked the foreigners into shape", and that he knew "how to handle them". He continued: "You have to make sure that the foreigners don't take over the club. If you let them, they behave like the Mafia". Naturally, distinctions are drawn between the various nationalities: "For instance, Czechs are easy to look after, whereas you have nothing but trouble with Yugoslavs and Turks". A player who earlier had praised the good team spirit, afterwards referred to the "stinking, untidy foreigners" who "take Austrians' jobs and homes". If anything, the 'foreign' players had an even stronger tendency than the Austrian footballers and managers to give socially adjusted responses. Only after the interviews did they begin to speak freely about their difficulties in getting to know indigenous players, about the prejudices they encountered, and discrimination during training and matches.

The strains between 'native' and 'foreign' players in the youth teams are unquestionably less severe, though the same tendency towards socially acceptable responses was apparent. Not only are language barriers clearly less of a problem but the young people also cope better with the situation. The small clubs are also particularly aware that, without the 'foreign' players, they would have to scrap their youth schemes. This results in a (more or less enforced) mutual tolerance.

However, the managers also made extremely negative comments about the 'foreigners' in the youth teams. In the first place, they are unhappy about the high proportion of 'foreign' children which — particularly in the youth teams in the lower divisions — can be as high as 90 percent. This gives rise to difficulties with Austrian parents, who do not wish to send their children to such clubs, thus exacerbating the situation. However, managers' attitudes are also associated with the Austrian football rules, under which there are special arrangements for youth teams, while the "foreigners clause", permitting the selection of only two or three 'foreign'players, is applied to the first teams.

The observed discrepancies in the responses themselves provide clear evidence of movement in attitudes to the "immigrant problem" in (and outside) football clubs. This is certainly a consequence of the direct contact and the common aim, which tend to erode prejudices. However, the fact that a debate has been set in motion tells us nothing about the course it will take. It is thus worth noting the problems that players, managers and officials repeatedly identify as the key issues:

• Independently of each other, and without prompting, both the managers and the 'native' players named a ratio of 70:30 of Austrians to 'foreigners' as desirable. Any share of 'foreigners' in excess of this percentage would inevitably, they felt, lead to conflicts.

- The language barrier was repeatedly named by the 'natives' as the greatest obstacle to social contacts outside the game. However, in this respect football at least in part lives up to its reputation as an integrative mechanism, as language problems play a subordinate role on the pitch.

- The 'foreign' players, for their part, highlighted the role of the manager as offering scope for improvement. They would like him not just to foster team spirit, but also to promote closer contacts outside the game, and to help the 'foreigners' deal with their specific problems (work, accommodation and citizenship).

Surprisingly, and in contrast to the findings in other European countries (Dunning, 1993; Penttilà and Olin, 1994), neither the interviews nor the subsequent conversations revealed significant differences between the 'foreign' stars of the League teams and the 'foreigners' who are accepted on sufferance in the lower divisions. The stars with their high price tags often face the same problems as the 'foreigners' in the lower reaches of the game, or indeed the youth scheme players — second- or even third-generation immigrants who start their careers in Austrian youth teams.

Racism in Austrian football

In addition to the presentation of our own findings, we would like to offer here a brief but critical account of an essay that appeared in Austria last year entitled, "Hostility towards Foreigners (*Ausländerfeindlichkeit*) and Racism in Austrian Football" (Lesny, 1995). A questionnaire was sent out by the Austrian Football Federation to the clubs of the first two divisions (26 clubs altogether) and to the Austrian players specifically. The response was as follows. Seven clubs returned a total of 69 questionnaires for a return rate of around 16% of the approximately 430 players in question. The survey concentrated above all on the players' personal experiences with, and attitudes towards, their 'foreign' colleagues. The study assumed that, given the competitive nature of the relationship between players, the attitude of the 'natives' towards the international players would emerge from the response to the survey as being rather one of rejection. The initial questions referred first and foremost to the general attitude towards the international players, to the "mercenaries". The majority of those surveyed, over 80%, viewed a ceiling on the number of 'foreign' players positively, though their reasons differed greatly. Approximately 40% felt that too many 'foreigners' would hinder the development of home-grown talent. Some 25% were of the opinion that a lifting of the restrictions on 'foreigners' would, in the end, lead to the demise of "Austrian Football"as such. Approximately half maintained that having 'foreign'players in the key positions of the club line-up was disadvantageous to Austria's national side.

All things considered, the evaluation of the 'foreign'players was predominately positive. Only 35% of those surveyed found that the naturalization of 'foreign'players proceeded too quickly (though taken in comparison to other sports, particularly ice hockey, the practice does not appear to be so frequent in Austrian football). Almost all granted that there were higher expectations of 'foreign'players than of local players; more than half held this view to be reasonable on the grounds that one would otherwise get by without the 'foreigners'. 'Foreign'coaches were judged rather more severely: 40% agreed with the statement that 'foreign'coaches showed preferential treatment to international players, a further 20% evaded the question by choosing to answer with "don't know". As far as contact with the 'foreign'players was concerned, the attitude of rejection was rather more obvious: only 13% had regular contact with their 'foreign'counterparts; half spoke of occasional contact; and the remaining some 35% had no contact whatsoever with the internationals in their own clubs. The 'foreign'players' inadequate command of the language was found to be at fault where the lack of contact between players was concerned. It was considered the responsibility of the 'foreigners' to amend the situation. However, this was held to be equally true of the clubs insofar as arrangements with regard to language courses were concerned. The 'foreign'players were nonetheless expected to make a signifigant contribution towards their integration through the acquisition of the German language. When questioned as to their own contributions towards improving the situation, a significant number of the Austrian players surveyed refused to reply; some 40% felt that, if at all, any activity directed towards relieving the situation should take place at an administrative level and/or on a personal, one to one, basis.

A further series of questions dealt with the expectations the players may have had in regard to the prospect of going to play in a 'foreign'country. Only 40% were not concerned about the possibility of discrimination. Some 50% were undecided.

As to acts of racism within Austrian football *per se*, four players indicated having been witness to a situation wherein a player was not signed due to his race, religion or place of origin, whereas some 70% considered such action to be inconceivable. With regard to racist conduct among the spectators, only 40% of the players reported having been witness to racist attacks on, or abuse of, 'foreign'players — the majority having added that they had not been in a position to do anything against such incidents when they occurred. Only 16% indicated having already noticed right-wing extremist agitation among the their club supporters whereas only half believed there was no chance of right-wing extremism spreading among their club supporters. Here the assessment of the fans is quite ambiguous: on the one hand they are looked upon as being susceptible to right-wing influence and on the other hand as being "good lads" as far as their actual conduct is concerned.

As to concrete possibilities for improvement, verbal willingness to act is relatively high. Three quarters of the players surveyed declared that they would be willing, in principle, to work together as players against racism and hostility towards 'foreigners', though the pressure of the demands of society must have had a considerable impact on this high percentage of consent. Some 6% nonetheless would refuse to participate in such positive action. Only half those questioned indicated having ever heard of players taking action against hostility towards 'foreigners', as opposed to the three quarters who described such action as being important and right, declaring their willingness to participate; 60% not only supported the hypothetical proposition that players go to schools in order to discourage racism and hostility to 'foreigners', but also expressed their willingness to do so.

The author of the essay, Günter Lesny, contrasted his results with an interview with a 'foreign'player in Austria and an analysis of the press coverage this issue has received. The interview brought to light long known prejudices against 'foreign'players and stressed above all the extent to which the judgement of 'foreigners' depends on their performance: the better he plays, according to the player interviewed, the better the relationship with his fellow players and so the less intense the hostility towards him, at least from the supporters of the team he is playing for.

The analysis of the media unearthed considerable differences between the individual news sources. It did however yield two basic conclusions: firstly, the problem has not been discussed at adequate length, having rather been played down and/or treated vaguely; and when a reference does occur it is rarely to be found in the sports section. Secondly, in the media generally, those on the receiving end are rarely given voice.

On the strength of his investigations, Günter Lesny comes to a positive conclusion overall: one we feel is too positive. Above all, the willingness of players to actively participate in a campaign against hostility towards 'foreigners' is given an inordinate value. In comparison with our own study, two parallels can be drawn: firstly, placing responsibility for initiating change on the shoulders of the 'foreign' players themselves, the clubs and the coaches; secondly, the enormous pressure created by the demands of society as this clearly predominates the question.

A third parallel can be drawn, albeit indirectly, and that is the complete disregard for that ever-present 'quiet racism' manifest throughout the stadium — though never truly vociferous, that is not now and again reduced to violence, nor that finds expression in demonstrations of disapproval — that continues uninterruptedly in private conversations before, during and after the game.

Conclusion

There is no doubt that the sport of football constitutes a highly complex system. In the Austrian context, and we assume not just here, it reflects the short-comings and xenophobic and racist traditions and attitudes of society. The data and findings discussed in this essay suggest that football does not provide an example of successful integration, as the problems are probably identical with those of society at large. The sole contribution that football can make is in initiating social contacts, which are otherwise frequently absent. The contra–dictory results of both surveys show that, for all concerned, uncertainty has replaced static prejudices. What follows this uncertainty will depend on factors external to football.

Notes

[1] "Second Republic" is a term widely used within Austrian society. It refers to the new democratic structure of the country after the liberation from Nazi rule in 1945. It is to be distinguished from the "First Republic", which lasted from 1918 to 1933.

[2] On February 5, 1995, four members of the Roma community of the small town of Oberwart were found dead at a crossing close to the Roma settlement at Oberwart. The bombing was obviously a racist attack by right-wing extremists, although up to April 1996 the murderers have not been found by police.

References

Abel, T. (1984) *Ausländer und Sport*. Köln: Pahl-Rugenstein.

Blain, N., Boyle, R. and O'Donnell, H. (1993) *Sport and National Identity in the European Media*. Leicester: Leicester University Press.

Bröskamp, B. (1994) *Körperliche Fremdheit*. Berlin: Argument.

Dunning, E. (1994) 'Sport and European Integration', Paper presented at the conference *'Macht und Ohnmacht in Europa'*, Vienna, May.

Flaschberger, L. and Supper, A. (1991) *Ausländerbeschäftigung 1991* (ed. Ministry of Social Affairs). Vienna.

Hausser, K. (1987) *Zum Identitätskonzept in der Ausländerforschung. Ausländerarbeit und Integrationsforschung*. Munich: DJI.

Horak, R. (1991) 'Things Change: Trends in Austrian Football Hooliganism', *The Sociological Review*, Vol. 39, No. 3.

Horak, R. (1994) 'Austrification as modernization: changes in Viennese football culture, in R. Giulianotti and J. Williams (eds) *Game without Frontiers: Football, identity and modernity*. Aldershot: Arena/Ashgate Publishing Ltd.

Horak, R. and Marschik, M. (1995) *Vom Erlebnis zur Wahrnehmung. Der Wiener Fußball und seine Zuschauer 1945– 1990*. Vienna: Turik and Kant.

Lanfranchi, P. (1991) 'Fußball in Europa. Die Entwicklung eines internationalen Netzwerkes' in R. Horak and W. Reiter (eds) *Die Kanten des runden Leders*. Vienna: Promedia.

Langisch, K. (1979) *75 Jahre ÖFB. Eine Dokumentation des Österreichischen Fußballbundes*. Vienna: ÖFB.

Leitner, H. (1983) *Gastarbeiter in der städtischen Gesellschaft. Segregation, Integration und Assimilation von Arbeitsmigranten am Beispiel jugoslawischer Gastarbeiter*. Frankfurt/New York: Campus.

Lesny, G. (1995) 'Ausländerfeindlichkeit und Rassismus im österreichischen Fußball', *Österreichische Zeitschrift für Soziologie*, Vol. 20, No. 3.

Lindner, R. (1983) 'Von sportsmen und einfachen Leuten. Zur Sozialgeschichte des Fußballsports', in R. Lindner (ed) *Der Satz 'Der Ball ist rund' hat eine gewisse philosophische Tiefe. Sport, Kultur, Zivilisation*. Berlin: Transit.

Marschik, M. (1994) 'Foreign Players in Football. Celebrated stars — tolerated workers', Paper presented at the *XIIIth World Congress of Sociology*. Bielefeld, July.

Natter, E. and Reinprecht, Ch. (1992) *Achtung Sozialstaat*. Vienna: Europaverlag.

Penttilä, M. and Olin, K. (1994) 'Globalization, Ethnoscapes and Social Integration'. Paper presented at the *XIIIth World Congress of Sociology*. Bielefeld, July.

Popp, F. (1987) *Sozialisations- und Akkulturationswidersprüche ausländischer Kinder und Jugendlicher in Österreich*. (Ph.D. thesis) Vienna.

Schidrowitz, L. (1954) *Geschichte des Fußballsports in Österreich*. Vienna-Wels-Frankfurt/Main: Traunau.

Schwind, K.H. (1994) *Geschichten aus einem Fußball-Jahrhundert*. Vienna: Überreuter.

Weber-Klüver, K. (1993) '"Neger raus" gegen "Zeugen Yeboahs", Fußball und Rassismus in Deutschland', in *Fußball und Rassismus*. Göttingen: Die Werkstatt, pp. 25-68.

Weiß, O. and Norden, G. (1994) 'Unter'm Sindelar hätt's das nicht gegeben', in. J. Skocek and W. Weisgram (eds) *Im Inneren des Balles*. Vienna-Stuttgart-Kiel: hpt.

Williams, J. (1991) 'Lick my boots. Rassismus im englischen Fußball', in R. Horak and W. Reiter (eds) *Die Kanten des runden Leders*. Vienna: Promedia.

FOOTBALL, RACISM AND XENOPHOBIA IN BELGIUM: RACIST DISCRIMINATION AND ANTI-RACIST RESPONSES

Bart Vanreusel

Introduction

Since the foundation of the independent Belgian state in 1830, Belgium has continually been confronted with conflicts between different population groups. The conflict between the Dutch-speaking Flemish and the French-speaking Walloons, with its historical, social, cultural and economic — and therefore political — background, has constantly dominated the development of Belgian society. Political reforms to create and guarantee a certain amount of autonomy for these two population groups have to date succeeded in maintaining a balance within the bicultural Belgium.

Today, however, in common with all other Western European nations, Belgium has changed within a few decades from a bicultural to a multicultural society. Whilst the original tension between two population groups was largely kept under control by democratic political means, new tensions and challenges are now being created by this rapid development towards a multicultural society.

These new tensions are focused on a polarisation between the indigenous and the minority ethnic groups, i.e. between Belgians and (im)migrants. A watertight definition of the terms "indigenous" and "non-indigenous" does not exist. Both concepts form part of a permanent psycho-social process of identity-formation and identity-allocation. It remains unclear how long individual migrant or minority ethnic groups continue to be seen as 'foreigners', and when and how they become 'indigenous'. In Belgium, even 'third-generation (im)migrants', with Belgian nationality, are still often regarded as 'foreigners'. These concepts should therefore be interpreted as changeable processes, both in the perspective of the life of the individual and in the longer perspective of the changing identity of population groups over generations.

Forms of discrimination based on ethnicity or geographical origin are the major elements in this tension between majority and minority ethnic groups in an increasingly multicultural society.

Sport as a very widespread form of popular culture has proved to be an area in which various forms of racist discrimination occur (Jarvie, 1991; Phillips, 1993; Beaujon, 1988). This issue has already been extensively studied with a strong focus on the relationship between blacks and whites in the United States (Nixon and Frey, 1996; Rees, 1991). Less attention has to date been devoted to sport and racist discrimination in Western Europe. In tandem with the rapid development of multicultural societies in the majority of Western European countries, however, attention there is also increasingly being devoted to racist discrimination in sport as a major form of popular culture. At the same time, however, it is pointed out that sport offers significant opportunities to combat racist discrimination and promote the integration of minority groups (Tolleneer *et al.*, 1995). Most Western European countries have initiated campaigns in which sport is used as a vehicle and means for integration and an example for non-discrimination (Knops, 1992). Similar initiatives are also being taken at pan-European level. The European Network of Sport Sciences in Higher Education, an umbrella organisation for institutions of Higher Education offering courses in the field of sport, discussed this issue during the 1995 forum in Bordeaux, and drew the following conclusions:

It is recognised that:

1. Migration, and consequently the need for individual and social integration will be permanent, 'normal' and crucial issues in the new Europe.

2. The development of multicultural societies has to be based on guiding principles of equal rights, non-discrimination and respect for different cultural identities.

3. Young (im)migrants, in particular, very often have to deal with problems of identity and problems of being underprivileged.

4. The concept of integration is difficult and sensitive. Integration policies have to avoid simplified interventionist and assimilationist approaches.

5. Sport, in its different forms and organisational frameworks, has great potential for contributing to a successful integration process.

6. Institutes for Sport Sciences in Higher Education have an important task with regard to the challenges of migration and integration in a changing Europe.

Recommendations:

1. Sport policies at all levels and all organisational frameworks should adopt the principles of equal rights, cultural identity and non-discrimination as basic guidelines.

2. Sports policies at all levels and organisational frameworks should develop affirmative anti-racist responses.

3. Institutes for Sports Sciences in Higher Education should adopt these principles as basic guidelines in their research and educational policies.

4. Institutes for Sport Sciences in Higher Education should develop a vision and a research agenda on the issues of integration, equal rights, cultural identity and non-discrimination. This research agenda has to include theoretical and applied perspectives and is preferably coordinated on a European level.

5. Institutes for Sport Sciences in Higher Education have to develop an educational curriculum for these issues which offer students research-based awareness, knowledge and methodology on the sport and integration issue.

6. Institutes for Sport Sciences in Higher Education have to develop a research-based policy on sport and integration in liaison with sport organisations. (Vanreusel, 1995: pp. 14-15)

The theme "sport and racist discrimination" requires that at least two key issues and questions be addressed. On one hand, sport is an area where racist discrimination occurs. On the other, sport is used as a means of combating racism and promoting the integration of minorities. This chapter seeks to offer a summary of sport in Belgium covering both aspects. Racism in sport is first examined at the various levels of sport, from top-level sport to non-organised, informal sport. Anti-racist initiatives in sport which have been introduced in recent years are then discussed. Before looking at the issue of sport and racism, the chapter first outlines the emergence and development of a multicultural society in Belgium.

Throughout this chapter I use the terms 'foreign' and 'foreigner' to refer to all those people without Belgian nationality, including EU and non-EU citizens. The use of inverted commas is intended to remind the reader of the problematic nature of this term as outlined by Mike Cole in Chapter 2 of this volume.

Immigration and the development of a multicultural society in Belgium

Various waves of immigration have altered the socio-demographic structure of the population in Belgium, particularly since the 1960s. The main forces driving this (im)migration were: an active immigration policy pursued by the Belgian government to attract cheap labour in the 1960s; the socio-economic draw of the Belgian welfare state and the relatively easy immigration procedures.

In 1991, 9.03% of the Belgian population of just under 10 million were 'foreigners' (i.e. persons who do not hold Belgian nationality) (see Table 1): 552,000 of these came from other European Union (EU) Member States, while 353,000 inhabitants had origins in non-EU countries. In 1993, this figure had increased to almost 10%. Table 1 also shows that the geographical distribution of 'foreigners' in Belgium varies widely.

Table 1:   'Foreigners' in Belgium (1991)

Region:	% of population:
Brussels region	28.47
Flemish region	4.49
Walloon region	11.38
Belgium	9.03

Source: National Institute of Statistics (NIS)

The Brussels conurbation has a much greater proportion of 'foreigners' than Flanders or Wallonia. The main countries of origin of (im)migrants in Belgium are Italy, Morocco, France and Turkey. However, substantial shifts have taken place in the proportions between the various nationalities (see Table 2). In the last two decades the number of EU citizens has declined while that of non-EU citizens has increased.

According to forecasts by the National Institute of Statistics (NIS), the number of migrants in Belgium is set to increase significantly over the next decades, though the increase will not spread evenly across the different regions (see Table 3).

Belgium proves to have a higher percentage of 'foreigners' compared with most other Western European countries. Moreover, the (im)migrant population in Belgium is very young. The socio-demographic structure of the Belgian population as a whole, like that in other Western European countries, indicates a pronounced ageing. However, the socio-demographic profile of the (im)migrant

Table 2:   Changes in population of 'foreigners' in Belgium

Origin	1970	1981	1991	% change 1981–1970	1991–1981
Italy	249,490	279,700	240,127	+12	–14
France	86,658	103,512	93,363	+19	–10
Spain	67,534	58,255	51,318	–14	–12
Holland	61,261	66,233	65,294	+8	–1
Morocco	39,294	105,133	142,098	+168	+35
West Germany	22,956	26,756	27,924	+17	+4
Greece	22,354	21,230	20,461	–5	–4
Turkey	20,312	63,587	85,303	+213	+34
Poland	18,370	7,642	4,871	–58	–36
UK	15,340	23,080	23,129	+50	+0
USA	12,676	11,536	11,502	–9	+0
Portugal	7,177	10,482	16,528	+46	+58
Luxembourg	7,018	6,013	4,646	–14	–13
Algeria	6,621	10,796	10,692	+63	–1
Zaire	5,244	8,575	11,828	+64	+38
Tunisia	2,201	6,871	6,316	+212	–8
Other	51,776	69,176	85,458	+34	+24
TOTAL	696,282	878,577	900,858	+26	+3

Source: National Institute of Statistics (NIS)

Table 3:   Estimated proportion of 'foreigners' in Belgium over the next decades

	1988	2000	2010	2020	2030	2040
Brussels region	26.2	33.9	39.3	43.8	47.7	51.2
Flemish region	4.0	5.1	6.0	6.9	7.9	8.8
Walloon region	11.7	13.6	15.2	17.0	18.8	20.7
Total for Belgium	0.7	10.8	12.5	14.3	20.7	17.8

Source: National Institute of Statistics (NIS)

population, however, illustrates a pronounced "young" pattern. Young people, i.e. aged under 18, form the majority of the (im)migrant population, and 22.5% of (im)migrants are aged under 15, compared with only 17.7% of the indigenous Belgian population. These specific socio-demographic features point to the importance of a successful integration process for young people.

There is one striking feature in the perception of (im)migrants in Belgium. The presence of a number of international bodies, such as the European Parliament and the European Commission, NATO and a large number of multinational companies, has a major influence on the number of non-Belgians in the population. These are people who reside permanently in Belgium and who have a specific, professional task. In the debate on immigration, however, reference is rarely if ever made to this category of (usually highly skilled) (im)migrants. The polarisation between Belgians and 'foreigners', between 'indigenous' and 'nonindigenous' citizens, appears to focus on that section of the non-Belgian population which is in a socio-economically and culturally underprivileged position. Racist discrimination is seldom aimed at the socio-economically privileged sections of the migrant population. The problems faced by the (im)migrants who are victims of discrimination occur in two areas which can be summarised as follows:

1. *Problems arising from socio-economic deprivation:*
   Many (im)migrants are confronted with a multi-dimensional deprivation problem, e.g. in the area of housing, employment, education and participation in socio-cultural life. This deprivation forms a serious obstacle to their integration in society.

2. *Problems arising from cultural identity*:
   The migratory flows in Europe have disrupted important traditional contributors to stable identities such as culture, nationality, ethnicity and geographic localisation. Socio-economically disadvantaged migrants are most severely exposed to problems and conflicts concerning their cultural identity. In many cases, though by no means always, migration is accompanied by loss of the migrant's existing cultural identity and difficulty in generating a new one.

Migration will undoubtedly remain a permanent and "normal" feature of a united Europe; by this we mean migration both within and beyond the borders of the European Union.

There is general consensus that the elimination of deprivation, the creation of equal opportunities on a social, cultural, economic, political and legal level, and the maintenance or development of a cultural identity are crucial elements in the process of successful integration of migrants.

The polarisation between Belgians and 'foreigners' has increased in recent years. This is most apparent from the increase in violent attacks and reports of discrimination. A number of factors have contributed to this increase of racism and xenophobia in Belgian society:

* Economic crisis and rising unemployment, which are felt most markedly among the economically weak groups such as migrants. Migration itself is in fact often the result of economic crisis. — The stigmatisation of migrants as a partial cause of economic crisis and unemployment.

* The rise of extreme right-wing parties in the political system, which promote and support racist and xenophobic ideologies.

* The rise of neo-nationalism and new forms of populist national or ethnic consciousness which reject and deny the reality of the multicultural society, and which arose in the first place precisely as a reaction to the growth of that multicultural society.

* The resilience of cultural prejudices towards other cultures and ethnic groups.

There is no doubt that racist discrimination is fed largely by feelings of fear, threat and uncertainty on the part of the discriminating section of the population, which focuses these feelings on that part of the population which suffers the discrimination.

Opposing the increased polarisation between majority ethnic and minority ethnic groups of the population, however, are those processes in Belgian society which aim to promote the integration of 'non-indigenous' groups through initiatives in education, in the political and legal sphere and in the areas of housing and employment.

Major initiatives have been introduced at the level of legislation to combat racist discrimination. In 1990 the "Centre for Equal Opportunities and Opposition to Racism" was set up as the result of a political decision by Parliament and government. This centre has been charged with the task of combating racism and xenophobia. It monitors compliance with the anti-racism legislation dating from 1967, with amendments in the 1980s and 1990s. In 1995 the Complaints Council of this institution handled 627 complaints about racism (Leman, 1996). Only six of these cases, however, concerned a complaint in the context of leisure, including sport. The majority of complaints about racism related to individual persons (77), municipalities (67), the Government's Aliens Department (60) and the police (50). This, however, does not mean that sport is free of racism. We shall argue later in this chapter that sport contains a great deal of hidden racist discrimination which does not come to light through complaints.

Sport and racist discrimination in Belgium

Like most other countries in Western Europe, Belgium has pursued a "Sport for All" policy for several decades. The democratisation of sport and thus access to active sport for the entire population has consistently been the primary aim of this "Sport for All" policy. In addition, this policy has continually focused on target groups whose rates of participation have been considerably lower than the national average — these were women, young adults and the elderly. The central plank of the "Sport for All" vision is therefore equality of opportunity. It is a remarkable coincidence that the development of the "Sport for All" policy coincides with the period in which the increase of minority ethnic groups was greatest: Belgium saw its greatest increase in the number of 'foreigners' in the 1960s and 1970s; moreover, the vast majority of these (im)migrants consisted of young people for whom sport is a very attractive activity.

Against this background, it might be expected that today, after more than twenty years of "Sport for All", the level of participation in sport by (im)migrants and minority ethnic groups would be no different than the average for the population as a whole, and could thus serve as an example of non-discrimination. And yet we would venture to put forward a hypothesis here which states precisely the opposite: *After almost 25 years of "Sport for All", the sports establishment in Belgium is still highly discriminatory towards (im)migrants and minority ethnic groups. Equal opportunity, the basic principle of "Sport for All", does not exist with regard to these groups. This racist discrimination in sport is reflected not so much in an open, incident-rich, extremist or aggressive manner, but occurs primarily in a hidden, implicit and inconspicuous — though nonetheless in a structural and systematic — way.*

This hypothesis requires further explanation.

(1) In the first place, the hypothesis claims that (im)migrants and minority ethnic groups participate in sport to a substantially lesser extent than other sections of the population. This lower representation is not based on the fact that these population groups do not wish to participate in sport. The hypothesis claims that the sports establishment, from the most senior and elite level, through competitive sport to informal and recreational sport, is insufficiently accessible to (im)migrants and minority ethnic groups. This high entry threshold to sport is, according to the hypothesis, caused not only by the socio-economic limitations of (im)migrants, but also and particularly by the socio-cultural and ideological characteristics of the sports establishment itself. We shall develop this hypothesis further and test it at various levels of sport.

(2) In addition, the hypothesis indicates the way in which racist discrimination manifests itself within sport. We are talking of creeping forms of racist discrimination which are so embedded in the system that they are barely recognised as discrimination at all. This does not, however, mean that there are no open racist incidents in sport: on the contrary, we are confronted on a regular basis with open forms of racism from members of the public, athletes, coaches, commentators, and so on. But it is precisely these incidents which take attention away from the more systematic, structural racist discrimination which exists in sport in the form of exclusion, deprivation and under-representation.

This distinction between open, individual discrimination and covert institutional discrimination is crucial for a differentiated analysis of racist discrimination in sport. The first, open form is more quickly recognised as racism and then frequently functions as a "lightning conductor" for the second, covert form of racism. Whenever the media and public discourses discuss the issue of racism in sport, the focus is placed almost exclusively on the first type of open and individual forms of racism. Racist behaviour by crowds at football matches directed at non-white players is the most obvious example of this type. With reference to the Belgian situation, it should be stressed that even these open forms of racism are barely discussed or criticised publicly. Racism in sport seems to be hushed up and played down rather than being brought out into the open. The social critic and Belgian football commentator Jan Wauters, as a privileged witness, summarises the attitude to open racism on and around football fields as follows:

> I have so far seen little evidence of a fight against racism. Open racism appears not to occur officially. Where is the problem then?... The spread of football hooliganism in the 1970s led to the poison of racism penetrating the ranks of supporters. Initially it involved poking fun, later hurling insults. The jungle noises echoed around the pitches whenever a coloured player (from the opposing team) had the ball. Few people concerned themselves about this, however. And things are still the same today. Another childish and shameful act is the throwing of bananas on to the pitch whenever a fast dribbler who happens to have a dark skin takes off with the ball. The fact that these dark-skinned players do not respond is a constant source of surprise to me. In the Netherlands a public debate was devoted to this issue. In Belgium people keep quiet about it. (Wauters, 1991: p. 48)

The following analysis of racist discrimination at the various levels of sport focuses mainly on the second, covert but structural and institutional forms of racist discrimination which have to-date still attracted little attention. This does not, however, mean that we ignore or underestimate the existence of open racism in sport.

Institutional racist discrimination in sport: a hypothesis-forming approach

Racism in sport is mainly — and rightly — associated with soccer and, more specifically, with the behaviour and chants of football supporters directed at 'foreign' players. This is a very incomplete image of racist discrimination in sport, however. The range of forms of sport stretches further than purely top-level competitive sport such as soccer. An analysis of institutionalised racist discrimination must also include other, less "mediagenic", but nonetheless popular forms of sport. The everyday human interactions and confrontations in other forms of sport are possibly just as — or even more — intense as in the "mediagenic" competitive sports such as soccer.

The following two examples clearly show that racist discrimination does also occur in other sports. We observed, for example, how racist behaviour and utterances occur very frequently in youth soccer among players aged from six to ten. It was not so much the players themselves as the spectators along the touchlines who exhibited racist behaviour. Furthermore, more racist abuses were observed after the match, e.g. in the changing rooms or canteen, than during the match itself.

Another example is gymnastics in Belgium. This sport is relatively popular, not so much as a spectator or televised sport, but rather in terms of the numbers of participants in the sport. The three gymnastics federations in Belgium together comprise hundreds of clubs and tens of thousands of members. In spite of this, the number of members from minority ethnic groups who join gymnastics clubs is extremely small (the gymnastics federations do not possess exact figures). Although membership is open to everyone and gymnastics is not economically elitist, few (im)migrants join these clubs. The reasons for this deserve further study. One possible explanation may lie in the cultural distance between gymnastics clubs and (im)migrants. Tolleneer (1990) showed how gymnastics clubs in Belgium have classically lined up with traditional ideas of nationalism and patriotism. In addition, gymnastics clubs also correspond with the traditional ideological divisions (Catholic, Socialist, etc.) in Belgian society. These two reasons make the cultural distance extremely large. It is arguable whether this explanation is correct, but it remains a fact that gymnastics in Belgium is much more an example of segregation than of integration.

Both examples demonstrate that a broad but differentiated perspective is needed in order to identify and analyse racist discrimination in sport. Therefore, five levels of sport participation were identified; together they cover the totality of sport in Belgium:

1. Olympic and international representative sport
2. national competitive sport
3. organised club sport
4. private sport on a commercial basis
5. informal, non-organised sport participation.

Each of these areas will now be considered separately and the major findings of our research summarised. Due to the exploratory nature of our research, some statements are speculative and require further investigation. Where already available, empirical data are used to back up our findings.

Olympic and international representative sport

In spite of several generations of (im)migrants with Belgian citizenship, members of minority ethnic groups are virtually absent from international representative sport in Belgium: to date, not one single (im)migrant has featured in an Olympic selection. While it is true that Olympic selections are based on objective performance, (im)migrants have evidently so far failed to penetrate the training/performance/selection process of top-level sport. The cause of this absence of (im)migrants and minority ethnic groups in top-level representative sport in Belgium is an issue which deserves further study.

Naturalised (im)migrants are rarely members of the national teams. If, in exceptional cases, an (im)migrant athlete is included in a national team, the athlete in question is also temporarily accorded Belgian identity. This "Belgian identity", however, disappears once the period in the national selection has ended. This construction and deconstruction of national identity in sport is clearly illustrated by the following example involving Josip Weber, a footballer of Croatian origin playing in Belgium.

Josip Weber was born in 1964 in Croatia in the former Yugoslavia, where he played soccer for Hajduk Split among others. He began playing in the Belgian football competition in 1988, where he carved out a notable career as a striker and top scorer. The popular media consistently placed the emphasis on his Croatian identity and his love of his country of origin. His humanitarian efforts on behalf of the civil war-torn Croatia were also a constant focus of media attention.

In 1994, just before the Soccer World Cup in the United States, Josip Weber was naturalised as a Belgian. This gave him the opportunity to be selected for the national team. However, his selection immediately generated a debate in the popular media regarding his national identity and the "genuineness" of his Belgian identity:

> ... we may wonder why the Croatian really applied for Belgian nationality.... Did Weber really want to become a Belgian or was it all a sort of sham?... (*Voetbalmagazine*, 1994: p. 46)

The press devoted regular attention to Weber's change of identity. Thanks to his excellent performance on the field, however, Weber came to be accepted more and more as a "genuine" Belgian in the press. Following excellent preparatory matches for the World Cup with the national team, Josip Weber was portrayed more and more as an "all-Belgian boy". His Croatian name Josip was replaced in the popular press by "Joske", a familiar and typical Belgian name which indicated that he had been accepted by the Belgians, that he was well-loved and was "one of us". The media, therefore, reconstructed the identity of Josip Weber in such a way that he was not only eligible to play for the national team under the official rules, but was also acceptable as a national symbol as "one of us":

> ...Can there still be any doubt that Belgian Joske will save the fatherland?
> ...It won't be long before he is murmuring the Belgian national anthem for the first time.... (*Voetbalmagazine*, 1994: p. 20)

> ...Of course I know the Belgian national anthem... I shall play football out of gratitude to this country!!! (Weber in *Voetbalmagazine*, 1994: p. 24)

Press reports of this kind were clearly designed to stifle potential resentment that a 'foreigner' was representing Belgium in international competition, even though his selection was completely legal and in line with the rules of the soccer establishment. The press assimilated Josip Weber to make him a Belgian. In fact, this manipulation of his national identity by the press confirms the implicit discrimination against individuals from minority ethnic groups in representative sport.

During the 1994 World Cup in the United States, however, Weber failed to meet expectations. He failed to score and missed out on selection for the basic team. These disappointing performances quickly led to a decline in his popularity. Moreover, they resulted in his identity as a Belgian player being dismantled in the press. After the championships, virtually no reference was made to Weber's Belgian nationality. His name was no longer "Joske" but had reverted to "Josip". Although he was officially a Belgian, the popular press once again began referring to him as "the Croatian Weber". In short, the identity of this footballer was reconstructed — or perhaps we should say deconstructed — in the press from Belgian to 'foreigner', despite his official status as a naturalised Belgian citizen.

The case of Weber illustrates the existence of implicit discrimination against members of minority ethnic groups in international representative sport. It is obviously difficult to accept that athletes of foreign origin can represent Belgium in international top-level sport. This observation is confirmed by the statements of other Belgian soccer internationals, who have declared that they were not in support of according Belgian nationality to players in order to enable them to play for the national team. They appear to be afraid that the Belgian public would then no longer identify with the Belgian team (*Voetbalmagazine*, 1994). When two naturalised Belgians (Oliveira and Weber) played for the national team in 1994, this was described by one of the coaches as a problem which would require a solution in the future (*Voetbalmagazine*, 1994). In summary, we claim that representative top-level sport displays clear xenophobic features and implicit forms of racist discrimination.

National competitive sport

In some areas of national competitive sport, such as soccer, we see an over-representation of 'foreign', non-Belgian players. At first sight this would appear to indicate successful integration. However, this strong presence of 'foreign' soccer players in the national competition is not a demographic reflection of the presence of minority ethnic groups in the Belgian population. On the contrary, the over-representation of 'foreign' players is the result of migrational flows of athletes in the professional circuit and of the purchase and transfer of international players (Bale and Maguire, 1994). Consequently, the phenomenon of over-representation of 'foreign' players is not a valid indicator for integration in sport. This can be illustrated with a few figures from soccer. In the Belgian First Division in 1995, 108 of 405 players were 'foreigners' — i.e. nearly 25% of the players were non-Belgians. The same percentage applied to the Second Division. In comparison, only 10% of the Belgian population are from minority ethnic groups. According to the Royal Belgian Football Association, the most common 'foreign' nationalities in the national football competition are:

First Division —   Brazil (11 players), Nigeria (10 players), Hungary
                     (8 players), The Netherlands (8 players), Zaire (6 players)
Second Division — The Netherlands (19 players), Brazil (9 players),
                     Zaire (8 players), Croatia (6 players)

Comparisons with the figures in Table 2 (p. 61) show that the distribution of 'foreign' footballers across the various nationalities is not a reflection of the minority ethnic groups in the Belgian population. Moreover, the number of 'foreigners' in football teams in the First and Second Divisions shows some other interesting features. For example, the Antwerp football club has the highest percentage (36%) of 'foreign' players, and yet Antwerp is the city where extreme right-wing and racist and xenophobic ideologies attract the highest number of votes in Belgian politics. Not a single 'foreign' player, however, comes from the (im)migrant community in and around the city of Antwerp.

On the other hand there is Tongeren, a club from the Second Division in the province of Limburg, one of the Belgian provinces with traditionally a high number of (im)migrants and minority ethnic groups stretching back three generations. In contrast to what we might expect, there is not one single 'foreign' or minority ethnic player at Tongeren football club.

In short, all the available data indicate that there is no correlation between the number of 'foreign' players in football and the degree of integration in society. The over-representation of 'foreign' players at the top end of the national soccer game is not a valid indicator of non-discrimination in the sport itself or in society as a whole.

Other competitive sports have few or no (im)migrants or minority ethnic groups at national level. Cycle-racing, an extremely popular sport in Belgium, numbers virtually no (im)migrants in its ranks. In this sport, too, the presence of participants of 'foreign' origin is determined entirely by the commercial circuit of buying and selling cyclists, and is in no way an indication of an integration process in the sport.

In conclusion, it should be stressed that the over-representation of 'foreign' athletes in certain sports is not an indicator for integration. Few if any integrated socialisation processes exist for bringing (im)migrants and minority ethnic groups into top-level competitive sport. On the contrary, a good deal of racist behaviour on the part of opponents and supporters is observed in national competitive sport, directed precisely against the sometimes large numbers of 'foreign' players. Moreover, national competitive sport acts as a breeding ground for racist stereotypes. In basketball, for example, it is argued with conviction, even by experienced coaches, that exceptional jumping power is a physical, biological characteristic of black athletes. This presumed characteristic is then accepted without question as an explanation for the superiority of black players in basketball. Racist stereotypes of this sort are still avidly propagated in sport and are accepted without criticism.

Organised club sport

Belgium has a dense network of sports clubs. In Flanders alone, with around six million inhabitants, there are an estimated 15,000 clubs. Every medium-sized town has around 200 to 250 sports associations, and the number of members of these clubs is estimated at 1.5 million. In addition the majority of municipalities, particularly the larger municipalities and cities, possess highly developed sports facilities and an infrastructure which helps to support this network of sports clubs. This dense network of organised sport is open to the whole population. Nonetheless, (im)migrants are strongly under-represented in this form of organised sport (Knops, 1992; De Knop *et al.*, 1994).

A case study in a municipality with a high proportion of (im)migrants and minority ethnic groups led Wijnands (1985) to the following conclusions:

> In spite of a well-developed network of sports clubs, sports facilities and infrastructure, there is a strong under-representation of (im)migrants in organised sport. Whereas 16% of the total population were members of a local sports association, the membership figure for (im)migrants was only 4%. This was in spite of the fact that interviews with young (im)migrants revealed a high demand for participation in sport. A majority of the integrated young people moreover belonged to the second generation of (im)migrants and had thus been born and raised in Belgium. (pp. 25-28)

In spite of being closely interwoven with local society, organised sport proves to be discriminatory towards (im)migrants and minority ethnic groups. Two possible causes should be mentioned here. The sets of norms and values in organised club sport can differ greatly from those of (im)migrants, possibly indicating a cultural gap between organised club sport and the (im)migrant population. Secondly, the network of clubs is less well developed precisely in those neighbourhoods where there is a large (im)migrant population, such as in the Brussels conurbation.

And yet a gradual revolution appears to be taking place with regard to participation in organised club sport. In a recent study of the participation in sport by young (im)migrants, De Knop *et al.* (1994) point out that the rate of participation in club sport among young (im)migrants has increased.

Nonetheless, he also observes that membership in the Brussels conurbation remains low. "Self-organisation" in the form of ethnic clubs for football, basketball, wrestling, etc., are also becoming more popular. Often, however, these clubs operate outside the framework of traditional organised sport, and their members are frequently the subject of racism.

Our conclusion is that organised club sport in Belgium is not openly but structurally discriminatory towards (im)migrants, although there are signs that racist discrimination in organised sport is declining. The dense network of organised sport, which has long effectively been a closed system, seems to be more accessible to (im)migrants and minority ethnic groups.

Private commercial sport

The emergence of a private sports sector operating on a commercial basis is a fairly recent development in Belgian sports. These sport centres and fitness studios form part of the leisure, tourism and health industry. According to our observations, there is a quasi-absence of (im)migrants and minority ethnic groups in this sphere of commercial sport opportunities. The financial cost of this form of sport appears to be too high for the socio-economically weaker groups, to which (im)migrants generally belong. Lifestyle and cultural differences may also contribute to this segregation. We suspect above all that the private, commercial sport and health sector is developing into an informal "apartheid" zone where (im)migrants and minority ethnic groups are not only kept out by financial hurdles, but also — and possibly particularly — by the norms and values which dominate this private sector.

The values in these centres which generally focus on individual health and fitness are strongly associated with a Western, white image, and the predominant body and fitness culture displays a dominant white and economically successful norm and value pattern. It is very likely that in this way the private sector is segregating itself culturally from (im)migrants and minority ethnic groups.

In a commercial climbing centre we observed how it was made clear to a group of young (im)migrants that they were not welcome, even though they had paid the same entrance fee as other customers. The manager explained afterwards that the "other" clients felt disturbed by the presence of the (im)migrants (Van Moffaert and Vanreusel, 1995: p. 30).

In short, not only does private commercial sport operate in a discriminatory way towards minority ethnic groups on economic grounds; our claim is that values and norms in the sports, health and fitness industry reinforce segregation in an implicit but clear way. Naturally, research is needed in order to test this claim.

Informal, non-organised sports participation

"Informal" sports participation refers here to participation in games, sports and recreational activities outside the traditionally organised and highly structured sports system. This includes public sports and games areas as well as local initiatives by organisations outside the sports establishment such as municipal youth facilities and youth movements, as well as informal forms of sports and games in local neighbourhoods.

According to our observations there is a very high proportion of young (im)migrants, the majority of whom grow up in neighbourhoods in large cities, with limited opportunities for participation in organised sport. The need for sporting activity is largely accommodated by informal forms of sports and games. These are practised largely in the participants' own neighbourhood; they are not expensive and are practised within the participants' own group. They therefore fit in with the immediate living environment of these young people. At the same time, however, participation in informal sports and games is largely segregated along racial lines. In this form of sport, too, contact between the members of the (im)migrant community and the "mainstream" population in Belgium is very limited.

Initiatives have been in place for several years in Belgium aimed at promoting informal, non-organised participation in sport by young (im)migrants. Most towns and municipalities with a high percentage of (im)migrants and minority ethnic groups are now setting up such initiatives.

An evaluation of thirty of these local sport initiatives, however, shows that to date they have had virtually no success in creating an integrational effect between 'Belgian' and 'foreign' young people (Van Moffaert and Vanreusel, 1995). Even though widespread and much encouraged, informal sports and games take place mainly in a segregated way, and often implicitly stimulate segregation between indigenous and non-indigenous participants. This segregated sports and games culture among young children could possibly determine the chances of success of a general integration policy. Anecdotal evidence of games and sports areas in the Brussels conurbation point to the existence of segregated sports and games "ghettos" rather than to any integrational effects.

In short, it is claimed that informal, non-organised sports participation is extremely popular, including among minority ethnic groups. At the same time, however, this informal form of sport and games takes place in a markedly segregated way and is thus once again an area open to racist discrimination. The influence of a segregated sports and games culture on the socialisation and integration process is something which undoubtedly deserves more attention from researchers. We would claim that forms of racist discrimination at this level are equally socially relevant, if not more so, as racist discrimination in spectator sports such as soccer, because the process of socialisation of young children takes place partly via games activities.

Sport and anti-racist responses

In the foregoing analysis we have clearly shown how sport in Belgium is an institution entailing structural racist discrimination on several levels. However, this approach would be one-sided if no reference were made to the initiatives which have been developed as anti-racist responses within and through sport. These initiatives will be examined critically in this section.

Anti-racist initiatives in sport occurred in two periods. The first runs until 1985, the year of the "Heysel tragedy" when, as a result of hooliganism, more than thirty football fans died during the European football match between Liverpool and Turin staged in the Heysel stadium in Brussels. Although hooliganism in Belgium was also associated with extreme right-wing ideologies, the Heysel tragedy was not in the first place a racist incident. It did however signify a turning point in the attention for the social problems surrounding football violence and in sport in general. The Heysel tragedy led to an acceleration in research into hooliganism (Van Limbergen and Walgrave, 1988), which also touched on racism. In the years following 1985, anti-racist and non-discriminatory actions were undertaken in a more systematic manner.

Before 1985 there were only a few individual, isolated initiatives based on a "sport as integration" view. In the province of Limburg, a region with a high percentage of 'first, second and third-generation (im)migrants' and minority ethnic groups, a number of sport organisations carried out a special campaign aimed at promoting sports activities among these population groups. A survey showed however that most of these initiatives failed to achieve their objective and had little or no success in encouraging young people from the (im)migrant communities to participate in locally organised sports (Naeyaert, 1982; Wijnands, 1985). The same author did however report the frequent emergence of ethnic sports associations. These often bore the name of a famous team from the country of origin and operated largely outside the existing sports network. A number of these ethnic clubs did however take part in existing competitions.

The largest meeting centre for (im)migrants in Brussels, FOYER, has for many years used sports activities as part of its integration programme. However, no data are available on the results achieved with this sports programme (Laga and Vanreusel, 1990).

These examples clearly illustrate that there was no structured anti-racist response within sport prior to 1985. The sports world was ruled mainly by ignorance and indifference with regard to racist discrimination and the issue of integration. A more fundamental criticism, however, relates to the conceptual underpinning of the few anti-racist initiatives in sport at that time. The implicit message underlying the earliest anti-racist campaigns pre-1985 was one of assimilation: non-discrimination and integration were understood as the assimilation of (im)migrants and minority ethnic groups into sport and thus into society. There was virtually no recognition in the sports world of cultural identity, equality and variety.

After 1985, more systematic, structured anti-racist responses got under way in Belgium, both within and through sport. These responses did not come so much from the sports establishment itself; sport was increasingly seen by external groups as a weapon for the battle against racism. The Koning Boudewijn Stichting (King Boudewijn Foundation) played a pioneering role here. In its fight against all forms of deprivation in Belgium, this Foundation not only launched its own anti-racist initiatives in sport; it also brought groups and institutions into contact with each other to enable them to conduct a coordinated and structured anti-racist sports policy (Knops, 1992). The three following examples illustrate the variety of campaigns launched since 1985.

The "*neighbourhood soccer*" initiative was aimed at instituting local, informal football competitions on the streets, squares and local football fields, and was targeted at economically deprived young people, particularly those from minority ethnic groups. This initiative was developed in conjunction with the national football association and was organised through the municipal sports services, though local youth services and "integration centres" in cities and municipalities were also involved in the project. The idea of neighbourhood sport specifically aimed at economically deprived groups is now being adopted in similar initiatives by the basketball and volleyball federations (Knops, 1994).

The "*local sports initiatives*" campaign supported existing small-scale projects focusing on deprived neighbourhoods containing (im)migrants and minority ethnic groups. One of the aims of this initiative was to create a bond between residents and their neighbourhood. The projects were targeted at those municipalities and cities with a high percentage of (im)migrants and where deprivation is worst. An evaluation of thirty such projects shows that a great deal of cooperation was established between local bodies which had formerly little or no contact with each other. Although participation in these local sports initiatives was very high, integration of majority ethnic and minority ethnic groups was hardly achieved (Van Moffaert and Vanreusel, 1994).

The "*sports clubs show their colours*" campaign arose from the observation that sport organisations themselves adopted a relatively passive response to calls to develop and implement a non-discriminatory policy. Moreover, as stated earlier the participation of (im)migrants in club sports was strikingly low. A campaign was therefore launched to encourage sports clubs to pursue an active non-discrimination policy and to adopt special initiatives aimed at integrating majority ethnic and minority ethnic participants. An intense information campaign about racism and discrimination against minority ethnic groups was targeted at sports clubs. In addition, clubs which develop active integrational initiatives are rewarded. Young people from the (im)migrant community are also given funding to enable them to undergo general sports training. The effects of the "*sports clubs show their colours*" campaign are not yet known (Knops, 1995).

These are just three examples of the many anti-racist activities which have been launched in sport. Together they indicate how the anti-racist response has taken on a more structured form, particularly since the start of the 1990s. While these activities will obviously need to be critically evaluated over the longer term, a number of comments can already be made:

1. The recent structured anti-racist responses of the world of sport has much less of an undertone of assimilation, of annexing minorities to the dominant majority culture, than earlier initiatives. In spite of this, there is still too little emphasis on preserving cultural identities and equality as well as multi-culturalism as guiding principles in anti-racist and integrational sports initiatives.

2. Discrimination is actively combated in these projects through integrational sports initiatives. The term "integration" mainly refers to attempts to increase participation in sports initiatives. It is however arguable whether a higher rate of participation in such initiatives is actually a good indicator of integration and non-discrimination in sport and society as a whole. Further research into the relationship between participation, integration and non-discrimination is therefore required.

3. Little is known about the transfer of attitudes, opinions and behavioural forms between sport and the wider society. The sports world displays a naive optimism regarding its actual contribution to the quality of life in society. It is an old cliché that sport is continually used as a panacea to heal all society's ills. It is too easily assumed that increased participation in sport has a non-discriminatory effect, and that integration and non-discrimination in sport work through to society as a whole. This generalisation requires a differentiated and critical examination.

4. The anti-racist responses through sport are aimed primarily at changing attitudes, opinions and ways of treating (im)migrants and minority ethnic groups. This takes place mainly through sports-oriented campaigns: in other words, sport is used as a socialising agent. The socialising impact of sport, and in particular its scope, are debatable, however. Admittedly, the target groups often adopt the activity pattern: they practice more sport, join a club, train and take part in competitions. Whether their attitudes, opinions and behaviour also change as a result of these sports initiatives is not clear, however. It has all too often become apparent with well-meaning initiatives of this sort that the actions are adopted but not the real, underlying objectives and motives.

Conclusion

Our aim in this summary of the situation in Belgium was to show that the relationship between sport and racist discrimination is twofold. On the one hand sport in its various forms appears as an institution which perpetuates discrimination. This claim is substantiated only partially by facts and is something which requires further inquiries. On the other hand, sport proves to be used intensively as a means of combating racism. These initiatives are hopeful and well-meaning as a response to racism. However, they are based on a "socialisation through sport" view which is not accepted without question by the scientific community. Close monitoring and evaluation of developments in the relationship between sport, racist discrimination and integration continues to be necessary.

References

Bale, J. and Maguire, J. (eds) (1994) *The Global Sports Arena: Athletic talent migration in an interdependent world.* London: Frank Cass.

Beaujon, E. (1986) *Minderheden in perspectief: Literatuurstudie.* Amsterdam: Instituut voor sociale geografie.

De Knop, P. (1993) *Onderzoek naar de integratiemogelijkheden van de georganiseerde sport voor migrantenjongeren.* Brussels: VUB Jongerenadviescentrum voor Sport.

De Knop, P., De Martelaer, K., Theeboom, M., Van Engeland, E., and Van Puymbroeck, L. (1994) *Sport als integratie voor migrantenjongeren.* Brussels: Koning Boudewijnstichting.

Jarvie, G. (1991) *Sport, Racism and Ethnicity.* London: Palmer Press.

Knops, G. (ed) (1992) *Sport als integratie: Kansen voor maatschappelijk kwetsbare jongeren.* Brussels: Koning Boudewijnstichting.

Knops, G. (ed) (1994) *Buurtvoetbal, een doelpunt voor integratie.* Brussels: Koning Boudewijnstichting.

Knops, G. (ed) (1995) *Sportclubs bekennen kleur.* Brussels: Koning Boudewijnstichting.

Laga, G. and Vanreusel, B. (1990) *Natuursport en kansarme jongeren (rapporten van de onderzoekseenheid sociaalculturele kinantropologie).* Leuven: Instituut voor Lichamelijke Opvoeding.

Leman, J. (ed) (1996) 'Racismeklachten', *Aanzet* No. 2 (Centrum voor Gelijkheid van Kansen en Racismebestrijding).

Naeyaert, D. (1982) 'Acculturatie van (im)migranten en hun vrijetijdsgedrag', *Vrijetied en samenleving*, Vol. 1, No. 1: pp. 23-48.

Nixon, H. L. and Frey, J. H. (1996) *A Sociology of Sport.* London: Woodsworth.

Phillips, J. C. (1993) *Sociology of Sport.* Boston: Allyn and Bacon.

Rees, I.R. (1991) 'Beyond contact: Sport as a site for ethnic and racial cooperation', in E. H. Katzenellenbogen and J. R. Potgieter (eds) *Sociological Perspectives of Movement Activity.* Stellenbosch: Institute for Sport and Movement Studies.

Tolleneer, J. (1990) Gymnastics and religion in Belgium (1882–1914)', *International Journal of the History of Sport*, Vol. 7, No. 3.: pp. 335-347.

Tolleneer, J., Vanreusel, B. and Renson, R. (1995) 'Kansen in de sport, herbronning en hertekening', in B. Pattyn (ed) *Wegen van hoop, universitaire perspectieven.* Leuven: universitaire pers. pp. 395-411.

Van Buggenhout, A. (1995) *Sport en racisme in de Nederlandstalige literatuur: Bijdrage tot het Europese onderzoeksproject "Euroracism and sport"* (licentiaatsverhandeling). Leuven: Faculteit voor Lichamelijke Opvoeding en Kinesitherapie.

Van Limbergen, K. and Walgrave, L. (1988) *Side, fans en hooligans: Voetbalvandalisme: feiten, achtergronden en aanpak.* Leuven: Acco.

Van Moffaert, K. and Vanreusel, B. (1995) *Lokale sportinitiatieven: Integratie in de praktijk.* Brussels: Koning Boudewijnstichting.

Vanreusel, B. (1995) 'Sports as an integrating factor among (im)migrants', *Network News* (European Network of Sport Sciences in Higher Education), No. 3: pp. 14-15.

Voetbalmagazine (1994) Vol. 13, Nos. 22, 23, 25, 26, 27, 34, 37.

Wijnands, A. (1985) 'Sportbeoefening en sociale integratie bij (im)migranten', *Sport* (BLOSO), Vol. 30, No. 4: pp. 25-28.

Wauters, J. (1991) *Racism, donker continent.* Brussels: NCOS.

FOOTBALL, RACISM AND XENOPHOBIA IN ENGLAND (I): EUROPE AND THE OLD ENGLAND

Scott Fleming and Alan Tomlinson

Introduction

The 1994/95 English football season might well be remembered for a number of high-profile scandals. There were allegations of 'match-fixing', irregular financial management of transfer deals (that is, 'bungs' to sweeten or clinch big-money signings); and several players were exposed as drug-users or drug-dependents. But Eric Cantona, Prima Donna of the English football stage, provoked the biggest and longest-running headlines of all. "The Shame of Cantona" (c.f. *Daily Mirror*: 27 and 28 January, 1995) is how one of the two most prominent tabloid newspapers put it, and media responses to the incident, across the quality or broadsheet as well as the tabloid press, featured widespread discussion of a deep-rooted moral decay in the fibre of the national game. The Cantona story was not only 'good copy'. It also threw into sharp relief some of the key themes and issues in the politics of the popular and of cultural identity that have characterised British football, and will feature prominently in some of the later sections of this review.

The social significance of football in Britain and throughout the world has been recognised in seminal studies of the roots of the modern game (on England, see Walvin, 1975; Mason, 1980; Fishwick, 1989; Wagg, 1984); and overviews of its growth worldwide and the expanding profile of the World Cup (Tomlinson and Whannel, 1986; Sugden and Tomlinson, 1994; Murray, 1994; Mason, 1995). The symbolic and cultural importance of football has been recognised in not just the social history and sociology of sport, but also in cultural studies (Critcher, 1982) and popular cultural studies (Redhead, 1987). Innovative sociological work on crowd violence in English football (Williams *et al.*, 1984) has been followed by cultural commentary on football style (Redhead, 1991), sociological work on worldwide football cultures (Giulianotti *et al.*, 1994), British football (Williams and Wagg, 1991) and football in Scotland and Ireland (Bairner, 1994; Moorhouse, 1995; Sugden and Bairner, 1993) and other specific cultures

(Redhead, 1993); and works in social psychology (Canter *et al.*, 1989). More literary and populist writing on the nature of football and the passionate responses it generates (Buford, 1991; Hornby, 1992; Davies, 1991; Kuper, 1994) has also raised the profile of the cultural analysis of football. A fascinating ambivalence characterises much of this writing, both academic and popular — celebratory as it is of the popular cultural bases of the game and of its global appeal, yet simultaneously aware of the reactionary values (manifest, for instance, in masculinist and nationalist terms) which are expressed by many of its adherents. Football can embody a popular aesthetic of collective endeavour, but it can also encourage prejudice, discrimination, stereotyping and ethnocentrism. It can bring different cultures together in common celebration, but it can also provide the basis for extreme, and very public, forms of xenophobia and racism. This latter dimension of the sport is explored here.

In the analysis that follows, we utilise the definition of racism developed by Cole (1996), in which social groups or collectivities are differentiated by the allegedly unchanging nature of their (biological and/or cultural) characteristics; and in which such perceived difference is a source of evaluated characteristics or stereotypes, which can distort and mislead, with "ultimately negative" effects (even if they at first appear to be positive). By xenophobia, we mean "the exaggerated hostility towards or fear of foreigners", which is, according to Klein (1993: p. 14), more psychologically than socially acquired, and is "the irrational fear or hatred of 'otherness'". These definitions should be kept in mind as the different sections of the paper offer examples, evidence and summaries of popular discourses, debates and research findings which shed light on these and related concepts.

The sources for the chapter are wide-ranging and eclectic. They include academic studies of the sociology, history, politics and culture of the game at its different levels, from participation in organised youth sport and amateur competition, through to the elite professional form; the everyday discourses of the print and the broadcasting media; player (auto)biographies; and studies of and reportage on fan cultures. In this chapter the following aspects are covered in six sections:

• general issues of xenophobia and racism as elements in the phenomenon of football fandom;

• examples of racist slurs and taunts as expressed in the professional game by players, managers, coaches and supporters;

• the responses of players to such expressions of racism, and of institutions to the recognition of such forms of racism;

• instances of xenophobia in the politics of world football, and in the depiction of the world game in an English football comic narrative;

- positive instances of cultural assertiveness as expressed in community-based forms of separatist sports culture;
- key overviewing themes and a research agenda for further study of xenophobic and racist discourses in supra-national European football culture, and of the media coverage of foreign players and issues of 'race'.

Xenophobia, 'race' and sport — some interconnections

"Off you go Cantona — it's an early bath for you."

In the television advertisements broadcast during the half-time break of the Coca-Cola League Cup Final between Liverpool and Bolton Wanderers at the beginning of April 1995, Manchester United's French footballer Eric Cantona and the England striker Les Ferdinand featured in an advertisement for their sponsors, Nike. They talked not about sports footwear, not about football directly but about playing the game free of prejudice and discrimination and the potential provocation which such attitudes and practices might generate. Nike used its slogan — "Just do it" — cleverly, linking pleas for racial tolerance and inter-cultural understanding to a sense of getting on with football for its own sake. This advertisement appeared within a couple of days of the successful outcome to Cantona's appeal against a prison sentence. He had been sentenced to two weeks in prison on conviction for "common assault", after assailing an English football fan with what the press rapturously labelled as a flying kung-fu kick. This incident occurred as Cantona was leaving the field of play, having been dismissed for violent play against the black Crystal Palace player Richard Shaw.

Differing versions of what happened have been peddled in the aftermath of this incident. What is certain is that after being dismissed from the field, Cantona was walking along the side of the pitch when he turned and lunged towards Matthew Simmons, the Crystal Palace supporter, and attempted to kick him, before trading blows. Inevitably, Cantona was widely condemned for his action, and there was, initially, quite a groundswell of popular opinion that he should be banned from English football for life. As the days passed, some of the initial reactionary rhetoric was superseded by more thoughtful analysis.

The case against Cantona was, reputedly, described by the victim of Cantona's attack:

> I thought I'd nip to the loo, I walked 11 steps down to the front. Everyone was jeering him. I yelled, 'Off you go Cantona — it's an early bath for you' and pointed to the dressing room… I do have a habit of swearing sometimes without realising it. I might have sworn at him, I'm not sure. (Syson and Lazzeri, 1995: p. 3)

This version of events[1] did not strike much resonance with the 'leader' writer of the *Daily Star* (28 January, 1995: p. 2) who suggested that, "As the French would say: *C'est merde*". The alternative 'truth' was that Cantona was provoked, and,

> Eye-witnesses reported that [Simmons] ran from his 11th row seat. He then screamed: "You dirty French bastard! F*** off back to France" before making a rude gesture. (*Daily Star*, January 27, 1995: p. 2)

If the reports of Cantona's own recollections are to be believed, Simmons also spat at him and added "You French mother****er" (Allen, 1995: p. 2). If this sequence of events even approximated to reality this would certainly represent significant provocation and perhaps even some sort of mitigation for Cantona's behaviour[2].

The ritual abuse of referees and opposing players and supporters is often characterised by the use of sexual terms, and as Holt (1989) observes, this often includes reference to "wankers" and "cunts". Yet football spectators often also engage in what might euphemistically be described as topical satire; and the 'scally-wag' terrace banter is a source of humour for some fans. When ethnicity or epithets associated with nationality are also used, the result is a form of insult that has been found to cause much offence (Kelly and Cohn, 1988); and which certainly displays "deep-rooted problems of nationalism and racism within the game" (Tysome, 1995: p. 5). In the Cantona case, the additional factor of the sexual innuendo in the term "motherfucker" appears to have been taken almost literally by Cantona himself, so compounding the insult. If this was indeed an accurate representation of what transpired, and if, as evidence suggests, this was not an uncommon outburst, then a sinister and disturbing xenophobic element is clearly present in contemporary football culture. This is especially the case when that culture can be seen to have some connections with and be effectively infiltrated by extremist political elements.

Football and the Far Right

As the character assassinations of Simmons in the national press stepped up a gear, it transpired that he had been involved in various 'hooligan' encounters in England and overseas, and that he was a lager-swilling soccer brawler (Towers and Mackay, 1995: p. 3). It was also reported that he had evidently been a sympathiser of the British National Party and of the National Front (Brough and Mackay, 1995: p. 1). The use of football matches as a medium for the expression of far right ideology is not new (Robins, 1984; Williams *et al.*, 1984), and in their examination of the English football hooligan on the European mainland, Williams *et al.* (1984) indicate that the impact of extreme right-wing groups has been considerable.

In Britain, National Front recruitment has been attempted at Chelsea, West Ham, Millwall and Arsenal, and the Front's youth paper *Bulldog* ran a regular football column 'On the Football Front' encouraging fans to support its racist aims. In the main these have been unsuccessful (Ward, 1989). But in spite of this, it is — at the very least — curious that the response of the football establishment to the spread of the extreme right was to suggest that it was 'just the latest fashion' (as reported in Hill, 1989: p. 21). Ethnographic accounts and investigative journalism have established that the link between far right political extremism and football cannot be dismissed so easily; and there is evidence — as Bill Buford (1991: pp. 147) indicates — that many members of the National Front were "drawn from the football grounds". He adds, "I had heard that the football grounds were ideal for recruiting new members".

The far right presence at football grounds was also prominent in the generation of the violence that led to the abandonment of the football international between the Republic of Ireland and England in February 1995. English football fans gave Nazi salutes and, after Ireland scored a goal, threw seats at the Irish supporters. Fans spilled on to the pitch to escape this attack, and fighting broke out. It emerged that the initiators of the violence were hard-core members of the political group Combat 18 (1 = the first letter of the alphabet, A; 8 = the eighth letter of the alphabet, H — the initials, of course, of Adolf Hitler). The television documentary World in Action (1995) made contact with a former member of Combat 18 who, having 'broken ranks', was now willing to talk about the group's beliefs. These included the extermination of Jews and a 'race' war. It appealed to football supporters to join it in its expression of values "against Niggers, IRA supporters and reds". Travelling Europe, group members had 'pissed about' at concentration camps on the way to Prague, and in one publication had announced that "the Holocaust is a load of bollocks".

Holt's (1989) historicized analysis of British football offers a view of the spread of the extreme right in and around football grounds:

> Chauvinism, local and national, lies at the heart of hooliganism and England fans seem to find in foreigners a convenient target for a vague resentment at Britain's diminished place in the world. Football has become a substitute for patriotism amongst disaffected, half-educated white working-class youth of a nation which only a generation ago was respected and feared throughout the world. (p. 343)

Racisms in Football

Combat 18 seeks to recruit extremists from within the fan base of football. There is also a less politically explicit yet equally important dimension to the xenophobic and racist element as expressed in football. A small survey of racism on the terraces of football grounds in England conducted by *The Guardian* at the start of the 1993 season (*The Guardian*, 1993) captured forms of the abuse that is directed towards African-Caribbean players — one 'terrace fan' hurling racist abuse at Southampton's Ken Monkou, "Someone sort the big nigger out, f***ing black twat", as heard by Randeep Ramesh. The influence of the Far Right in football grounds is through an everyday racism which is mobilised along more explicit lines, and white working-class masculinity has been vociferous in its racist invective against black players. Other rivalries — of region or locality, for instance — are transcended as the evaluated characteristics of 'race' are brought to bear in a situation. In April 1994 at an English Endsleigh League match between Fulham (a West London club) and Burnley (a North-east Lancashire club in the North of England), a robust challenge by one of Burnley's black players on one of Fulham's white players incensed some spectators in the front row of seats. One of them rose to his feet, gesticulated aggressively at the Burnley player, and shrieked "Fuck off back up North, you fucking Northerner". One of his companions immediately added: "He ain't a fucking Northerner, he's black". This distortion of history and humanity has been far from unusual at English football matches, and this particular instance of it reveals the complexity as well as barbarism of some forms of cultural affiliation in football. In the labelling of the Other, the vilification of the threat of difference, the difference of region ("Northerner") is collapsed in a perception of the more fundamental "difference" of 'race'.

One of the ironies of the Cantona situation is that the very racism that black players in Britain have been subjected to for many years is now being used as 'a stick with which to beat' Cantona:

> Editorial (*Daily Mirror*, January 27, 1995: p. 6):
> There is little doubt that he was provoked. But many other players are cruelly taunted, too — week after week after week. Black players have suffered particularly harshly. They do not respond as Cantona did. Most of them are sensible enough not to react at all.

It is to the issue of racism(s) in football that the discussion now turns — and there is no shortage of evidence. On one level, although the 'stacking' of black players in certain positions on the field of play (with them significantly over-represented, in USA sports, in the non-central playing positions) has been reported in English football (Maguire, 1988), black players have become prominent in all positions. But the absence of black people in the management, coaching and boardrooms of football clubs is in stark contrast to their prominence on the field of play. These are the kinds of manifestations of racism that can be understood through the use of the notion of 'institutional racism' (c.f., Abercrombie *et al.*, 1984). The important challenge is to identify the reasons for their existence, and such a task would require a rigorous longitudinal study. There are, though, other widespread and more easily identifiable forms of racism in football of a more 'personal' kind; that is to say, they are direct, overt and individual. A montage of typical examples is illustrative.

From players —

Stoke City striker Mark Stein punched an opponent who racially abused him at the end of a second division promotion match, a jury heard yesterday... "There was simply ugly and abusive language and Stein was giving as good as he was getting." ...Mr Stein then turned towards Mr Gannon and said: "What is the fucking score then?". Mr Gannon called Mr Stein "a short, ugly, black wanker"... (*The Guardian*, October 27, 1993: p. 7)

From managers, coaches and administrators —

John Bond [televised comments on Dave Bennett before 1981 FA Cup final] illustrates some traditional football attitudes towards black players: "... like a lot of coloured players in this country... you pull your hair out with them... they drive you mad... he's got so much ability and so much potential". (Redhead, 1987: p. 28)

Ron Wylie commented to Garry Thompson, "I think you're a coward. All you people are". (Cashmore, 1982: p. 193)

When invited to contribute to the TV documentary Great Britain United, one First Division football manager responded: "What do I think about the black bastards you mean?". (Wilson, 1991: p. 41)

Dick Wragg, ['Chairman' of the English FA's International Committee] commenting on the issue of racist chanting at a Sheffield United v Newcastle United game: "They're so used to seeing all-white football teams, that they don't like to see darkies introduced ... I'll tell you this, a lot of my friends don't like to see a lot of black people in the teams. But as far as I'm concerned, I tell everybody this, knowing the English players, and our own dark players, they are normally better dressed and better spoken than seventy-five per cent of the white people. The dark fellows who come into the England team, they're tremendously well-behaved, they really are". (Davies, 1991: p. 94)

From the boardroom —

I don't think too many can read the game... You get an awful lot, great pace, great athletes, love to play with the ball in front of them... when it's behind them it's chaos. (Hill, 1991: p. viii)

When you're getting into midwinter in England you need ... the hard white man to carry the artistic black players through — Ron Noades. (Wilson, 1991: p. 41)

From spectators —

Ian Wright: There's a team in South London, which I won't name, where I wouldn't take my family. The fans there throw peanuts on to the pitch. (*The Guardian*, August 13, 1993: p. 20)

Letter to the Everton fanzine *When Skies are Grey* in May 1991:
I speak for the majority of blues when I say Everton are white and should remain so. Quite simply we don't want any coons, pakis, wops, dagos or little yellow friends pulling on the royal blue shirt... Everton are a club of great tradition and we do not want to see any banana chewing wogs at Goodison. Quite simply the majority say keep Everton white.
Colin English, Maghull
PS The police don't clamp down on racist abuse because they agree with it.

National Front "thugs" following England's 1984 tour in Brazil, when John Barnes scored a marvellous individual goal: "these people (who took the same flight as the squad from Montevideo to Santiago, and barracked Barnes all the way) said the score was only 1-0, because 'Nig goals don't count'". (Davies, 1991: p. 244)

Elsewhere —

The ex-Manchester United star [George Best] outraged dinner guests by describing the Brazilian ace [Pele] as "not bad for a nigger" (Rowe, 1993: p. 9); and more recently, during 'An Evening with George Best and Rodney Marsh', Best was asked about the sale of Andy Cole. His reply was, allegedly: "£7 million is a lot to pay for a nigger".[3]

Amongst spectators—

When Raj Dhandsa thinks back to April 3, 1984, his memories are ... [of] the fellow Spurs fan who pulled a knife on his brother and called him a "black bastard" ... The story — one of many we came across — is an example of the racism that seems all too common inside many of Britain's football grounds. (Taylor, 1994: p. 36)

Responses

Players' coping strategies

Players have reported different ways that they respond to various kinds of racist abuse:

> [Brendon] Batson took a bite out of one of the bananas thrown at West Ham: "The worst thing you can do is react angrily. So you join in and have a laugh" (Hill, 1989: p. 14).

> George Berry: "I blow kisses at them when they get at me. I can see 'em bursting at the seams" (Cashmore, 1982: p. 181).

> Bob Hazell: "The barracking makes you concentrate as hard as possible 'cause you know that if there's one slip, the crowd's wanting to get at you for anything at all … If someone says 'you black bastard', I say something equally as personal and that usually subdues them" (Cashmore 1982: pp. 181 and 183).

> Viv Anderson: "'Go and call him a white bastard, then kick him back,' was Clough's robust response to racial taunts on the field" (Longmore, 1988: pp. 46).

> John [Barnes] combats it [racism] with humour. He turned up at the players' Christmas party dressed as a Ku Klux Klansman: "I wanted to go as a banana but I couldn't find a banana suit" (Kennedy, 1988: p. 21).

Brendon Batson's remarks to Dave Hill (1989) are also illustrative of other analyses of the experiences of these players:

> We are conscious of it. Because if any person is going to be subjected to ninety minutes of abuse, you'd have to have a hide thicker than a rhinoceros to say it didn't affect you. I always remember going to places like Leeds and West Ham where they used to hurl bananas at us and what have you… and it is so insulting. But what do you do? Do you react to it, then maybe throw your game completely, and then be subjected to more of it? You've literally got to grin and bear it, everyone thinks, "oh, well, you're accepting it". But I can assure that black players don't accept it. (Hill, 1989: pp. 36-37)

Importantly too, this is a comment about self-control on the field of play, and is interesting in terms of the Cantona incident. For Cantona had crossed the boundary between performer and onlooker, expelled from the field of play. Barnes has claimed that in the thick of the fray, it is not possible to pick out individual comments or even songs from the crowd. As Cantona left the field, he was no longer in the 'thick of the fray', but very close to an easily identifiable xenophobic extremist and racist abuser. Without the protection that anonymity in the crowd would usually afford, Simmons offered himself as a focused target for Cantona's response.

'Let's kick racism out of football'

In 1991, Walsh (1991: p. 26) remarked that:

> The football authorities, for example, have never formulated a policy on racism. This should not surprise us. Such a move would be tantamount to admitting there is a problem which needs tackling, and, since racism is an issue which has consistently been ducked and denied, it has always been an unlikely step. It has been a bit of a taboo subject.

At that time, the real initiatives had been left up to the fans themselves either under the auspices of the Football Supporters Association or through the actions of lobbying groups of activists (e.g., Leeds Fans United Against Racism). Since then, aware of the prevalence of racism in football, the Commission for Racial Equality (CRE) launched a campaign entitled "Let's Kick Racism Out of Football". Of all the clubs in the F. A. Premiership and the Football League, only York City have not embraced the scheme. Important steps forward have been made by clubs that have had notoriously vociferous racist elements in their crowds — especially Leeds United and Millwall (Wainwright, 1994; Ouseley, 1994).

Other interventions have helped to create a climate of increasing intolerance to racism. Some clubs have imposed bans on spectators who abuse black players: for example, Newcastle United, Oldham Athletic and Blackburn Rovers (Harris, 1994). The effective penalty against racist fans might be not so much prosecution by the law as expulsion by the football club.

There is also a clause under the Football Offences Act of 1991 that makes racist chanting illegal, yet in spite of good intentions and purposeful interventions, football grounds free of racism are still some way off. The racist chanting persists, and the police have not been successful in enforcing that particular element of the Act; for example, one fan who had allegedly made monkey noises and sung offensive songs could not be convicted because it was successfully argued that chanting required the involvement of at least two people, and the prosecution had failed to prove that others were taking part (Taylor, 1994). More worrying still are the stories of spectators who, on complaining to the police about racist abuse on the terraces, are themselves then threatened by the police with ejection from the ground (Taylor 1994); and it would certainly be true to say that all clubs have not been as proactive as they might have been in their attempts to deal with racism on the terraces. Keith Alexander, one of the first black football league managers (since sacked by Lincoln City) commented:

> I think at certain clubs there will always be racial chants. We played at Colchester first game of the season not long after every club in the league had had the directive about trying to eradicate racism in football — blah, blah, blah. And they were chanting every time Steve Mardenborough touched the ball. Eventually, midway through the second half, there came an announcement over the tannoy — anyone shouting racial abuse would be kicked out of the ground. You know? But it was too late. (Avery, 1994)

"The whole crowd was singing it": institutionalising racism

When one football fan was accused and convicted of calling Andy Cole a 'black bastard' he was sentenced to a 3 month ban from football grounds and a £100 fine (Taylor, 1994). His excuse that "The whole crowd was singing it" raises an important point about the extent to which racist abuse of black footballers has become institutionalised. It may be that it has become so entrenched and widely practised that it has become a kind of institution in itself: "regularly and continuously repeated, ... sanctioned and maintained by social norms" (Abercrombie, *et al.*, *1984*: pp. 110-111).

The football ground has offered a forum for the normalizing of otherwise untolerated behaviours; a social and cultural space literally and symbolically out-of-bounds of mores and conventions of everyday life. It can render the intolerable and the abnormal routine, institutionalizing in the anonymity of the crowd what would be unspeakable on many levels of individual conduct. Elements of blame clearly lie with the media, whose responses often feed stereotypes and negative evaluations rather than countering them.

'We like big tits, but we don't like wogs' (Sweeney, 1988: p. 62)

Sweeney's telling caricature of the editorial policy of the tabloid press illustrates the racist attitudes of the press itself. But it would be wrong to condemn only the tabloid newspapers for this; for whilst the BBC is arguably less concerned with the exploitation of the female body, it has not been dynamic in challenging racism as manifested at football grounds. When literally thousands of spectators have 'racially' abused black footballers, some football commentators have remained rather silent on the matter (Whannel, 1992; Klein, 1993). Others have offered a rather odd perspective on the matter; for instance, the way John Barnes was abused by the Everton crowd was described variously — Ray Clemence: "Good-natured banter"; Jimmy Hill: "Not a place for anyone with a faint heart or nervous disposition"; Trevor Brooking: "The atmosphere is electric as always" (cited in Hill, 1989).

The nearest that television[4] commentators seem to get to openly acknowledging and condemning racism in football is exemplified in commentator John Motson's words: "A few boos being directed there at John Barnes. We could do without that" (Hill, 1989: p. 146). Hill concludes:

> The BBC's presentation of the match was an object lesson in the way television's production values effectively sanitize football and largely exclude reflection of the social issues connected with it... The result was that an entire, central element of a major footballing occasion — the violently racist behaviour of Everton fans — went utterly unremarked. (1989: pp. 141-142)

Sport and ethnicity present a paradox for broadcasters, for as Whannel (1992: p. 191) explains: "television celebrates nationalism and national identity, and mobilises viewer identification with British chances". But it is not a great leap from espousing nationalism through sport to the identification of supposedly national characteristics — which are often value-laden. John Hargreaves (1986: p. 157) begins to unravel the complexity of this in the kind of language used by commentators and the sorts of adjectives that they apply:

> The major motivating signifiers here are hair and skin colour: 'Latin' connotes 'fiery' and also 'bad' (cynical, dishonest, dirty — the England football manager Alf Ramsey's celebrated castigation of the Argentineans as 'animals' partakes of this kind of discourse)[5]. 'Nordic' is 'cool' and 'good' (professional, open, disciplined).

Xenophobia and Euroracism — sports politics and popular culture

An ethnocentrism bordering on and not infrequently spilling over into xenophobia underpins much supporter banter and 'hooligan' ethos when football fans travel the world (Williams, *et al.*, 1984: p. 184):

> 'We'll show the Krauts why they lost the last war'
> 'Two world wars and a world cup too, doodah, doodah'

For Eric Cantona, the public debate over his actions has in part been cast in xenophobic terms: "Eric's mad say Frogs..." (*Daily Star*, January 27, 1995:

p. 2). And even when the comment is more restrained, the message is one based on cultural stereotypes: "I'm not defending what Eric did. But he'd just been sent off and he's got a Latin mentality" (Cable, 1995: p. 5). The 'scallywag' popular humour has not been slow to leap on the bandwagon too. Following his other sending-off only days before, the 'joke' about early baths was predictable:

HA HA
QUESTION: Who is the only Frenchman in recent times who is known to have had TWO baths in just one week?
ANSWER: Eric Cantona. (*Daily Star*, January 28, 1995: p. 7)

Here, the popular stereotypical notion of the foreigner as the contemptible unwashed is played on by the tabloid press. In the 1994-95 season, too, a scallywag kind of humour was directed at players by the fans of the struggling Everton Football Club, eventual FA Cup winners. Daniel Amokachi, star of the Nigerian side in the 1994 World Cup in the USA, found life difficult at Everton at first, in a poor side lacking in confidence. Everton fans, whose club was reputed to operate — however implicitly — racist policies and practices, soon embraced the African player with their terrace wit: "Question: What's big and black and carries lots of passengers? Answer: Daniel Amokachi", pronounced "Ama Taxi". Although this is actually a football joke against the rest of the team, it is easy to see how some might see elements of racism — rather than merely innocent Merseyside literalness and banter — in the joke.

Football has been a powerful force for international contact and, potentially, understanding. But its competitiveness and its nationalistic basis have perpetuated cultural stereotypes and institutional prejudices. When the world governing body, the Federation Internationale de Football Association (FIFA) was formed, England initially stayed out, displaying an arrogant superciliousness towards the seven European countries which founded FIFA in 1904. The English joined the following year, with an Englishman taking over the Presidency "with a clear mandate 'to regulate football on the Continent as a pure sport'" (Tomlinson, 1994: p. 15). Over half a century later, the Englishman Sir Stanley Rous succeeded another Englishman as President of FIFA in 1961, and held the post until the Brazilian João Havelange defeated him in 1974. Havelange mobilised the Third World nations, and during his Presidency has sought to promote the game worldwide and broaden the base of the World Cup. The English football journalist Brian Glanville has been an outspoken critic on this, writing in 1984 that Havelange has "ruined the World Cup, has sold it down the river to the Afro-Asians and their ilk" (cited in Tomlinson, 1994: p. 23). This Eurocentric prejudice constitutes a form of xenophobic arrogance.

FIFA itself has been accused of racism. The 1995 World Youth Cup was to be hosted by Nigeria, and £50 million was spent in achieving the facilities and infrastructure demanded by FIFA. For obscure reasons concerning health, safety and alleged insurance problems for European nations, and then the state of Nigerian politics, the event was postponed, cancelled, then rescheduled to take place in the Gulf State of Qatar (Radnege, 1995: p. 50). The Nigerians were far from happy about this, as was reported in *The Observer*:

> FIFA said it cancelled the tournament because of an outbreak of cholera and meningitis in Nigeria. The Nigerian FA Chairman Emeka Omervah said: "FIFA are being political. They don't want any black country to host the competition". (*The Observer Sport*, February 12, 1995: p. 2)

The politics of the situation are clearly complex. The global stretch of FIFA's influence in Havelange's regime might well have overcome some xenophobic constraints upon the growth of the world game, but there is clearly a belief among some of FIFA's members that it is racist in some of its current policies and practices.

One of the joys of sport is its capacity to symbolize a culture and the aspirations of a culture. But this of course can lead to a conservative and reactionary politics of identity. Examples of this can be seen in the British football comic, where the foreigner is seen as not just an adjunct to the adventure narrative, but as different and unreliable. The right-winger (positional, not political) Pierre Dupont is presented in one *Roy of the Rovers* adventure in the comic *Tiger* as "a queer character … always going off on mysterious jaunts" (*Tiger — The Sport and Adventure Picture Story Weekly*, 22 December 1956: no. 120). Players from other countries are often presented as ruthless cheats, lacking core qualities of fair play and sportsmanship. A defender for Portugal's Corados in Melchester Rovers' European Cup Winners' Cup Final in the 1972-73 season is presented as cunningly pretending not to speak English, and as 'patronising' and provoking — a foreigner playing in a fashion alien to the true sporting spirit of English football (Acton and Jarman, 1994: pp. 87-91). In Summer tours abroad Melchester players are kidnapped, threatened, abused, in strange-sounding countries by sinister-looking characters. For almost 40 years from September 11, 1954 to March 20, 1993, when the comic closed, English football was presented to generations of new readers as honest, gritty, fair, and world-conquering — in contrast at many points to the football cultures and values of other countries and nations. The short life of the *Roy of the Rovers Monthly* publication from Summer 1993 to Winter 1994/95 could never relive these past glories, though to its credit it did take on board issues such as racism and profiled black players very prominently and urged its dwindling readership to oppose all forms of racism in the game.

Cultural difference and cultural identity — some positive contributions of football

Xenophobia as the irrational fear of the other and as the denigration of difference must be opposed in any open-minded and civilised society and culture. But the collapsing of all difference would be absurd, and would be a sham. But how can ethnic and cultural differences be celebrated without perpetuating racist stereotypes or cultivating xenophobic values? Football's role in asserting cultural distinctiveness is a reminder of the complexities of this question.

In 1851, 220,000 of the 400,000 population of the English industrial city of Manchester/Salford were born elsewhere, and the ethnic and cultural communities within the society made sense of their new environment by (to paraphrase Mike Cole) defining *themselves* as "structured by specific cultural characteristics" and forming "differentiated social collectivities". Networks of immigrants interconnected, forming separate yet mutually respectful Irish, Jewish and Italian communities, for instance. The former professional footballer, Irish writer Eamonn Dunphy writes revealingly on this in his book on Matt Busby and Manchester United:

> Manchester *was* different. There were more minorities than in most other English cities, all in their own way victims of prejudice ... Manchester had the feel of a place where things weren't yet decided, where identity could be determined by the kind of person you were — and things you did — rather than the tribe you belonged to; Manchester was still working out its identity. Football had played a significant role in the creation of the city's image of itself. (Dunphy, 1991: p. 94)

This capacity of football to generate and not merely reflect a cultural identity is sometimes neglected in well-intentioned attempts to play down ethnic and cultural differences.

The Accra Football Club in Brixton, South London is an exclusively black club (Morgan, 1995). One of its members tells how he asked a steward directions at a professional football game: "'You better find your way back to Heathrow Airport', the steward replied" (Morgan, 1995: p. 22). In the light of reactions such as this it is understandable why the club stays exclusively black. It is seen by one of its organisers as a valuable social institution which can help prepare young black men for the difficulties they are likely to encounter in a racist society. The club can help them build self-confidence, and to express themselves through sport in ways that will be beneficial in other spheres of life. It is also about a distinctive cultural assertiveness, a pride in being black. That a search for positive cultural identity develops in such a separatist form as the Accra Club is understandable, yet is also a cause for concern — however admirable the motives of the organisers, such an initiative must also be recognised as a classic form of moral intervention-ism, scarcely challenging of the social context which is generative of the problem in the first place. Such a cultural separatism is, too, primarily excluding, violating as it does the principle of equality of access which drives the meritocratic motor of much of modern competitive sport.

Concluding reflections and issues for further research

Sport has been a major factor in breaking down racial and religious barriers; long may it continue to pioneer this cause. Sport can bring about a situation of one-ness regardless of colour. For some, it has continued to epitomise the true spirit and brotherhood of "man" (Hamilton, 1982: p. 10). But the idealised capacity of sport to promote such universalised values is counterbalanced by other tendencies.

The most repeated song on one football trip to Bilbao was a revamped version of the official Spurs Wembley song. The new version expressed the following sentiments (Williams *et al.*, 1984: p. 58):

> Spurs are on the way to Auschwitz. Hitler's gonna gas 'em again.
> You can't stop 'em, The yids from Tottenham,
> The yids from White Hart Lane.

The Cantona affair, and the context in which it occurred — alongside, in the same month, the extremist political hooliganism which caused the abandonment of the Republic of Ireland-England international in Dublin — exposed the deep-lying roots of an Anglo-British racism and xenophobia. That such roots can co-exist with the capacity of football to act as a source of cultural expression, and celebratory but non-threatening national identity, is one of the sport's enduring fascinations and dangers.

Chronicler of the Cantona affair, Ian Ridley, ultimately reads the affair as an indictment of the darker side of the game, Cantona as victim of a residual extremist nationalism, and comments: "The anti-racist, anti-violence, anti-drugs campaigns ... do need to be stepped up. We must be brave enough to speak up, with support from other decent supporters, when we encounter ugliness" (Ridley, 1995b: p. 200). And, as Ridley also reports, the Cantona incident did prompt the English FA to speak out against "the increasing levels of abuse that footballers have to suffer", in Chief Executive Graham Kelly's words (Ridley, 1995b: p. 38).

In April 1996 Eric Cantona was awarded the title of Footballer of the Year by the English football press/writers, to add to his 1994 award of Player of the Year which he received from his peers. This was remarkable testimony of the rehabilitation of Cantona, after his long suspension from the game. The previous footballer of the year in England was Jürgen Klinsmann. It is telling to note that both these 'foreign' stars received the English accolade after transforming themselves — from the media's portrayal of them as arrogant, ruthless, cheating German, and haughty temperamental Mediterranean Frenchman, respectively — into models of the English gentleman and sportsman. When such transformations of image are not so easily effected — in intolerant forms of xenophobia and expressed forms of racism, cultural evaluations operate to unacceptably negative effect.

In reviewing the range of sources and themes above, the following five negative and three more positive points arise concerning the question of Euroracism, xenophobia, cultural identity and football:

*   players and fans have to tolerate persisting forms of racism in the public culture of the football ground;
*   racist aspects of extremist far-right politics are worryingly compatible with established elements in British football culture;
*   personalised racism is widespread in the everyday discourses of football culture;
*   xenophobia and racism are characteristic of governing bodies at national and international levels;
*   popular culture, in forms such as the comic-book football narrative, perpetuates cultural stereotypes and xenophobic values.

On a more positive side:

*   the passion of football can be celebratory of difference without being denigrating of it;
*   'race'-based cultural separatism, and ethnic distinctiveness, can find valuable expression in a sport such as football;
*   football is a source for the articulation of complex 'race'/place dynamics, which translate into shifting expressions of identity.

In Britain racist prejudices run deep, and despite all the institutional interventions in the world the misplaced cultural pride of dominant racist groups continues to promote unacceptable types and levels of racist discourse and practice. Nick Hornby (1992) has written of his wish that fans, players, and commentators would express their disgust at and opposition to racism. There is a fine balance between cultural caricaturing, offensive stereotyping and a damaging xenophobia — but there *is* the possibility of a pre-offensive non-threatening balance. A xenophobic element connected to a racist disposition — a not uncommon cocktail in British football culture — is, though, a threat to the standards of a civilised society and a culturally tolerant international community. It is for this reason the football community must be castigated — at all its levels, from the terrace fan to the world governing body — for its complacency and its naïveté in either denying the extent of racism in the game, or hoping that it will simply go away.

Recommended further research

*   Systematic research on the life-histories of black and 'foreign' players, particularly those who have played in several European countries;
*   Analysis of the policies of national associations and the international ruling body, in terms of their stances on racism and their approach to issues of national identity and cultural affiliation;
*   Analysis of the coverage and presentation of non-nationals in the English press;
*   Comparative ethnographic study of terrace and club fan cultures in different European countries, with detailed investigation of special cases such as Northern Ireland and Catalonia.

Acknowledgements

Many thanks to: Dr Mike Cole for his comments on the early drafts of this paper; Dr John Sugden for his detailed analytical response to the extended second draft of the paper.

Notes

1   The full picture of the case against Cantona has been added to by the allegations that Cantona had constantly flouted authority in a turbulent career, and that he had had many disciplinary problems. Psychologists were invited to diagnose the problem with Cantona's psyche, and some even speculated that this behaviour was a product of being under-appreciated as a child by his father, and/or a direct consequence of his diminished self esteem resulting from a childhood speech impediment. In contrast Simmons was initially portrayed in the tabloid press as a 'nice young man' who lived with his mother and lived for Crystal Palace Football Club.

2   As the stories and counter-stories began to gather momentum, it was revealed that Simmons revelled in the nickname of 'Psycho' in local league football, that he had been a spanner-wielding service-station raider with a conviction for 'assault with intent to rob', and that he received £20,000 for his story from the News International group — which includes *The Sun* newspaper (Ridley, 1995a). As the weight of public opinion began to at least understand, if not condone Cantona's violent outburst, Jimmy Greaves reflected:

Who does he think he is, Mr Cholmondley-Warner?... A measly ten quid does not give you permission to abuse, taunt, spit, lob coins, make rude gestures, throw missiles and generally behave in a way that would get you locked up if you repeated it in the High Street. (Greaves and Samuel, 1995: p. 4)

The pendulum of public opinion swung Cantona's way and his punishment of community service in the form of football coaching for local children was not so much a punishment as a further chance to restore his status as superstar and idol. One former player and journalist saw this early on in the process: "Eric Cantona has in England become a cult hero, marketing thuggish behaviour with impunity" (Dunphy, 1995: p. 8).

3 Could it be that the fact that Best is an East Belfast Protestant (or "Prod") is significant here? To a white working-class Protestant from East Belfast to call someone a "nigger" is a fact of everyday life. We are grateful to John Sugden for suggesting this connection.

4 The only condemnation that Hill (1989) notes was from radio commentators, Alan Green and Dennis Law on BBC Radio 2, and Clive Tyldesley on Liverpool's local commercial radio station.

5 This depiction was comically exposed as fraudulent on Channel 4 Television's "Fantasy Football" on Friday, 12 April, 1995, when the English team's own style of play could be seen to be less than pure.

References

Abercrombie, N., Hill, B. and Turner, S. (1984) *The Penguin Dictionary of Sociology*. Harmondsworth: Penguin.

Acton, P. and Jarman, C. M. [compiled by] (1994) *Roy of the Rovers — The Playing Years*. Harpenden: Queen Anne Press.

Allen, D. (1995) 'It was an unforgivable act and I regret what I did', *News of the World*, 29 January: p. 2.

Avery, R. (1994) B. Sc. (Hons.) Sports Science. Undergraduate dissertation, University of Brighton.

Bairner, A. (1994) 'Football and the Idea of Scotland', in G. Jarvie and G. Walker (eds) *Scottish Sport in the Making of the Nation — Ninety Minute Patriots?*. Leicester: Leicester University Press, pp. 9-26.

Brough, G. and Mackay, D. (1995) 'Cantona's victim is thug', *Daily Mirror*, 27 January: p. 1.

Buford, B. (1991) *Among the Thugs*. London: Secker and Warburg.

Cable, A. (1995) 'Is he barmy or what? Genius is next to madness — Cantona on the couch', *The Sun*, 27 January: p. 5.

Canter, D., Comber, M. and Uzzell, D. L. (1989) *Football in its Place — An Environmental Psychology of Football Grounds*. London: Routledge.

Cashmore, E. (1982) *Black Sportsmen*, London: Routledge.

Cole, M. (1996) '"Race" and Racism', in M. Payne (ed) *A Dictionary of Cultural and Critical Theory*. Blackwell: Oxford.

Critcher, C. (1979) 'Football Since the War', in B. Waites, T. Bennett and G. Martin (eds) *Popular Culture: Past and Present*. London: Croom Helm, pp. 219-241.

Daily Mirror (1995) 'Comment', 27 January: p. 6.

Davies, P. (1991) *All Played Out — The Full Story of Italia '90*. London: Mandarin.

Dunphy, E. (1991) *A Strange Kind of Glory — Sir Matt Busby & Manchester United*. London: Heinemann.

Dunphy, E. (1995) 'Lament for a lost game', *Independent on Sunday*, 19 February: p. 8.

Fishwick, N. (1989) *English Football and Society*, 1910-1950. Manchester: Manchester University Press.

Giulianotti, R., Bonney, N. and Hepworth, M. (1994) (eds) *Football, Violence and Social Identity*. London: Routledge.

Greaves, J. and Samuel, R. (1995)*The Sun*, 28 January: pp. 4-5.

The Guardian (1993) 'Soccer's true colours', 16 August: pp. 2-3.

Hamilton, A. (1982) *Black Pearls of Soccer*. London: Harrap.

Hargreaves, John (1986) *Sport, Power and Culture: A Social and Cultural Analysis of Popular Sports in Britain*. Cambridge: Polity Press.

Harris, H. (1994) 'Fash in Everton race blast', *Daily Mirror*, 11 May: p. 25.

Hill, D. (1989) *'Out of his skin': The John Barnes Phenomenon*. London: Faber and Faber.

Hill, D. (1991) 'The race game', *The Guardian Guide*, 31 August: p. viii-ix.

Holt, R. (1989) *Sport and the British*. Oxford: Oxford University Press.

Hornby, N. (1992) *Fever Pitch*. London: Victor Gollancz Ltd.

Kelly, E., and Cohn, T. (1988) *Racism in Schools — New Research Evidence*. Stoke-on-Trent: Trentham Books.

Kennedy, P. (1988) 'Private joy of John Barnes', *Daily Express*, 8 March: pp. 20-21.

Klein, G. (1993) *Education Towards Race Education*. London: Cassell.

Kuper, S. (1994) *Football Against the Enemy*. London: Orion.

Longmore, A. (1988) *Viv Anderson*. London: Heinemann Kingswood.

Maguire, J. A. (1988) 'Race and position assignment in English Soccer: A preliminary analysis of ethnicity and sport in Britain', *Sociology of Sport Journal*, Vol. 5, No. 3: pp. 257–269.

Mason, T. (1980) *Association Football and English Society 1863-1915*. Sussex: The Harvester Press.

Mason, T. (1995) *Passion of the People — Football in South America*. London: Verso.

Morgan, A. (1995) 'Racism won't affect our goals', *The Independent*, 25 January: p. 22.

Moorhouse, H. F. (1995) 'One state, several countries: Soccer and nationality in a "United Kingdom"', *The International Journal of the History of Sport*, Vol. 12, No. 2: pp. 55-74.

Murray, B. (1994) *Football — A History of the World Game*. Aldershot: Scolar Press.

Newman, D., Hudson, D. and Lancaster, S. (1994) 'Vinny wants a word boyo', *Daily Star*, 21 December: p. 1.

Ouseley, H. (1994) 'Do I not like that … rooting out the racists', *Independent on Sunday — Sport*, 25 May: p. 10.

Radnege, K. (1995) 'Qatar to the rescue', *World Soccer*, Vol. 35, No. 8 (May): p. 50.

Redhead, S. (1987) *Sing When You're Winning: The Last Football Book*. London: Pluto Press.

Redhead, S. (1991) *Football with Attitude*. Manchester: Wordsmith.

Redhead, S. (ed) (1993) *The Passion and the Fashion — Football Fandom in the New Europe*. Aldershot: Arena/Ashgate Publishing Ltd.

Ridley, I. (1995a) 'Game needs to win back respect', *Independent on Sunday — Sport*, 29 January: p. 3.

Ridley, I. (1995b) *Cantona: The Red and the Black*. London: Victor Gollancz, Ltd.

Robins, D. (1984) *We Hate Humans*. Harmondsworth: Penguin Books.

Rowe, D. (1993) 'Pele slur gets Best red card', *Sunday Mirror*, 16 May: p. 9.

Sugden, J. and Bairner, A. (1993) *Sport, Society and Sectarianism in a Divided Ireland*. Leicester: Leicester University Press.

Sugden, J. and Tomlinson, A. (1994) (eds) *Hosts and Champions — Soccer Cultures, National Identities and the USA World Cup*. Aldershot: Arena/Ashgate Publishing Ltd.

Sweeney, J. (1988) 'Hop off you hacks', *Observer Magazine*, 7 August: p. 62.

Syson, N. and Lazzeri, A. (1995) 'I could see the whites of his eyes — Cantona kick victim tells of terror', *The Sun*: pp. 2-3.

Taylor, D. (1994) 'Walking away from football', *Sports Magazine*, March, 36-38.

Tomlinson, A. (1994) 'FIFA and the World Cup: The expanding football family', in J. Sugden and A. Tomlinson (eds) *Hosts and Champions: Soccer Cultures, National Identities and the USA World Cup*. Aldershot: Arena/Ashgate Publishing Ltd., pp. 13-33.

Tomlinson, A. and Whannel, G. (eds) (1986) *Off the Ball — the Football World Cup*. London: Pluto Press.

Towers, M. and Mackay, D. (1995) '20 pints and a good punch-up', *Daily Mirror*, 28 January: p. 3.

Tysome, T. (1995) 'Cantona clash linked to football racism', *The Times Higher Education Supplement*, 10 February: p. 5.

Wagg, S. (1984) *The Football World: A Contemporary Social History*. Brighton: The Harvester Press.

Wainwright, M. (1994) 'Leeds tactics kick out worst troublemakers on terraces', *The Guardian*, 11 May: p. 2.

Walsh, M. (1991) 'Coming through the hard way', *Sport and Leisure*, Vol. 32, No. 5: pp. 26-27.

Walvin, J. (1975) *The People's Game*. London: Allen Lane.

Ward, C. (1989) *Steaming In — Journal of a Football Fan*. London: Sportspages.

Whannel, G. (1992) *Fields in Vision — Television Sport and Cultural Transformation*. London: Routledge.

Williams, J. and Wagg, S. (eds) (1991) *British Football and Social Change — Getting into Europe*. Leicester: Leicester University Press.

Williams, J., Dunning, E. and Murphy, P. (1984) *Hooligans Abroad*, 2nd Edition. London: Routledge.

Wilson, P. (1991) 'The black man's burden', *Observer Sport*, 22 September: p. 41.

FOOTBALL, RACISM AND XENOPHOBIA IN ENGLAND (II): CHALLENGING RACISM AND XENOPHOBIA

Jon Garland and Michael Rowe

Introduction

There is a certain irony in that one of the legacies of the 'English disease' of football hooliganism is that there seems to have been a greater academic investigation into the nature of football and its fans in Britain compared to elsewhere. Coupled with the efforts of supporters' groups and the football clubs and authorities, these inquiries have meant that a concern about and desire to tackle the problem of racism and xenophobia has developed in Britain in recent years as efforts to tackle the wider problem of hooliganism have continued. It seems that the hooliganism phenomenon has produced, as if in accord with Newton's third law, an equal and opposite reaction.

Although parallels can be drawn between the British and the continental European experience of football and hooliganism, it must not be assumed that the British case can be discussed as if it were either typical or universal. Neither are we suggesting that British attempts to deal with these problems can be replicated in other contexts. As other contributions included in this volume indicate, situations in the various countries are so disparate that even finding common terminology is problematic. This chapter does no more than offer a brief account of the history of racism in British football and an evaluation of some of the key anti-racist initiatives. If some resonance with other experiences is perceived, then so much the better.

One of the central reasons for examining racism and xenophobia in the context of football is that, in certain respects, this sport presents a mirror (although arguably a distorted one) to society and reflects back deeper processes therein. Given this, it is impossible to divorce one from another or even to understand the nature of racism and xenophobia in football apart from the social context in which it develops. Although often employed as an excuse

Racism and Xenophobia in European Football

for inaction, there is some truth in the claim that racism and xenophobia are society's problem, not football's. The recent campaign to 'kick racism out of football' (discussed below), was initiated by, amongst others, the Commission for Racial Equality, who have begun to develop a more campaigning role in British society. It is such particularities of the English experience which will be outlined here.

Ironically it has been the success of black footballers that has made the need for such anti-racist strategies more apparent. In the 1970s, when black footballers such as Viv Anderson, Brendon Batson and Laurie Cunningham first appeared in the English game in any significant number, the degree of racist abuse that they endured was often regarded as no more significant than the abuse that all players, of whatever ethnic background, received from opposition fans. It is to the game's credit that this complacency is being challenged, although it has certainly not disappeared completely. There are other developments in the attitudes towards the issue of racism and football which are also welcome and encouraging. That is, the growing recognition that racism is a problem for the fans themselves, and not just the players. Just as football clubs are beginning to court a family-friendly image (largely as hooliganism, at least within grounds, is declining), there are signs that the clubs are beginning to realise that racism is also alienating their potential *customers* from the minority ethnic populations. Alienating customers is clearly as unwise for the football clubs as it is for any other enterprise.

On a European scale the problem of xenophobia becomes increasingly salient. As European integration develops, the question of reducing xenophobic stereotypes, prejudices and misconceptions becomes an issue of technical and practical, as well as moral, significance. In this sense football is elevated to a position where its competition becomes a metaphor for national rivalry. The old xenophobic English response to German football, which reminds the fans of 'two World Wars and one World Cup', illustrates this point very well. As the member states of the European Union attempt to forge new partnerships at different levels (political, cultural, and economic, for example) football should be encouraged to reduce xenophobic mistrust and misrepresentation and not be allowed, largely via the media, to run counter to these broader developments.

Following the outline of the history of racism and xenophobia in football in Britain, the remainder of this chapter is structured in the following way. Firstly, we present a brief outline of our methodology. We then examine the trends identifiable from our various interviews and surveys. A variety of anti-racist initiatives are then analysed, before a discussion of these findings concludes this chapter.

The issue of 'race' in British football: an outline

Contrary to popular belief, there have been minority ethnic[1] footballers in Britain for at least a century. It has been suggested[2] that the first professional black player was Arthur Warton, who signed for Darlington FC in 1889; and Celtic reserves fielded an Indian, Abdul Salim, in the 1930s. In the 1960s Clyde Best of West Ham and Albert Johanneson of Leeds United became the first *high profile* black players in the English league by playing successfully in the top division. As in other areas of British history, the presence and contribution of minority ethnic groups is often marginalised or forgotten. Laurie Cunningham, Brendan Batson, Viv Anderson and those others who were heralded as 'ground-breaking' black professionals in the 1970s were not, in fact, without antecedents.

What does seem to have changed in the last few decades is the number of African Caribbean professionals in English football. Whereas the presence of a black player was worthy of note thirty years ago, it is now unusual to watch a team that has none at all. Recent England squads have included black players such as John Barnes, Andy Cole, Les Ferdinand, Paul Ince (the first black player to captain England), Paul Parker, Trevor Sinclair, Des Walker, and Ian Wright. When England played San Marino in November 1993, no less than six members of the 16-man squad were black, as were all of the scorers of England's seven goals.

Recent years have also seen an increase in the number of players from other European countries. In the 1970s the Dutch players Arnold Mürhen and Franz Thyssen played in the top division in England; Jan Molby joined Liverpool in the 1980s. More recently, internationally-renowned players such as Eric Cantona, Jürgen Klinsmann, Ruud Gullit, and Denis Bergkamp have joined English clubs. The reaction to their arrival has been mixed in many respects and has included xenophobic attitudes and stereotypes. Before Klinsmann's arrival at Tottenham Hotspur, for example, the media often portrayed him as a cynical player prepared to cheat. It was only when Klinsmann deflated this image by performing an exaggerated dive to celebrate his debut goal that the press and fans began to treat him as a hero. The discussion of the 'Cantona incident' (outlined in Fleming and Tomlinson's contribution) often referred to his 'Gallic temperament' by way of understanding his otherwise inexplicable behaviour.

Although there are now significant numbers of black players in Britain there is only one professional from an Asian background. Many explanations for this from within the game repeat familiar racist stereotypes (suggesting that

Asians are physically unsuited to a harsh game) that were also propagated about black players in the 1970s[3].

Others claim that Asian people are not interested in the game for cultural reasons, preferring to play other sports. Although less pejorative than arguments about physique, this claim seems equally untenable. Football is played in many Asian countries: it is even the national game of Bangladesh. In Britain there is evidence that Asian people do play the game. A study conducted in 1991 (Verma, *et al., 1991*) found that a higher proportion of the Bengali community played football than any other group (including whites).

One reason why this high-level of involvement does not translate into professional circles may be related to the nature of the leagues and teams in which Asians play. For various reasons it seems that Asians are often playing football in a different environment from that which the scouts of professional clubs turn to in their search for fresh talent. Every year, for example, several dozen teams from the Patel community (originally from the Gujerat and Mahrastra regions of India) participate in their own competition which is watched by several thousand supporters. Also, over 30 teams compete in the Laurentian Life Asian Football League.

Some club officials are beginning to recognise that the scouting procedure may be inadvertently over-looking possible talent. The Community Liaison Officer at Leicester City recognises that:

> ... scouts don't look for Asian players because they have not been regarded as likely pros. They watch the two or three non-League clubs where we traditionally get pros from, not the Asian teams, even though many of them are very good... (Brown, 1995: p. 15)

Whilst football clubs, authorities and fans have taken various steps (as discussed below) to counter racism in the game, it appears that the problem is still conceived as one which affects black people. Clearly the position of other minority ethnic groups requires greater attention.

Attempts to tackle racism and xenophobia in British football have evolved alongside moves to counter the broader problem of football hooliganism. A detailed history of this problem cannot be given here. Instead we give a brief outline of one of the key ways in which the problems of racism and of hooliganism intersect, namely the activities of Far Right groups at football. Extreme right-wing groups in Britain and elsewhere have regarded football crowds as potentially fertile recruiting grounds since at least the 1930s, when the British Union of Fascists tried to attract the young working class male supporters into their brigade of uniformed 'stewards'. During the late 1950s the

White Defence League sold their newspaper *Black and White News* at various grounds in London.

It was not until the 1970s, though, that the problem of football hooliganism drew attention to the role of Far Right groups such as the National Front. The Front's magazine *Bulldog* included a regular column about football and encouraged the throwing of bananas at black players. *Bulldog* also carried a regular 'League of Louts' and encouraged hooligan groups to compete for the title of 'most racist ground in Britain'. Whilst particular clubs had reputations for strong fascist elements during the 1970s — for example, Chelsea, Leeds United, and West Ham United — it seems that the presence of such groups at the club-level has waned more recently as we discuss below. However, there is anecdotal evidence which suggests that Far Right groups are now commonplace at England fixtures and some suggestion that Combat 18 were involved, to some extent, in the violence at the aborted Ireland-England game in February 1995.

Various attempts to confront the problem of football hooliganism have been made during the last few decades, not all of which can be outlined here[4]. Many of these have concentrated on improving the policing of football crowds and controlling their travel arrangements so that separate groups of fans do not come into contact before the game. Fences were erected at most grounds during the 1970s and early 1980s so as to physically prevent hooligans from confronting their opponents[5]. The police have also concentrated on gathering intelligence about the activities of the hooligan 'firms' which represent the hard-core of the problem. The National Football Intelligence Unit was established in 1989 and now regularly monitors such groups as well as liaising with forces in other countries where international fixtures are concerned.

The introduction of closed circuit television (CCTV) into most major grounds has helped to reduce the levels of hooliganism within stadia. Footage recorded by CCTV has been successfully used in prosecutions and means that perpetrators can be identified and arrested sometime after the actual incident has passed. That CCTV deters fans from misbehaving is evidenced by one football intelligence officer who went so far as to suggest that, of the fans of the club he polices:

> ... they are now very wary of cameras. Point a camera at our lot and they don't like it. And that's true about a lot of the 'top lads' from other teams, because a lot of them have been convicted by the use of CCTV.[6]

There is less certainty about whether this development has led to an absolute decline in levels of violence or just that the location for such incidents has been displaced from the ground to city centres, railway stations, and so on.

Trends in the level of racist abuse at football matches

Methodology

Trends in the level of racist abuse in football during the last five years were identified through the analysis of the results of a questionnaire and interviews we conducted. During December 1994 120 questionnaires were distributed to 'fanzine'[7] editors. Of these, 49 questionnaires were completed: a response rate of 41 per cent. Fanzine editors associated with a wide range of clubs from all divisions responded. The *Carling Premiership Fan Surveys 1993/1994*[8] were used in order to support the evidence from the questionnaire. Interviews were conducted with representatives of the Commission for Racial Equality (CRE) and various football bodies. These included representatives from the Football Association (FA), Football Trust, Football Supporters Association (FSA)[9], Professional Footballers Association (PFA) and with the players and officials of six clubs.

Racism in Football

All respondents felt that there was racism in football, to varying degrees (see Figure 1). A clear majority (79 per cent) of respondents felt that there were elements of racism throughout football, while only 2 per cent believed that racism was a serious problem. The remaining 19 per cent of respondents, along with many players interviewed, felt that racism was a problem which was only associated with a handful of clubs (Chelsea, Everton, Leeds United, Millwall and West Ham United, amongst others, were cited in this respect).

Figure 1:　The perception of the pervasiveness of racism in football

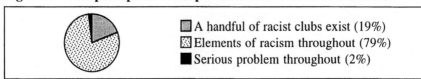

☐ A handful of racist clubs exist (19%)
▨ Elements of racism throughout (79%)
■ Serious problem throughout (2%)

Extent of Racist Abuse

The *Carling Surveys* report that 26.1 per cent of respondents have heard racist abuse at their home ground. However, the CRE believes that this figure under-estimates the actual level of racist abuse at football matches. The very nature of racist remarks may mean that they are not widely heard even when they are made, a point often overlooked by those trying to quanitify such activity (see, for example, Holland, 1995). Racist chanting is a more public phenomenon.

Our questionnaire asked editors about the different forms of racist abuse they had witnessed at football matches. Table 1 illustrates their responses relating to their experiences during the previous year.

Table 1:　Evidence of abuse over the past year

	At every home game	At most home games	Half of home games	A few home games	Never	Total
	(%)	(%)	(%)	(%)	(%)	(%)
Racist chanting	0	4	4	51	41	100
Throwing objects at players	0	0	0	8	92	100
Activity by right-wing groups	0	2	0	21	77	100
Racist remarks	0	2	0	25	73	100
Racist violence	0	0	0	2	98	100
Racist graffiti	0	2	0	33	65	100

The most striking feature of the responses is the perception that racism is not a pervasive feature at football matches. Only a small minority felt that there were problems at most home games. However, racist chanting, such as the infamous 'monkey chant', is the most common form of racist abuse reported at football matches with 51 per cent of respondents having witnessed such abuse at a few home matches over the past year. Although the most common form of racism witnessed, it appears that it is unusual to hear mass racist chanting. Only 8 per cent of respondents were aware of this form of abuse at over half the home games or more. The relative rarity of this type of racism is further emphasised by the fact that 41 per cent of respondents had not heard any racist chanting over the previous year.

A quarter of respondents (25 per cent) were aware of racist remarks made by individuals at a few home games during the past year. Many supporters believe that being racially abusive is no different from abusing, for example, a player who is overweight or losing his hair. It is the common perception by both players and supporters that racist abuse is a part of the game and that black players should accept it or not bother to play. For instance, Steven Morrow of Arsenal said that players have to "accept that we are going to get abuse of some sort, during or after the game"[10]. However, Holland (1995: p. 575) suggests that black players receive more abuse (whether racist or otherwise) than their white counterparts.

That only 25 per cent of respondents were aware of racist remarks made by individuals is a likely underestimate of the extent of the problem, for a variety of reasons. For instance, less racist abuse may be heard in the family section than in other parts of the ground. It must also be noted that levels of abuse vary from club to club. Other research suggests that the ethnic background of the respondent is also an important factor. The *Carling Surveys*, for example, state that 29.0 per cent of non-white supporters had heard abuse at their home ground compared with 24.9 per cent of white supporters.

The majority of respondents to the questionnaire (77 per cent) had not seen any right-wing activity over the past year at their home stadium. A sizeable minority (21 per cent) had witnessed Far Right activity at a few home games. It is clear that right-wing groups, such as Combat 18, are numerically small but have a disproportionate level of influence. Indeed, in 1994 Combat 18 attacked members of the Chelsea Independent Supporters Association after they had begun an anti-racism campaign (World in Action, 1995).

Although there is evidence that the Far Right targets football matches in order to try and recruit supporters (as mentioned above), there is some debate as to how successful they have been. The relatively large numbers of Far Right sympathisers at England matches does not appear to be mirrored at club level. Indeed, apart from a presence amongst fans at a handful of grounds, their influence amongst club supporters in general is believed to be minimal. As the National Football Intelligence Unit suggests:

> We are aware that certain right-wing parties have been looking at football hooligans because they see them as an organised group and try to recruit them for this purpose with, I have to say, fairly limited success ... It has been seen as an opportunity by many, but I don't think it has been a dramatic success, there is no evidence for that.[11]

It appears that throwing objects at black players is rare, with only 8 per cent of respondents having witnessed this at a few home games during the past year. Similarly, there appears to be little racially motivated violence aimed at spectators. However, this may be related to the fact that there are few Asian or black spectators and that "football has still got the image of white men between the ages of 18 and 35, going to football in groups"[12]. This can be illustrated by the ethnic make-up of the respondents to the *Carling Surveys*: 99 per cent of their respondents were white, 0.4 per cent were Asian, 0.2 per cent were Afro-Caribbean and 0.4 per cent were from other minority ethnic groups[13].

There are also examples of black players being racially abused by their fellow professionals. For example, Stuart Pearce allegedly racially abused Paul

Ince in the match between Manchester United and Nottingham Forest in December 1994. It appears from interviews conducted for this research that the attitude of most players is to treat the abuse as a joke or to explain it in terms of a 'heat of the moment' reaction.

Perceived trends in the level of racism

Figure 2 illustrates the perception of the respondents to our questionnaire concerning the level of racism in football over the last five years.

Figure 2:   Reported trends in racism in football during the last five years

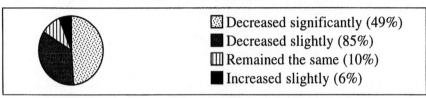

Decreased significantly (49%)
Decreased slightly (85%)
Remained the same (10%)
Increased slightly (6%)

Our results suggest that the level of racist abuse is declining. This finding was echoed by nearly all of the administrators, players, and officials interviewed.

Overall, 84 per cent of respondents believed that the levels of racism at football matches had declined over the past five years. 49 per cent of these respondents felt that there had been a significant decline, while 35 per cent felt that such a decline had been minimal. Further, a general improvement in the atmosphere at matches is cited by 51 per cent of respondents. These results are supported by the *Carling Surveys* where 78.2 per cent of respondents believed that the level of racist abuse was less than a few years ago.

Factors cited in the perceived decline of racist abuse

Figure 3 (following page) illustrates those factors that respondents felt have been influential in the decrease in the levels of racist abuse at football matches (note: the figures total more than 100 per cent because respondents could cite as many reasons as they wished).

As previously mentioned, our questionnaire was completed by fanzine editors. Accordingly we feel that the two most commonly cited factors shown in Figure 3 may have been disproportionately selected. 90 per cent of respondents who felt that fan-based initiatives had been successful attributed this to the fact that such campaigns were organised by and for supporters. The CRE shares this belief that supporter-led campaigns are the most effective method of combating racism because the CRE "can't stop racism by campaigning, it is only individuals who can do this"[14].

Figure 3:   Reasons cited for the perceived decrease in racism at football matches

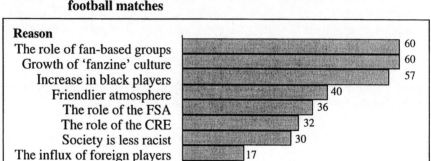

A majority of respondents (60 per cent) was aware of fan-based anti-racism groups such as *Leeds Fans United Against Racism and Fascism* (Leeds United supporters) and *Foxes Against Racism* (Leicester City supporters). The *Leeds Fans United Against Racism and Fascism* campaign (discussed below) resulted in a reduction in the levels of racism at Elland Road and forced Leeds United and West Yorkshire Police to take a strong stand against racism and fascism. Ian Wright of Arsenal FC spoke of the impact of *Leeds Fans United Against Racism and Fascism*, saying:

> ...we went to Leeds the other week — it was brilliant! They've got this thing down there petitioning against the nazis and the racial abuse black players take. I think it's a giant step because Leeds were really bad ... it's changed a lot. (Brown, 1994: p. 10)

Broader changes in the culture of football supporters (also associated with possible declining levels of hooliganism) were also cited. 'Fanzine culture'[15] was seen as instrumental, with 60 per cent of respondents listing this as a factor in the decline of racism in football. Many fanzines actively campaign against racist abuse. For instance, *When Skies Are Grey* (an Everton fanzine) began their campaign during the 1992/93 season in response to the racist abuse directed at black players.

More than half of the respondents (57 per cent) felt that the increase in the numbers of black professional footballers was another factor in the decline of racism. In 1995, approximately a quarter of professional players in England are black and there are very few clubs with no black players, whilst at many clubs such players have achieved heroic status amongst supporters. Thus, it would seem that racism in football has decreased as the number of black professional players has increased.

The improvement in atmosphere at football stadiums was regarded by 40 per cent of respondents as a factor in the decline in racist abuse. This has much to do with the improvement in the behaviour of supporters and the upgrading of facilities after the Hillsborough disaster. The Football Trust argues that:

...it is in no-one's interest if having created these new stadiums they become centres for menace, violence and racism.[16]

It has been argued that since Millwall moved to a new stadium there has been a noticeable decline in racial abuse and Far Right activity[17]. However, two black Derby County players, Gary Charles and Paul Williams, were substituted during a match at Millwall's new stadium (May 1994) because of racial intimidation from the crowd and fears for their safety.

There is of course an "issue which is more important than racism in football, which is racism in society"[18]. Presumably, if society as a whole were less racist then this would also be reflected in football. Reduced levels of racism in society was cited by 30 per cent of respondents who felt that racism had declined within football[19].

One commonly-held view of those interviewed and respondents to our questionnaire was that the anti-racism initiatives of the CRE and the FSA were relatively ineffective in reducing the levels of racism. 36 per cent of respondents who felt that racism had been reduced at football matches thought that the FSA's *United Colours of Football* fanzine (discussed below) had contributed to this situation. This was despite the fact that 78 per cent of respondents were actually involved in that particular fanzine.

Approximately one-third (32 per cent) of respondents who felt that levels of racism had declined cited as a factor the CRE's *Let's Kick Racism Out of Football* campaign (discussed below). Many of those interviewed also expressed the view that the initiative had been relatively ineffective. However, all the respondents were aware of its existence and 44 per cent of respondents felt that it had raised peoples' awareness of the problem. 18 per cent of respondents felt that the success of the campaign was that it forced clubs to address the problem of racism in their grounds. Despite 91 out of 92 clubs offering their support in season 1994/95, the CRE estimates that only one third of participating clubs are genuinely committed to the campaign and have developed it further[20].

Suggestions for the improvement of future campaigns

Figure 4 illustrates the most cited suggestions made by respondents to improve future anti-racist campaigns. There was no general agreement among respondents on how to improve future anti-racist initiatives. The most popular suggestion was for greater club and player participation, with 27 per cent of respondents suggesting this. It can be argued that if a campaign is "not specifically geared towards your own supporters, it is likely to have less impact"[21]. Individual club campaigns, such as *Rams Against Racism* (Derby County) and *Red, White and Black at the Valley* (Charlton Athletic) have been effective in combating racism (as we discuss below).

Figure 4:   Most cited suggestions to improve anti-racist campaigns

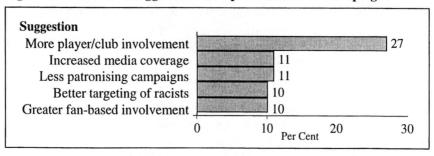

A small number of respondents (11 per cent) felt that future campaigns should receive greater media attention. This view was echoed by many of those interviewed who were critical of *Let's Kick Racism Out of Football* because it was unable to sustain a high profile throughout the season.

10 per cent of the respondents felt that the campaigns failed to target racists. Indeed, some of the Community Officers interviewed were more concerned with educating children than campaigning to reach adults. 11 per cent of respondents believed that anti-racist initiatives were patronising in tone. It may be that fanzine-led campaigns (discussed below) will be more effective in this respect.

Anti-Racist Initiatives

It seems likely from the evidence discussed in Section 3 that the level of overt racism in football has declined in recent years. There are several factors that may account for this trend. It may be that nationwide anti-racist football initiatives (such as the CRE's *Let's Kick Racism Out of Football* project) have had an effect, whilst the results of our survey suggest that independent supporters' efforts have also played a significant role in this perceived decrease.

Other measures, such as club community schemes and legislation such as the 1991 Football (Offences) Act may also have helped. This section will outline and analyse such recent initiatives in order to ascertain their efficacy.

Let's Kick Racism Out of Football

To coincide with the start of the 1993/94 football season the CRE and the PFA launched the nationwide *Let's Kick Racism Out of Football* campaign, with the aim of highlighting anti-racist and equal opportunities messages within the context of football. It was developed by the CRE's Campaigns Unit (formed in the summer of 1993), who recognised that football provided a useful conduit for anti-racist schemes:

> The first campaign we did was a football campaign, *Let's Kick Racism Out of Football*, because we looked at the whole area of young people and how to get to them, what medium we could use which would hold a message against racism and for equal opportunity and would also speak very clearly and directly to all people.[22]

The campaign received enthusiastic support from the PFA, who suggested that the CRE should get all of the 92 professional clubs to support its anti-racist strategy outlined in the '9-point plan'. By the time of the launch over 40 clubs had agreed to declare their support for the campaign and its aims in their matchday programmes.

However, despite the enormous blaze of publicity that the launch generated, not all clubs were enthusiastic about *Let's Kick Racism Out of Football*. Some viewed it with suspicion, claiming that the campaign, by highlighting racism within the game, would only bring negative publicity to football. Others claimed that racism was not evident at their ground, or that if it was then publicly supporting the measures would only bring attention to the problem and therefore make matters worse.

Another significant development was the production of the glossy and colourful *Kick It!* magazine which outlined the aims of the initiative, and looked at other issues such as the history of black players in the game, and the lack of Asian professional footballers. The magazine was part-sponsored by the Football Trust, which for the first time became actively involved in the revitalised campaign with a donation of £50,000.

Equally important was the participation of the FSA, who, with money from the CRE, produced *United Colours of Football*, a fanzine containing anti-racist articles, statements and cartoons. On the opening day of the 1994/95 season, 110,000 copies were distributed free to fans at nearly all football grounds.

The success of the Campaign

Let's Kick Racism Out of Football was, in many respects, a success. All of the football authorities and all but one of the professional clubs in England supported it, a factor which raised the campaign's media profile and helped to increase awareness of the issue of racism amongst supporters (indeed, all of the respondents to our survey of fanzine editors knew of it). It prompted several clubs to initiate substantial schemes of their own and compelled many clubs (who may otherwise have remained inactive) to take the minimal steps of issuing anti-racist statements.

However, the campaign had its weaknesses. Putting the CRE's posters up and issuing statements was as far as many clubs went. Indeed, frustration at the apparent inactivity of Leeds United caused a spokesperson from the Leeds United supporters' organisation *Leeds Fans United Against Racism and Fascism* to state that there has been:

> ... nothing in the programme, on the tannoy, in the media ... it's about time they [the club] did a bit more and took a little less credit. (Labour Research, 1995: p. 149)

It was this approach by some clubs that caused many people in football to doubt whether a campaign of this nature could be truly effective. As the Community Officer of a well-known London club commented:

> I think that if you hope to educate people then you've got to have one-to-one contact with kids and fellow supporters. I can't see that sticking up a poster is going to achieve very much.[23]

At the start of the 1995/96 season, however, the campaign appeared to be addressing some of the above criticism by becoming more proactive. The campaign aimed to work with a variety of organisations[24] in a multi-agency context in order to develop a more comprehensive and strategic approach. Furthermore, the CRE developed detailed plans designed to implement the broad aim of removing racism from the game. Previously there was a suspicion that the campaign was little more than a slogan that clubs could easily endorse: the intention now is that concrete steps be taken. At this early stage it is not possible to predict whether or not the campaign will develop as intended.

However, to expect the campaign alone to change attitudes and the atmosphere within grounds significantly is perhaps to misunderstand its nature, and the role of the CRE in general. The CRE argue that:

We can't enforce legislation on them. We can only act as a catalyst to get them going[25].

It should be remembered that the CRE is an independent campaigning body who regard their role in this context as awareness-raising rather than legally-oriented. Several clubs have taken up the lead given to them by the CRE, and have developed and expanded the original campaign in the context of their local community. Probably the two biggest schemes of this kind are Derby County's *Rams Against Racism* and the Leyton Orient initiated play *Kicking Out*, both of which are discussed below.

Kicking Out was the brainchild of the Community Officer at Leyton Orient, a relatively 'small' club from London's East End. The Officer's motivation was that:

I wanted to look at the campaign and take it a stage further and make it more relevant to our local community. This is probably what the CRE wanted clubs to do. The two issues that I thought were important here were (a) why don't the Afro-Caribbean/Asian community come and support us? and (b) why are there no Asians in the professional system?[26]

It was decided that the best way to tackle these problems would be through educating local school children about some of the myths and attitudes that exist around the involvement of minority ethnic groups, and Asians in particular, in football. To this end, *Kicking Out* was produced to tour secondary schools. A variety of public and private sources of finance were utilised and the Arc Theatre Ensemble was commissioned to perform the piece. Launched at the House of Commons in November 1994, *Kicking Out* is based around an ethnically mixed youth 5-a-side team that eventually tackles and defeats the racist attitudes of its coach. By the end of its first run, the play had been performed to an estimated 70,000 children.

As stated above, *Kicking Out* appeared as a result of a club community officer wanting to take *Let's Kick Racism Out of Football* further, and therefore the original campaign can also take credit for the play's undoubted success. It has provided a framework within which clubs and concerned organisations can act, and has undoubtedly boosted independent supporters' campaigns. Above all, it has demonstrated what clubs can achieve if they have sufficient will and enthusiasm (and no little expertise), and shows that the campaign was not just a success at raising awareness. As the CRE suggest:

[The campaign's] ... got a lot of people thinking about it, lots of media publicity and most heartening is the fact that there are about ten clubs who are making a tremendous effort which you would have been astounded at five or ten years ago.[27]

Anti-racist fan-based initiatives

Supporters have played a prominent and important role in combating racism in football during the last decade. One of the most important developments has been the growth of the independent FSA. The activities of the FSA have always had a strong anti-racist element, and it has taken several steps to combat racism and xenophobia amongst England supporters abroad. For example, during the 1990 World Cup in Italy the FSA organised 'embassies' for England fans, in order to promote better relations between them and the local population. Similar schemes have been held at other tournaments involving the England team, and are being developed for the 1996 European Championships.

More recently, the FSA outlined its desire to reclaim England fixtures for non-violent, anti-racist fans, and to decrease the influence of the Far Right at international matches. It arranged a message of support for the Irish football community, signed by representatives of many English fanzines and supporters' groups, in the hope of demonstrating that the vast majority of supporters of the English national team condemned the actions of those who rioted in Dublin in February 1995.

Another initiative organised by the FSA was the *United Colours of Football* fanzine, part of the CRE's *Let's Kick Racism Out of Football* campaign (discussed earlier). Whilst the extent of the success of these schemes is hard to quantify, the FSA has undoubtedly contributed to a context in which supporters have formed local groups to fight racism.

Fan-based anti-racist groups

The first fan group formed specifically to fight racism was the Leeds United fan group *Leeds Fans United Against Racism and Fascism (LFUARAF)*. Several other campaigns have followed their example, in places as disparate as Newcastle in the north of England and Torquay on the south coast, but it is to this first influential campaign that we will turn first.

Leeds Fans United Against Racism and Fascism (LFUARAF)

LFUARAF is an independent supporters' organisation that was formed in 1987 to combat the influence of the Far Right at Leeds' Elland Road ground. During the mid-1980s, the National Front (NF) and British National Party (BNP) openly sold their papers at the club's home matches. The incidence and levels of racist chanting inside the ground were sufficient to give Leeds United's supporters one of the worst reputations for racism in the country.

Deciding that 'enough was enough', a group of Leeds fans produced anti-racist leaflets that were distributed by over 100 sympathisers outside Elland Road before a home match. This was the first step in a campaign that had the short-term goal of challenging the dominance of the Far Right coupled with the long term ambition of ridding the ground of racist chanting and abuse.

Despite initial hostility from the club and the police, the campaign gained momentum, and in 1988 contributed to *Terror On Our Terraces* (Leeds Trades Union Council and Leeds Anti-Fascist Action, 1988), a report detailing the involvement of the Far Right amongst the crowd at Leeds. This evidence prompted the club to issue an anti-racist statement signed both by players and management, a factor which gave further credence to *LFUARAF* amongst fans. Within a few months, the number of Far Right paper sellers at matches had started to dwindle, as their influence became increasingly marginal. The situation at Elland Road is now much improved according to *LFUARAF*:

> Looking at Elland Road today, it's hard to imagine what the atmosphere was like in 1987. The NF sellers have disappeared, driven away by hostility and lack of sales. Racist abuse has almost disappeared, as has violence. We believe we can take some of the credit for having kept going over a five year period. (Thomas, 1993: p. 19)

The contribution that fan-based initiatives can make is demonstrated by the success of *LFUARAF*. Whilst schemes such as *Let's Kick Racism Out of Football* are important in raising awareness amongst supporters, the campaigns by local fans also have a crucial influence.

Football fanzines

The explosion in the production and popularity of fanzines has been a characteristic of British football in the post-Heysel era. From their basis in the first roughly produced efforts of the mid-eighties, football fanzines have now developed to such an extent that almost every club has at least one associated with it, many of which are professionally produced and of a high quality.

One of the crucial aspects of fanzines is that they have been, almost exclusively, anti-racist in their slant. The popular national fanzine *When Saturday Comes* frequently carries articles discussing racism in football and how to counter it, and gives publicity to anti-racist initiatives and periodically has editions with whole sections devoted to the issue of racism in football[28].

Club-based fanzines, because of their stance and popularity, have also been influential in combating racism. There are currently several fanzines that devote much of their space to anti-racism — two of which, *Marching Altogether* (Leeds United) and *Filbo Fever!* (Leicester City) are produced by the anti-racist fan-groups *LFUARAF* and *Foxes Against Racism (FAR)* respectively[29]. According to *LFUARAF*, the fanzine was an ideal way to counter entrenched racist views of fans:

> What we needed was a long-term campaign. So we launched our fanzine *Marching Altogether* ... we wanted to communicate with all the fans, especially the younger ones who might easily fall into racially abusing black players and fans. (Thomas, 1995: p. 99)

Marching Altogether, which is given away free at Leeds' home games, has the usual fanzine mixture of serious and amusing football articles, and although it carries an anti-racist message, is by no means solely about racism in the game. It pitches itself at the average fan, and, by not lecturing or posturing, has proved popular over the last seven years. It has undoubtedly played a part in the success of the Leeds groups' campaign.

Other club-based fanzines, whilst not being produced by anti-racist fan groups, have nevertheless carried anti-racist articles and publicly supported campaigns. These include *When Skies Are Grey* (Everton), *Our Day Will Come* (Celtic/Manchester United), *Bluebird Jones* (Cardiff City), *The Leyton Orientear* (Leyton Orient) and the *Chelsea Independent* (Chelsea). Some of these fanzines have actively and effectively campaigned against right-wing infiltration into their respective clubs. The Community Officer at Leyton Orient, outlined how the BNP were combated in the late 1980s:

> The fanzine campaigned very hard to stop that [right-wing activity]. I think it was the BNP that came and leafleted outside the West Stand. I think the club was driven on by the fanzine *The Leyton Orientear*, who are a very well established organisation. They put a stop to this very quickly.[30]

It is often argued (as the producers of *Marching Altogether* do) that fanzines are mainly produced and read by those who already hold anti-racist views, and therefore fanzines carrying articles condemning the problem are merely 'preaching to the converted', and have no tangible effect on racist fans who tend not to buy fanzines. It is for this reason that *Marching Altogether* is given away free at matches.

Therefore, those who claim that fanzines do have an effective role to play in combating racism may well have a point, and it is perhaps no coincidence that the rise in popularity of fanzines amongst fans has been apparently mirrored by a simultaneous decrease in racism on the terraces.

Club-based initiatives

Community Schemes

Community schemes are initiatives run by clubs and designed to bring clubs and their local community closer together. They began in 1986 when it was generally recognised that football had lost touch with sections of the population who, put off by decaying stadia and rampant hooliganism, had turned their backs on the sport. Other sections were hostile to clubs, viewing them as being 'closed' organisations that solely represented the white community.

The first 'community officers' were sponsored by the PFA and had the unenviable task of persuading the public, and particularly those who lived near grounds, that clubs were genuinely interested in them and had much to offer them. Nine years later, a number of these schemes have been extremely successful, and have played their part in helping to increase attendances nation-wide[31].

Many of these schemes are funded by clubs with contributions from local authorities, the PFA and local businesses. Nearly all clubs have a community officer, although some clubs place a greater emphasis on this side of their operations than others. Some, such as Everton's, are large and run on a non-profit making basis. However, other Premier League clubs charge for coaching courses, and it has been suggested that some clubs operate their schemes with the sole intention of bringing in revenue.

One of the biggest and most enterprising schemes is run by Leyton Orient. This scheme was initiated by the local authority, Waltham Forest, who employ a Community Officer to work under the auspices of the club to liaise with local people. The Council recognises the value of the scheme:

> [it] was enabling youngsters, girls, people with disabilities to get involved in a whole range of things [the community officer] started to develop and take further with the club. [The community officer] also, in a sense, educated the club along those lines. So, not only were the community getting involved outside the club, but within the club they were starting to provide facilities for people with disabilities, and family groups and so on. The Council, for a limited contribution, was getting all of this done.[32]

So, in return for an initial grant of £12,000, the officer was performing several very useful roles for the Council. Four years on, the scheme, now funded jointly by Waltham Forest and Hackney Boroughs, runs over fifty projects for all sections of the community, covering a range of activities. It has won several awards, and undoubtedly helped to integrate club and community.

As to whether the scheme could help encourage minority ethnic communities to attend matches, the officer himself offered this reason as to why they refrain from spectating:

> I suggest the most important reason is that we have not won their confidence yet. [Football] can be very threatening for an Asian woman with two kids.[33]

Leyton Orient try to combat this by targeting sections of the local population with free match tickets, and by developing a family section to encourage parents from all communities to bring their children. However, it has been suggested that the best way to attract people to come to matches is to produce a winning team, a fact acknowledged by the Football in the Community Officer:

> If you are at Tottenham and your crowds go down by 5,000, then you just go and spend £3 million on a player and the 5,000 will come back again. I'm sure that Klinsmann's transfer to Tottenham in the summer [of 1994] put more people on the gate than the best community scheme in the world.[34]

As we have seen in the previous section, the response from football clubs to the *Let's Kick Racism Out of Football* campaign has been mixed. Whilst some clubs have taken giant steps to further the campaign (for example, Leyton Orient's play *Kicking Out*), other clubs appeared to content themselves with placing a few posters around the ground, and there must be a measure of doubt as to whether many would have acted at all if they had not been prompted into doing so. However, there are a number of clubs who have started anti-racist programmes of their own, and have achieved a measure of success with them.

Rams Against Racism – Derby County

The idea to dedicate a home matchday to the cause of combating racism came out of a liaison between Derby County (nicknamed the "Rams"), the club's Football and Community Development Officer and the Racial Equality Council based in the town. This idea involved displaying anti-racist banners, carrying campaign messages in the match programme, getting the players to make a public stand against racism and at the same time distributing 250 free tickets to local children. These initiatives were brought together under the banner *Rams*

Against Racism (RAR), and the first match given over to the scheme was against Millwall in the Spring of the 1993/94 season.

The day turned out to be a success, with *RAR* gaining much media attention. The club decided to continue the initiative with several long-term measures, including much work within schools with the aim of encouraging local Asian footballing talent. Early in the 1994/95 season, a second fixture was designated a *RAR* game.

It is nevertheless difficult to ascertain how successful *RAR* has been in encouraging the local Asian community to attend Derby's home games, but, the club's Press Liaison Officer argues[35] that one outcome has been the strengthening of links between the two parties.

Red, White and Black at the Valley – Charlton Athletic

In 1993 London's Charlton Athletic launched the leaflet *Red, White and Black at the Valley* in conjunction with the police, the local Racial Equality Council, Greenwich Council and Charlton's Supporters' Club. The idea behind the leaflet was to promote Charlton Athletic as a club that people from all disadvantaged minorities could attend without worry of harassment from other supporters. The club followed this up by producing posters and issuing statements in the matchday programmes. Significantly, players also participated by visiting local schools and colleges.

Whilst it is difficult to measure how successful *Red, White and Black at the Valley* has been generally, a concerted effort by the police (acting on a tip-off from the club) to remove racist fans from one end of the ground was effective. Further, Charlton continues to demonstrate the club's opposition to and intolerance of racist chanting in a poster displayed prominently at the Valley.

Many other clubs have taken measures to promote their clubs as 'safe' places for people from minorities to watch football. For example, Leicester City has turned reserve team matches, traditionally sparsely attended, into 'Family Night Football' — events where children's entertainment is provided in the hope of encouraging those who would not normally attend. So far, the scheme has been a success in that thousands of children go to these games, although whether those from minority ethnic groups can be persuaded to attend first team games on a regular basis is certainly difficult to ascertain.

Nevertheless, even if only small numbers of minority ethnic families attend such events, Leicester City are helping to counter fears that minorities may have about attending events held at soccer grounds. That minority groups may actually have a fear of being racially abused at football was graphically illustrated by Brian Holland's 1992 study of the local Asian community living near Burnden Park (home of Bolton Wanderers). He found that:

> ...85 per cent felt either uncomfortable about, nervous about, or fearful of football fans visiting Bolton Wanderers' ground. (Holland, 1993: p. 17)

This is a point that is appreciated by some clubs. At First Division Millwall, the club offers the use of its stadium's pitch for the local Asian community to use. As their Community Officer says:

> Once they are comfortable with us we can give them tickets and they can come to a game. But, to start with the idea for a lot of people in coming to the club is that they can't come, because of this stigma of being a racist club which is attached to us. So we need to break that down before we can get them to a game.[36]

Whilst it may be encouraging that the club is attempting to develop links with local groups, the above quote suggests that the reasons that Asians do not attend is because they are uninterested in football. Asian hockey teams may well wish to make use of the New Den, but it seems equally plausible that Asian football teams would welcome the opportunity. As has been argued above, it is a myth that Asian people are absent from the professional game because they are culturally uninterested.

Millwall was also one of the first clubs to build a completely new, state of the art' stadium in the wake of the recommendation in the Taylor Report (Taylor, 1990) that all stadia in the top two divisions be made all-seater. Millwall's previous home 'The Den' was a dilapidated venue, notorious for its violent supporters, that seemed to epitomise the state of many grounds at the time. However, several recent incidents of disorder involving Millwall fans indicate that better facilities at the 'New Den' do not appear to have improved the behaviour of the violent minority of supporters associated with the club.

On a broader scale, the effect of improved facilities on fans' behaviour is hard to gauge. If the perception of a downward trend in the levels of racist abuse is correct, then it could be argued (as 40 per cent of respondents to our survey who agreed with that assumption did) that the improved atmosphere at the revamped grounds has played a part in this. Perhaps it will take several seasons before minority ethnic groups truly believe that there has been a significant change in the behaviour of fans, and start coming to matches in larger numbers.

The 1991 Football (Offences) Act

Although the use of 'obscene and foul language' at football games had already been outlawed by the 1989 Football Supporters' Act, racist chanting was not explicitly made illegal until the advent of the 1991 Football (Offences) Act. One of the intentions of the Act was to make fans realise that football grounds were not places where they could go and be as racist as they liked, without any fear of prosecution. Thus the Act decreed that 'chanting of an indecent or racialist nature' was an offence, and that anyone caught doing so could now be prosecuted.

However, there is a loophole in the way the legislation is framed that makes prosecutions for racist abuse difficult. If an individual is caught being racially abusive they cannot be convicted under the Act because they are not behaving 'in concert with one or more others' as the wording of the Act requires. Prosecutions of individuals have broken down because of this loophole. Other laws may be used against offensive behaviour but it is unfortunate that such a high-profile piece of legislation is flawed in this respect.

The results from our survey showed that of those fanzine editors who believed that there had been a decline in racist abuse, only 15 per cent believed that the Act had been a factor in this decline — the smallest percentage for any of the ten explanations listed (see Figure 3 above). This reflects a lack of confidence in the Act, and also a lack of conviction on the part of supporters that those in charge of crowd management at matches, and in particular stewards, take the action they should when fans are being racist.

Conclusion

There is a widespread belief that the amount of racism has decreased in British football in recent years. There is a concern that this belief may mask the fact that a less public form of racism is still widespread at football matches. Whilst National Front paper-sellers are no longer a common sight and 'monkey chanting' is now rare it is less certain that racist comments or threats have also disappeared. The lack of supporters from minority ethnic backgrounds suggests that there is still at least a perception that football is a white domain. For financial and other reasons clubs have tried to develop strategies to encourage a more diverse audience. Most of this effort has been concentrated on attracting a 'family' crowd, and there seems to have been some success.

This research discovered a variety of reasons thought to have played a role in this decline in racist chanting, throwing objects at black players, and campaigning by Far Right groups. Certainly the most high-profile of these anti-racist initiatives has been the CRE's *Let's Kick Racism Out Of Football* campaign. Others mentioned include the widespread change in the culture of football supporters (witnessed by the growth in fanzines and supporters' groups) and the increasing number of black players.

Although the CRE campaign has received a certain amount of criticism from respondents to this research, it seems that this largely stems from mistaken expectations rather than a failure in its own terms. The respondents to our survey did not rate the CRE campaign highly compared to other anti-racist efforts from the FSA or the general change in the atmosphere of football matches and the growth of fanzine culture. Several interviewees claimed that the campaign was little more than a symbolic gesture, and one that most clubs could hardly refuse. There is a perception that, for many clubs, the campaign was taken no further than this and remained largely a matter of public relations. This report has outlined some cases where clubs have taken further initiatives, but these remain the exception rather than the rule. That this is the case seems to add weight to claims that *Let's Kick Racism Out of Football* has been superficial. However, this may not be the fault of the campaign itself but rather due to the conservative nature of many football clubs. The CRE intended to raise awareness of the problem of racism in football as part of developments in the organisation itself towards a consciousness-raising role. That all of the respondents to our survey (although not representative of supporters as a whole) were aware of the campaign suggests that the campaign has achieved its limited goal. As mentioned, a revised and strengthened version of the campaign was launched for the 1995/96 season, but at the time of writing it is difficult to predict the extent to which this will have succeeded.

A national initiative such as this is perhaps more effective where local factors are such that they can combine with and build upon the broader developments. This may mean that national measures such as those of the CRE give weight to a group of local campaigners, club or local authority officials who are keen to develop anti-racist initiatives. The high profile CRE campaign gives these groups a convenient opportunity to apply pressure for resources and support for locally-based schemes. It seems that national campaigns are most effective when they complement fan-based local activities. This reflects a commonly held belief in the importance of 'grass-roots' involvement in anti-racist initiatives which enable a more effective dialogue with football fans. The anti-racist fanzines deliberately include a range of articles, cartoons, etc., about a wide-range of football-related issues. This is designed to make their anti-racist arguments palatable to fans who may not be easily reached by other means.

A more fundamental problem also exists. As has already been suggested the growing importance of financial success for the top clubs since the advent of the Premier League in 1992-93 season has led to increasing concern to attract a wider (more affluent?) audience. If the presence of racism at matches runs counter to this aim then clubs clearly have an interest in preventing racism in football. Supporters from minority ethnic groups who experience broader socio-economic disadvantages may be marginalised by commercialisation (and increasing ticket prices) and actually be less likely to attend games. Thus football may find itself with a relatively minor problem of racism but still attract an overwhelmingly white audience.

Notes

1   Defining ethnicity is always a problematic exercise, but for the purposes of this paper the term 'black' refers to those of African or Caribbean descent, and 'Asian' refers to those of South Asian descent.

2   Vasili, P. (1993) 'Men Out of Time', in Lyons, A. (ed) *When Saturday Comes*, No. 80: pp. 8-9.

3   An un-named official at West Ham United said, "You hear about Asians stopping practice to say their prayers. They're different from us, have a different culture". Quoted in *The Sunday Times, 7* January 1995, Section 1: p. 3.

4   For a fuller discussion of football hooliganism see Murphy *et al.*, 1990.

5   Following the Hillsborough Stadium disaster of 1989 (when 96 fans watching Liverpool vs Nottingham Forest in the semi-final of the FA Cup died as a result of a crush) most grounds have now removed these fences because of the dangers that they pose.

6   Interview conducted for this research 19 October 1995.

7   Fanzines (independent club-based football magazines produced by supporters) have their roots in those produced in the punk rock era of the late seventies.

8   *Carling Premiership Fan Surveys 1993-1994*, hereinafter referred to as the *'Carling Surveys'*.

9   Formed by two Liverpool fans in the wake of the Heysel Stadium disaster in 1985. The FSA has been a campaigning group that has fought for the rights of football supporters. It has organised several high profile protests, and was instrumental in defeating the government's controversial identity card proposals during the late 1980s.

10   Interview conducted with players from Arsenal Football Club, 13 February 1995.

11   Interview conducted for this research 6 June 1995.

12 Interview conducted with Football in the Community Officer, Leyton Orient, 19 January 1995.

13 The 1991 Census indicates the following ethnic breakdown of population of Britain: 94.5 per cent white; 1.6 per cent black; 2.7 per cent Asian, and 1.2 per cent Chinese and 'other'.

14 Interview conducted with CRE Campaigns Unit, 9 December 1994.

15 'Fanzine culture' is a difficult concept to summarise. Fundamentally it emphasises that the game belongs to the fans and that clubs, players, officials, etc., should be more accountable to supporters.

16 Interview with Football Trust, 8 December 1994.

17 Interview with Football in the Community Officer, Millwall, 23 February 1995.

18 Interview with Football in the Community Officer, Leyton Orient, 19 January 1995.

19 There is some evidence of a more widespread belief that general levels of racial prejudice have declined. For example, an ICM survey conducted for *The Guardian* (1995) revealed that 40 per cent of white Britons polled believed there was a lot of prejudice towards black people in Britain. This figure showed a decline since 1983, when 50 per cent believed there was a lot of prejudice.

20 Interview conducted with CRE Campaigns Unit, 6 December 1994.

21 Interview with Football in the Community Officer, Millwall, 23 February 1995.

22 Interview conducted with CRE Campaigns Unit, 6 December 1994.

23 From an interview conducted for this research, February 1995.

24 The 1995/96 campaign is sponsored by the Commission for Racial Equality, the Football Association, FA Premier League, Football Trust, Professional Footballers' Association, League Managers' Association, Football Supporters' Association, National Federation of Football Supporters' Clubs and the Association of Metropolitan Authorities.

25 Interview conducted with CRE Campaigns Unit, 6 December 1994.

26 From an interview conducted with Football in the Community Officer, Leyton Orient, January 1995.

27 Interview conducted with CRE Campaigns Unit, 6 December 1994.

28 *When Saturday Comes,* first published in March 1986, now sells over 200,000 copies per month (source: *Race and Class* No. 4 April-June 1995).

29 Other fanzines produced by anti-racist fan groups include *You Wot!* (Gulls Against Racism – Torquay United), *Red Attitude* (Man Utd Anti-Fascists) and *Doon by Gorgie* (SCARF – Hearts).

30 From an interview conducted with Football in the Community Officer, Leyton Orient, 19 January 1995.

[31] In 1985/6 season total attendance in the Football League was 16,488,577. By 1994/5 this had increased to 21,796,332 and attendances had risen during each of the preceding seven years, the first time this has happened since 1945. (Figures from Rollin, 1994).

[32] From an interview conducted with Arts and Leisure Department, London Borough of Waltham Forest, 3 March 1995.

[33] From an interview conducted with Football in the Community Officer, Leyton Orient, 19 January 1995.

[34] *Ibid.*

[35] From an interview conducted with Press Officer, Derby County, 23 February 1995.

[36] From an interview conducted with Football in the Community Officer, Millwall, 23 February 1995.

References

Ansari, L. and Frow, M. (eds) (1994) *Kick It!*. London: CRE.

Anti-Fascist Action (1994) *Fighting Talk: Football Special*. Issue 9. London: Anti-Fascist Action.

Brown, A. *et al.* (eds) (1994) *The United Colours of Football*. Liverpool: Football Supporters' Association.

Brown, M. (1995) 'Asian Games', in A. Lyons (ed) *When Saturday Comes,* No. 80, London: WSC Ltd.

Davies, P. (1990) *All Played Out*. London: Heinemann.

Ennis, G. (1993) 'Black and Blue', in A. Lyons (ed) *When Saturday Comes,* No. 72, London: WSC Ltd.

The Guardian (1995) 'Most white Britons say racial prejudice lives on', 20 March, p. 1.

Hill, D. (1989) *Out of His Skin: The John Barnes Phenomenon*. London: Faber and Faber.

Holland, B. (1993) 'Colour field', in A. Lyons (ed) *When Saturday Comes,* No. 72, London: WSC Ltd.

Holland, B. (1995) 'Kicking racism out of football: An assessment of racial harassment in and around football grounds', in *New Community*, Vol. 21, No. 4. London: Commission for Racial Equality.

Labour Research (1995) 'Kicking racism out of football', in C. Ruhemann (ed) *Labour Research,* Vol. 84, No. 4, April, London: LRD Publications.

Leeds Trades Union Council and Leeds Anti-Fascist Action (1988) *Terror on Our Terraces: The National Front, Football Violence and Leeds United*. Leeds: Leeds Trades Union Council and Leeds Anti-Fascist Action.

Murphy, P., Dunning, E., and Williams, J. (1990) *Football on Trial*. London: Routledge.

Office of Population, Census and Surveys (1993) *1991 Census of Great Britain*. London: HMSO.

Rollin, J. (ed) *Rothmans Football Yearbook 1994/95*. London: Headline Book Publishing.

Scoon, R. (1995) 'Reclaim the game', *Campaign Against Racism and Fascism*, April/May 1995, London: CARF.

Sir Norman Chester Centre for Football Research (1994) *Carling Premiership Fan Surveys 1993/1994*. Leicester: Sir Norman Chester Centre for Football Research.

Sunday Times (1995) 'Asian Stars Ignored by "Racist" Football Clubs', 7 January, Section 1: p. 3.

Sunday Times (1995) 'The Complete Statistical Guide to the 1994/95 Season', 21 May, Section 2: p. 22.

Taylor, Lord (1990) *The Hillsborough Stadium Disaster (15th April 1989) – Enquiry by the Rt Hon Lord Justice Taylor, Final Report*. London: HMSO.

Thomas, P. (1993) 'Leeds by example', in A. Lyons (ed) *When Saturday Comes*, No. 72, London: WSC Ltd.

Thomas, P. (1995) 'Kicking racism out of football: A supporter's view', *Race and Class*, Vol. 36, No. 4 (April/June), London: Institute of Race Relations.

Varma, G. K., Macdonald, A., Darby, D. and Carroll, R. (1991) *Sport and Recreation with Special Reference to Ethnic Minorities, Final Report*. Manchester: University of Manchester, Centre for Ethnic Studies in Education.

Vasili, P. (1993) 'Men out of time', in A. Lyons (ed) *When Saturday Comes*, No. 80: pp. 8-9. London: WCS Ltd.

Williams, J. (1992) *Lick My Boots: Racism in English Football*. Leicester: Sir Norman Chester Centre for Football Research.

World in Action (1995) 'Combat 18', 27 March, Granada TV.

FOOTBALL, RACISM AND XENOPHOBIA IN FRANCE: THE STATUS OF 'FOREIGNERS' IN AMATEUR FOOTBALL — A CASE-STUDY OF MARSEILLE*

Jean Marc Mariottini

Introduction

This chapter begins with a brief and fairly general[1] account of the history of immigration in France and the means of acquiring French nationality and will, finally, set out to analyse the present situation of minority ethnic groups and 'foreigners' in this country, particularly in amateur football.

Background

Although France has historically been widely open to 'foreigners'[2], their presence greatly increased with the advent of migrant workers at the beginning of the 19th century, but really took wing between 1850 and 1880 with the coming of the industrial revolution. Then, within a little more than a century, different migratory waves followed one another more or less steadily, interrupted only in periods of crisis — in particular during World Wars I and II. Thus during the 1851-1982 period, the population of minority ethnic groups and 'foreigners' in France rose from 380,000 to over 3.5 million people.

The permanency and duration of this trend offers a whole gallery of immigrant portraits. In the first stage, these migrant workers came predominantly from Northern Europe (Belgium, Germany, Switzerland, the United Kingdom) and among them some were highly skilled workers, such as the English mechanics who participated in the installation of spinning mills. In the second stage, this migratory flow increased dramatically[3], at first much 'latinised' with Italians, Spaniards, Portuguese, with the exception of Belgians and Poles[4], then 'african-ised' with Maghrebians and Black Africans, to end up with the more traditional and almost stereotypical image of migrant workers — poor, unskilled wretches destined to carry out toilsome tasks in agriculture and industry.

Naturalization in France

As long as migrants confined themselves to the role of temporary migrant workers, acquiring French nationality was hardly, if ever, an issue. They stayed in France only for the duration of a job, and usually on their own, which pre-supposed their return to their families and countries of origin after a certain period of time. The issue is, however, different if migrant workers intend to settle for a longer time, either by having their families join them or by starting a new life. In this context, it is important to consider the conditions and policies which enable such permanent immigration, with special attention to the relations between the local people and the newcomers, and the perception each group has of the other — all elements very often proving to be key issues[5].

Although French law, as far as nationality and citizenship is concerned, gives priority to the principle of *"jus sanguinis"* (blood rights) — anyone who has one French parent is French — it also gives weight to the principle of *"jus soli"* (soil rights), since anyone born in France will be able to, if they wish, acquire French nationality either (a) at birth if their parents, though they are 'foreigners', were born on French soil[6], or (b) automatically[7] at 18 years of age, if their parents were not born in French territory. The principal modification, introduced by the Pasqua Law of July 1993, prevents the automatic acquisition of French nationality. Thus since 1 January, 1994, any young 'foreigner' must demonstrate an intention to become French[8] and is no longer automatically awarded French nationality. Finally, anyone who can claim neither of these rights — that is, those born abroad of 'foreign' parents — may nevertheless apply to acquire French nationality. In 1992, for example, 39,346 individuals were nationalized by decree, whilst in the same year 32,249 persons acquired French citizenship by declaration (i.e. marriage to a French national).

The relative flexibility of French law in this matter makes differentiation be-tween French nationals and 'foreigners' very difficult as available statistics lack the reliability one might expect of official reports and thus fail to reflect ade-quately the reality of 'foreign' presence on French soil. Indeed, one may find new-ly naturalised people who are still so imbued with their culture of origin that they are still perceived by French nationals as members of 'foreign communities'. This applies particularly to Maghrebians and Black Africans, and in regions where the concentration of immigrants is high (e.g. in Paris, Nord-Pas de Calais, Lorraine, Rhône-Alpes, Provence). In some of these areas the housing structures have led to a residential segregation. Large housing projects at the edge of towns, host-ing predominantly migrants, emphasise their foreignness and status as migrants or newly naturalised citizens and hamper their integration into French society.

How then should these 'foreigners' be considered and referred to? As French nationals, in spite of the gap between their standard of living and that of the average original French? Or as 'foreigners', despite their status as French citizens? This is still a matter of debate. As a consequence of our preliminary investigation concerning this fundamental question, when we tried to identify and weigh the importance of 'foreignness', we concluded that it is more suitable to define as 'foreigners' those who are migrants of foreign nationality and to include those who have acquired French nationality but have foreign origins. This is the approach we followed in our field work, where this was a crucial issue. Although we still find it unsatisfactory, it does appear to reflect reality more accurately.

Size, structure and geographical distribution of the 'foreign' resident population in France

According to the 1990 census[9] there was a 'foreign' resident population of 3.6 million (6.4% of the total population of 56,651,955). Over a third came from countries of the European Union (EU); the rest came from non-EU countries or from other continents. This population has increased at the rate of approximately 135,000 new permanent immigrants annually. If we add seasonal workers to that figure or others staying for a short period of time, the figure rises to about 200,000[10] annually. Of this expanded figure, only one quarter originate from member states of the European Union, with the remaining non-European immigrants coming mostly from Africa and Asia. Of this 'foreign' population, proportionally fewer are in paid employment (36.26%) than the total population (39.31%). The distribution of workers is as follows:

retail services	39.5%	non-retail services	10.3%
heavy industry	26.2%	agriculture	3.4%
building/construction	20.6%		

These figures are averaged across all nationalities, although variations do occur. For instance, the Turks work more in industry and the Algerians more in retail services.

In terms of geographical location, the immigrant population is distributed as follows: Ile de France, with 12.8% of the total population, comes far ahead of all regions; it is followed by Corsica (10.2%), Alsace (8.1%), the Rhône-Alpes Region (8%), Provence or PACA, (7.2%), Franche Comté (6.6%), and Nord-Pas-de Calais (6.6%).

There are further variations within "*départements*" of the same region: in 1990, the Bouches du Rhône numbered 118,407 'foreigners' (about 6.6% of the total regional population) out of 1,797,165 inhabitants:

Algerians	37.6%	Black Africans	4.6%	Portuguese	3.3%
Moroccans	12.0%	Italians	8.0%	Asians	2.7%
Tunisians	11.9%	Spaniards	6.5%	Turks	1.5%

In the city of Marseille, the "*département*" town of the Bouches-du-Rhônes, the ratio rises to 7.54% (56,102 'foreigners' out of 743,747 inhabitants). In Marseille the proportion of Maghrebian immigrants is higher than elsewhere: Algerians (43.7%), Tunisians (12.9%), Italians (7%), Moroccans (6.5%), Spaniards (3.7%), Portuguese (2.6%), Turks (1.6%).

But as already mentioned, these official statistics reflect the 'reality' less than adequately. For if we add the 54,098 people who acquired French nationality to the 56,102 'foreigners' who live in Marseille, then their total number amounts to 14.8% of the total population of Marseilles[11].

The case of Amateur Football in Marseille

Among our fields of research in ethnology we have long been committed to sports, and more particularly to football[12], both as a cultural practice and as a spectacle. In this vast area we recently investigated issues of racism, xenophobia and the integration of 'foreigners' in football, particularly amateur football in Marseille. Whether and to what extent football is an integrating or an excluding factor for young members of minority ethnic groups was our key research question. Beyond the personal affinities which induced us to deal with that subject matter, the choice of amateur football was full of potential — a space devoted to a dominant[13] cultural practice deeply rooted in the popular, indigenous, local culture.

Methods

Amateur football includes a large variety of football practices ranging from the most informal to the most formal organisational structures. Street and courtyard football, football played in front of or between blocks of flats or in parks belong to the former type. The latter, the official football, is commonly practised within a club; its form and status may differ from one club to another, and within the framework of particular football associations — FFF[14], FSGT[15], FGSPF[16], UFOLEP[17], Corporative[18], etc. which run specific championships in which the clubs can participate.

In this paper, we shall particularly deal with the status of minority ethnic players in Marseille's clubs affiliated to the South-East League of the French Football Association. 95 clubs belong to this category in Marseille as of this writing, but we have deliberately limited our survey to the clubs whose first senior teams[19] belong to the élite local football culture —19 teams which play at the 4 higher levels of amateur football. From top to bottom, these are:

- *3 teams in "Division d'Honneur Régionale" [DHR]:* 1er Canton[20], SMUC-7ème (Stade Marseillais Université Club, a multisports students' club, here associated to the 7th "canton's" club), JSA-St Antoine (Jeunesse Sportive Arménienne de Saint Antoine, the Armenian youth of the parish);
- *2 teams in "Division d'Honneur"[21] [DH], the regional championship of Provence–Côte d'Azur:* l'Olympique de Marseille, and Montredon-Bonneveine (after the name of two parishes in Marseille);
- *6 teams at "Promotion d'Honneur A" level [PHA], a départemental level, also called "District"[22]:* Ste Marthe, Vivaux-Marroniers, Burel, Consolat, (all named after parishes), Amicale ("association"), and UGA. Ardziv (Union Générale Arménienne-Ardziv, an Armenian club).
- *8 teams at "Promotion d'Honneur" level [PHB]:* La Cayolle, Félix-Pyat, St Gabriel, Endoume, Mazargues, Carmes-Belzunce (parish names), JSA St Antoine (Jeunesse Sportive Arménienne, the Armenian sporting youth of this parish), ASPTT (Association Sportive des PTT, the French Post).

The data we have collected derive from computerised listings of clubs and players and contain information such as the player's name, age and nationality. Additionally, we have carried out follow-up investigations with each club in order to analyse the problems of integration more closely and over a longer period of time.

For each of these clubs we have taken into account the 13 players who usually play for the first team, thus amounting to 247 players altogether. This group is made up of players whose ages range from 18 to 35, but — as both young talents of under 20 and veteran players are rather few — the majority of them range from 20 to 30 years of age.

Results

Firstly, we observed that 'foreigners' constitute a relatively low proportion (5.2%) compared to their share in the total population of Marseille (7.5%). Yet if one considers the sons of 'foreigners' as well, their proportion is much higher: almost 30% of the total number! Second generation immigrants, who represent 14.8% in Marseille's population, are over-represented in Marseille's amateur football leagues, or at least among the clubs that we have studied. Further, the majority of those players are Maghrebians and Black Africans, 65% and 29% respectively.

But if 'foreigners' (or sons of 'foreigners') amount to 30% of all players, this figure only represents an overall average estimate, as they are unevenly distributed among the various clubs. Thus in 4 clubs (Félix-Pyat, La Cayolle, Consolat, Carmes-Belsunce), the ratio of 'foreign' players (or sons of 'foreigners') reaches almost 70%. In 7 other clubs, the ratio varies between 23% and 46%: Burel has 3 players of 'foreign' origin in its team; SMUC-7ème: 4; Ste Marthe, St Gabriel,

Endoume, Mazargues, and Montredon-Bonneveine: 5 each; JSA St Antoine: 6. In other clubs, the ratio is below 20%; some teams have only 1 'foreign' player: e.g. Vivaux-Maronniers, ASPTT, UGA Ardziv.

This discrepancy must be related, of course, to the socio-demographic characteristics of the various parishes where the clubs are based. Thus the 4 clubs with the largest proportion of 'foreign' players have their headquarters mostly in working-class areas and council estates where the immigrant ratio is particularly high. In sharp contrast, the clubs with the fewest 'foreign' players are generally found in middle-class residential districts. So one may conclude that, from this angle, the various clubs reflect the social structure of their district or parish, and that players usually join their parish club, which is the nearest one. Yet the number of players of foreign descent that play in a club is not always strictly proportionate to the population of foreign origin in the parish where it is based. As we will see, other factors are equally important.

The status of the 'foreign' player is closely related to the geographical location of the club. On the one hand, there are teams with very few players of 'foreign' origin. These are based in the middle class districts, in which the proportion of minority ethnic groups is low. These are also the "great clubs" with a long list of successes and ambitions going beyond the local area which compete at a regional or national level. Their headquarters are in the parish, although they do not necessarily stand as the identifying medium of the parish, but rather as that of a larger unit, e.g. the city of Marseille: the 1er Canton team actually represents the Marseille local council.

In order to fulfil this role — that is, maintaining their prestige through success — these clubs follow a recruitment policy which is widely open and goes well beyond the boundaries of the parish. Players come from everywhere, from all parishes in the city, to play for Burel, Mazargues or Les Caillols. They usually come from the greater Marseille area, if not from the whole of Provence, to play for Olympique de Marseille, the widely celebrated team of Marseille, idol and champion of Southern France. And it is against this background and within this framework that particularly talented players of 'foreign' origin are recruited.

In many cases the 'foreign' player is perceived according to the model used in professional football: he is the "star" who plays for the team, devoting his skills to achieving a collective goal. Should differences concerning the colour of his skin or his cultural practices be commented upon, it is in jest rather than with malice. For his team mates, the team management, even the supporters, his 'difference' does not seem to entail any consequences — as long as he performs his role.

At this level of competition, the time devoted to playing football is very important indeed: the 'foreign' player will be close to his team mates and the club staff during regular training sessions and matches. In addition, his participation in the team's activities goes beyond the sporting dimension to include, for example, parties run by the club and leisure time spent with team mates. Indeed, such opportunities to socialise seem to contribute to the 'foreign' player's gradual separation from his original culture and his parallel adaptation to the society he finds himself in.

This integration into the local group is promoted by a variety of mechanisms. In order to sign a talented player, the common practice for "great clubs" is to offer him a job, plus the usual perks and benefits — a common trend nowadays, even at the amateur level. Of course, this prospect is very attractive for young players of foreign origin who are generally low-qualified and without professional skills. On the other hand, there are clubs in which the number of 'foreign' players is high. These clubs are predominantly located in socially disadvantaged urban areas where minority ethnic groups are well-established (such as in the Northern districts of Marseille).

Contrary to the "great clubs" from the Southern middle class districts, they are "small clubs" — that is, with generally a short history, a small trophy cabinet, and whose ambitions are limited to the local area. They are more in rivalry with the other clubs for local supremacy than for a wider one. They are the real district or parish clubs, true representatives of the local identity — at least from a sociological point of view — and when the districts are made up of council estates such a club may represent one of them: that is, a much reduced and homogeneous urban unit. This is the case for 2 clubs in particular: both include the highest proportion of 'foreign' players and come from such estates, and after which they are named. Finally, their recruitment policy tends to stress the development of their own human resources, by training the young from the district, rather than recruiting from outside — which they could not afford.

Within such clubs, one may immediately observe that a 'foreigner problem' does not exist[23]. But it does exist outside when, through competition, they meet other teams with fewer or no 'foreign' players.

Just like the population they represent, these clubs live in closed circles where the social setting reinforces the original culture rather than encouraging its adaptation to the values of the 'host society'. In fact, rather than preserving the original culture, it would be more appropriate to speak of expressing the district's or the suburb's culture, that of young gangs — a minority culture on the fringe of the majority mainstream culture. In fact, the interviews conducted for the survey reveal that the club's life is part of the district's life. There are also some special cases that are very revealing — e.g. the 'ethnic' or 'foreign' clubs whose names refer directly and openly to a 'foreign' nationality. The 2 Armenian clubs, the JSA

St Antoine (the Armenian Sporting Youth of St Antoine) and the UGA Ardziv (the Ardziv Armenian General Union) belong to this type.[24]

The UGA-Ardziv has 10 players of 'Armenian' origin in its squad; the few other positions are occupied by players of French origin (1 player) or Italian descent (2 players). However, if one investigates the 'Armenian' players in more depth, their origin is found to be distant rather than recent. In fact, most players are only grandsons or even great-grandsons of Armenian immigrants. Just as the Armenian community is currently well-integrated into Marseille's population — its immigration goes back to 1920 — its young players do not share the characteristics that can be found among more recent immigrants. For instance, the oldest of them are well established in their area and in their trade, and their membership is in no way the expression of a cultural or social isolation. As members they certainly celebrate their Armenian background and identity, and assert their difference; but this process is more about the re-appropriation of a cultural inheritance — a somewhat folklorist trend — than about a self-chosen withdrawal caused by exclusion. This bears testimony to how one may remain a 'foreigner' to some extent, while being well integrated in the wider society.

Curiously enough, things are different with the other 'Armenian' club where, apart from the management and administrative staff, there are today no players of Armenian descent. Does this mean that the club has abandoned its national and cultural origins? Contrary to the former Armenian club, which is more representative of both the local and regional community, the JSA St Antoine (the Armenian Sporting Youth of St Antoine) has a very limited local appeal. It is a parish club — that of St Antoine, a Northern parish in Marseille — which since its inception has been the standard bearer of Armenians living in the parish. Local representation usually entails a relationship between the composition of the team and the socio-demographic composition of the parish: it is at this level that things have changed. Although this parish had long played a crucial part in the settling and integration of new Armenian immigrants, this is no longer the case. The second generation of Armenian immigrants has moved to more middle class areas in the city and more recent immigrants from other countries have taken over the available accommodation in this particular suburb. Actually, the first team of the JSA acts almost as a melting pot made up of 3 players of French origin, 4, 2, and 1 players respectively of Italian, Spanish and Portuguese descent, plus 3 players of Maghrebian origin. In this case, the national identity gave way to the local identity, that of the parish. If considered from a purely sporting angle, one may say that the higher the team plays — which is the case for this club compared to the former one — the more the technical abilities and skills of players are valued by the club when recruiting, rather than national origin.

We shall close this section by briefly mentioning those clubs in which 'foreigners' and 'natives' are well-balanced. Clubs of all sorts may be found in this category. Some are "small parish clubs" with a strong local base (St Gabriel, Ste Marthe, Sport Athlétique de St Antoine). The particular composition of those teams clearly reflects the socio-demographic composition of the parish.

Others may be clubs of greater regional importance, e.g. the Association Sportive de Mazargues. Initially, this club from a Southern middle-class parish was among the regional élite; it has now dropped 4 divisions during the last 6 seasons. Today it is trying to stop this dramatic decline by changing its recruitment policy, and is now recruiting players on a multi-ethnic basis, setting a new atypical trend for clubs of this kind.

This is what we can say today of the status of minority ethnic players in amateur football clubs in Marseille. It is a sort of snapshot of the present situation, supporting a view we believe to be objective. The survey would be worth extending to the other clubs, and to other age groups.

Conclusion: objectivity vs subjectivity, or how to measure integration

This case study shows the discrepancies that are revealed when the same 'reality' is viewed from opposing, and with selective, perspectives. From one point of view, the signs of racism and xenophobia are neither fewer nor less apparent in Marseille than elsewhere, and are just as deeply rooted in everyday attitudes and discourse. Minority ethnic groups such as Maghrebians and Black Africans are often pointed at and described in degrading terms: "darkies", "mongrels, "rats", and so on. In Marseille, this latent racism and xenophobia has taken a more structured shape, appearing as a more collective form of expression. Thus, at local polls a quarter of Marseille electorate voted[25] for JM Le Pen, the top candidate of the *Front National* (the extreme right wing party) whose ideology is summarised in the slogan "*Les Français d'abord*" ("The French first"). Yet, from the opposite perspective, one may notice that members of minority ethnic groups are active participants in local social and cultural activities — and not only in marginal ones, but in highly popular areas deeply rooted in local and national culture. Of course, football stands out as one of the best examples we can think of.

What conclusions can be drawn? How should this discrepancy be interpreted? Should we only take into account the objective evidence — the actual presence of 'foreigners' in any activity, and their participation, rejecting the racist and xenophobic attitudes as spontaneous, short-lived, circumstantial, having little effect on the objective process of integration? Or, on the contrary, should we give all the credit to these racist and xenophobic manifestations, and assign them enough significance so that the racism of our society can be evaluated and measured? If we return to the case of amateur football, with its 5.2% of immigrants and almost 30% of sons of 'foreigners' on teams — although each group only globally represents about 15% of the total Marseille population — one would conclude that today in Marseille football is widely accessible to members of minority ethnic groups. And that says a lot.

It means that the 'host society' accepts the presence of minority ethnic groups, and integrates them in its own activities. This can also be seen in the game's own regulations governing the numerical participation of 'foreigners': 3 'foreign' players can participate in amateur football teams (with a derogation of 5) and 2 in professional teams. That means, according to the letter of football law, one seventh of a team[26] could consist of 'foreigners' — a higher percentage than their actual proportion in society. Besides, one can assume that laws and regulations, in a democratic society where the laws of the state prevail, represent on the whole the collective will and consciousness of its people, or at least of its majority.

On the other hand, this situation demonstrates that minority ethnic groups actually benefit from this opportunity, which was not evident at first. It also provides evidence of such players' refusal to segregate themselves, if not a desire to be integrated. Playing in the structure of a club is first and foremost accepting a set of rules that any players must obey, along with the rules of the game — that is, the club's regulations and those of the Football Association[27]. In short, one may think that accepting this disciplined framework, and beyond it the culture of the receiving country, is a starting point of socialisation into and adaptation of that culture. Even in most extreme cases, that of clubs characterised by a large proportion of players from minority ethnic groups (which could lead to exclusions), there are nevertheless signs of players accepting local norms, if only through their participation in competition.

These two conditions, therefore, will enable the players, whatever their origin is, to at least establish a relationship through the sharing of a common cultural practice and the contact between majority ethnic and minority ethnic groups, which remains the minimum pre-condition of all integration. Thus, shouldn't this presence of 'foreigners' in various activities be considered as a first stage of integration, a kind of starting point for the process, a level at which integration could actually be measured?

In our opinion it is only later that the study of racist or xenophobic manifestations should be carried out. According to that point of view, racism and xenophobia appear as indigenous responses in conflict with the obvious state of things (shall we call it reality?). As far as we can really identify different racist or xenophobic acts or slurs, for which a few classifications can be established, these manifestations will then become objects of analysis. But the observer and researcher will have to be careful to treat them precisely only as objects of analysis, not to assign to them more meaning than they might in fact contain. Indeed if one discounts the characteristic manifestations whose significance is particularly obvious (for example physical aggression or other acts aimed at the exclusion of the 'foreigners'), a new problem — that of interpretation — will arise for all the other behaviours, and notably those pertaining to the domain of the discourse (in fact most of them).

Now we shall return to football, professional football this time, to look for an example likely to illustrate the opacity of facts, the difficulty one has when interpreting them. So, as we have witnessed several times[28], when a player from a minority ethnic group plays for his team, the public will adopt a rather appreciative attitude towards him. In fact when this player is outstanding they will even idolise him. Conversely, when that same player plays for the other side[29] the same audience may easily give way to uttering racist or xenophobic slurs. For instance, he will be greeted with bananas and any of his actions will be punctuated with monkey cries. What should be thought of such an audience, of such contrasting attitudes — a sort of double-standard circumstantial racism? Are these 'public racists' xenophobic? Certainly not, for if they truly were, they would in the same breath reject the 'race' and the 'foreignness' of the player, whether he plays for their team or not. On the other hand, associating Black African with monkeys proceeds from a racist attitude — since this is the only word we have at our disposal to signify this. Then what?

What this example seems to reveal is that reactions to foreign and minority ethnic players are, after all, little grounded on reality, on firmly established and long-lasting values or convictions, but that they closely depend on the general environment and situational factors. As we can see from this example several factors play a role in the relationship between the 'foreign' and the 'indigenous' population: (i) his attitude towards the majority ethnic group in that society — does he act for it or against it?; (ii) the social distance separating them[30]; and (iii) the overall economic situation of the surrounding community — all elements which, in some cases, may place him as a rival to the local people.

The problem and the difficulty one has to face when tackling such significant issues as racism, xenophobia and integration is semantic. Such words as racism and xenophobia, are very often overloaded in their connotations to denote a concept adequately and univocally. Using these notions unduly, in the wrong way and at the wrong moment — and even with the intention of being politically correct — may lead to aberrations or effects exactly opposite to the ones desired at the beginning[31].

During our research on the participation of 'foreigners' in Marseille's amateur football, we realised the necessity of a cautious attitude. Indeed this case study allowed us to pinpoint what dangers a one-sided approach might bear. We wished to show that by starting with a crude objective quantitative estimation of the phenomenon —measuring the actual presence of 'foreigners' — we could avoid at least some of the excesses which might result from an approach based from the beginning only on abstract terms and theorisation.

Notes

1   Historians and specialists of migration, or lawyers (more particularly on the code of nationality) would, of course, give a more detailed and in-depth analysis of this context.

2   François Rabelais, the French humanist, had already alluded to this: *"Mais comment voudriez-vous la France abandonner, quand tous les étrangers veulent séjourner!"* ("How could France be abandoned, when all foreigners want to sojourn there?").

3   And so much so as to reach a rise of some 25% within five years in 1880.

4   The former continued to provide farms with labour in the North of France; the latter began flowing in after the first world war, mostly to work in collieries.

5   As Maurice Garden puts it "the foreign worker, isolated if not lonely, living in a workers' home or sharing a furnished room, sending his savings to his family that has remained abroad, is considered as a passing sort. He is looked upon differently when he lives at home with his family in the same new residential estate, with his children attending the same school" (Lequin, 1988: p. 457).

6   We include in this category, along with metropolitan France, overseas "départements" and territories, and also Algeria prior to 3 December, 1962

7   And provided that the applicant has lived in France for 5 years, that s/he can speak French fluently enough, and can be given a certificate of good character — all conditions of little constraint as we can see, and usually rather easy to meet. Further, voluntary enlistment in the French forces is another way of acquiring French nationality automatically, even before the age of 18.

8   This demonstration of one's intention consists in completing a form and signing the declaration it contains, a procedure which can be carried out in front of any of several authorities (magistrates' courts, local councils, préfectures, sous-préfectures, gendarmeries, and consulates abroad). It is open to any foreigner born in France, from 16 to 21 years of age, provided they have continuously stayed in France for 5 years, they have not been subject to an expulsion order, they have not been condemned for terrorism or sentenced to over 6 months' imprisonment for any other offence.

As previously specified, enlisting in the French forces is considered as a demonstration of one's intention of becoming French.

9   This is from the latest general population census.

10   204,963 incomers in 1992, for instance.

11   In fact this ratio should be considered as minimal, as our estimation of individuals of 'foreign' origin only takes into account those born in France who automatically acquired French nationality at their 18th birthday.

12   *"Le match de football"* (Bromberger, *et al*).

13   Football is the first sporting activity in the Bouches-Rhône with 44,587 registered players, ahead of tennis (38,272) and bowling (21,779).

14   *Fédération Française de Football*, the French Football Association, is the most important organisation; it runs the professional and top-level football competitions.

15   *Fédération Sportive et Gymnique du Travail*, initially launched by trade unions in corporations and firms.

16   *Fédération Gymnique et Sportive des Patronnages de France*, combines church youth clubs and catholic associations.

17   *Union Française des Oeuvres Laôques d'Education Physique* combines non-catholic youth clubs and cultural associations.

18   The corporative championship run by the FFF combines corporate clubs from both public and private sectors.

19   Football players are divided into 6 official age groups: *Poussins* (8-10 years), *Pupilles* (10-12 years), *Minimes* (12-14 years), *Cadets* (14-16 years), *Juniors* (16-18 years), *Seniors* (above 18 years), *plus Vétérans* (old boys' teams). The biggest clubs usually enter several teams in each category, but on the whole each challenges its rivals at a different level: *Excellence*, *Pré-Excellence*, or *Honneur*. Thus the first team in each category is theoretically the best, and competes at the highest level.

20   The *"canton"* is an administrative division of a French *"département"*; in towns it is made of one or several districts.

21   The *"Division d'Honneur"* level is immediately below the national level.

22   This term of French football organisation must not be confused with the English administrative "district" or parish.

23   Apart from possible rivalries which, within the club, may oppose foreign groups of different origins.

24   In Marseille, 12 clubs altogether, among those affiliated to the only FFF, assert a foreign national filiation through their very name, such as Algerian, Comorian, Tunisian, Cape Verdian, West Indian (Antillais), Guyanian. They play at all (championship) levels, not necessarily the highest. These clubs may, if they wish, have 10 'foreign' players in their first team, as long as they are of the nationality to which the club's name refers. Concerning their reference to their original identity, it can be national,

ethnical or regional (Algerian, Tunisian, Armenian, "Antillais", Corsican, etc.), though these categorizations may arouse much discussion.

25   One of the highest returns in France.

26   And at best almost half of it.

27   Regulations he might easily escape, for example, by playing football the informal way.

28   During our enquiries on stadium audiences, especially in Marseille, but also in Italy.

29   As noticeable recent examples, the cases of 2 famous Black Africans who wore the legendary light blue OM jersey (it used to be white earlier on!) and, another season, that of OM's opponents, in the temple of the Velodrome Stadium: Basile Boli played for Auxerre before he was recruited by OM, and Joseph-Antoine Bell played for Bordeaux before and for Toulon later.

30   Isn't it strange that it is particularly in popular districts, precisely those in which the populations share lots of characteristics with the immigrants — residence, professional status, cultural level — that the xenophobic political discourse is best heard? Contrarily, social, economic, cultural, in a word sociological, distance seems to favour a tolerant attitude.

31   If we well understand the necessity to denounce racism whenever and wherever it lies, we should do it at least with discrimination. Has anyone ever wondered what effects an over-exploitation of such terms as "racism" — and especially by the media — might have on public opinion in association with events which manifestly had nothing much to do with it?

Bibliography

Anglade, J. (1976) *La vie quotidienne des immigrés en France*. Paris: Hachette.

Birnbaum, P. (1992) *Le peuple et les Gros*. Paris: Pluriel.

Bromberger, C. (*et al.*) *Le match de football*. Paris: EMSH.

Dubet, F., and Augustin, M. (1993) *Sports de rue et insertion sociale*. Paris: INSEP.

Donzelot, J. (1991) 'Face à l'exclusion', *Esprit*, Paris.

Glazer, N. (1983) *Ethnic dilemmas*. Cambridge MA: Harvard UP.

Guillaumin, C. (1972) *L'idéologie raciste*. Paris: Mouton.

Lequin, Y. (*et al.*) (1988) *La mosaïque France*. Paris: Larousse.

Marsh, P. (1978) *The rules of disorder*. London: Routledge and Kegan Paul.

Noiriel, G. (1988) *Le creuset français*. Paris: Seuil.

Touraine, A. (1991) 'Face à l'exclusion', *Esprit*. Paris.

Weil, P. (1991) *La France et ses étrangers*. Paris: Calman-Lévy.

Wieviorka, M. (1992) *La France raciste*. Paris: Seuil.

FOOTBALL, RACISM AND XENOPHOBIA IN GERMANY: 50 YEARS LATER — HERE WE GO AGAIN?

Udo Merkel, Kurt Sombert and Walter Tokarski

Introduction

In 1995 Germany had a population of 81 million, of which almost seven million were not in possession of a German passport. This number has increased from about 600,000 in 1961 to the seven million today. There is no doubt that Germany has become one of the most popular immigration countries in the second half of the 20th century. However, migrants in Germany are disadvantaged in respect to their legal status and they experience many forms of discrimination. In addition, they have, particularly in the 1990s, increasingly become the victims of criminal attacks by offenders with a right-wing political background. The main targets are migrant workers, as well as asylum seekers and their hostels. Consequently, the growing readiness of some members of the population to commit acts of violence against minority groups has become the subject of much debate.

Sport, and in particular football, is characterised by a high degree of ambivalence in terms of the meanings it provides for the people involved in it. Football provides a source for national identities and pride, but this tends to go hand in hand with exaggerated forms of patriotism and discriminatory behaviour. On one hand, due to its global appeal it is one of the most popular games around the world, whilst on the other, it embodies and provides an outlet for nationalistic, ethnocentric, racist and xenophobic attitudes. It is this latter perspective which we explore in this chapter.

In the analysis that follows we use the definition of 'racism' as outlined by Mike Cole in the chapter on nomenclature in this volume. Jarry and Jarry (1991: p. 709) define 'xenophobia' as "an exaggerated hostility towards or fear of foreigners", which we feel is most suitable and applicable to the German context since it covers the wide range of xenophobic attitudes and patterns of behaviour we encountered when we did the research for this project.

Although the German Aliens Act provides a precise definition of the group of persons to be referred to as 'foreigners', in reality the division between 'Germans' and 'foreigners' becomes increasingly unclear. It is important to recognise and to take into account that the old 'foreigner' cliché (i.e. uneducated, low skilled, working class males from Mediterranean countries, doing the 'dirty' and low-paid jobs) needs to be replaced by a more differentiated approach. Consequently, we find that the use of the term 'foreigner(s)' in the German context is both inadequate and incorrect since the majority of those referred to by this term have lived in Germany for decades, and many members of the so-called 'second' and 'third generation' of migrant workers were born and brought up in Germany. For lack of a suitable alternative, we will predominantly use the term 'migrant(s)' as it has become a customary international term, and use inverted commas in association with the term 'foreigner(s)' in order to mark its problematic nature.

These brief notes on terminology indicate the complexity of the migrant population in Germany. To disentangle this complexity is the aim of the following section, which is followed by a description of the development of right-wing extremism which has become a serious challenge to the German state over the last five years. The subsequent section will then focus exclusively on racism and xenophobia in the area of sport and leisure, with detailed reference to soccer which is generally considered to be the major German game. The fourth section will then deal with both the counter-measures introduced to combat racism and xenophobia through sport and leisure, and the use of sport as an instrument for the promotion of social and cultural integration. The final section sets out to draw some conclusions.

Size, structure and the development of the 'foreign' resident population in Germany

In its post-war history, Germany has experienced three major types of migration: the migration of workers (the so-called *Gastarbeiter*), particularly from Turkey as well as other Mediterranean recruitment countries; the influx of refugees (*Flüchtlinge*) and asylum seekers (*Asylbewerber* or *Asylanten*) from politically unstable countries such as the former Yugoslavia, particularly in the first half of the 1990s; and the return of many Germans who had left the country and settled in Eastern Europe or had stayed in those parts of pre-WW II Germany which after the War became Polish or Russian territory, or were ordered by the Soviets in the aftermath of World War II to be transported to parts of the ex-Soviet Union (*Aussiedler*).

Some quantitative data

Currently, migrant workers from within and outside the European Union comprise almost seven million people, accounting for about 8.5% of the German population. This figure falls midway in the range of European countries. The vast majority (97%) live in the former West Germany, a tiny minority (3%) live in the former East Germany. Approximately one migrant in four (22.3%) originates from a member state of the European Union. 27.9% are Turkish (1.92 million); 13.5% are from Ex-Yugoslavia. There are also large communities from Italy (563,000), Greece (352,000), Poland (261,000), Austria (186,000), Romania (163,000) and Spain (133,000).

About 25% of all migrants have lived in Germany for longer than 20 years; about 40% longer than 15 years, and about 50% longer than 10 years. In 1993 about 100,000 babies were born to migrant parents. In addition, at the end of 1993 there were about 2 million political refugees and asylum seekers living in Germany. Due to the 'moral panic' caused by this large number, Article 16 of the German constitution (Right of Asylum) was changed in July 1993 to reduce and restrict the number of refugees entering Germany.

A key feature of migration in Germany is that the various groups (migrant workers and their dependants, citizens of the European Union, refugees and asylum seekers) are not treated as equals to German citizens with respect to the legal situation. There are a number of basic rights to which only Germans are entitled, e.g. Article 8 (Freedom of Assembly), Article 9 (Freedom of Association), Article 11 (Freedom of Movement), Article 12 (Freedom of Choice concerning Trade, Occupation and Vocation), Article 33 (Eligibility for Public Office). In addition, numerous laws and provisions make clear distinctions between different kinds of 'foreigners', and their prospects of remaining in the Federal Republic and being integrated into German society also vary widely.

Post-War labour migration

By July 1955 there were already 80,000 migrant workers, of whom 10% were Italian, and by July 1960 the overall figure had increased to 280,000, of whom 44% were Italian. This was partly due to the conclusion of a recruitment agreement with Italy (1955), followed by many others between 1960 (with Spain) and 1968 (with Yugoslavia). This post-war labour migration was driven by economic considerations and gradually increased during the 1960s and early 1970s. The November 1973 stop in recruitment induced a slow decrease, and, since 1975, numbers of migrant workers have been oscillating between 1.8 and 2 million, leading to a resident 'foreign' population of 5.2 million in September

1990. This development shows that the initial official assumption that worker migration would be a temporary phenomenon was mistaken. The German *Gastarbeiter* population has not returned to their countries of origin as anticipated by politicians, but has settled in Germany permanently with their families. Various attempts to reduce the 'foreign' population were more or less doomed to failure and there is now no doubt about the fact that Germany is a country of immigration.

The clearly visible change from worker migration to family settlement is shown by the fact that 44% of the resident 'foreign' population are women. Many of these are, of course, EU nationals with consequent rights of settlement and movement, but the largest number of 'foreign' residents in Germany are undoubtedly the 1.92 million Turks.

Returning Germans

A particular aspect of the German situation is the growing number of 'original Germans' (*Aussiedler*: often referred to as 'ethnic Germans' in the English language) who have been re-admitted over the last years, on average about 200,000 people annually. Considered as Germans, they are granted citizenship in a quasi-automatic way. Consequently, they are not included in the above figures — but such immigrants are, at least initially, in a similar economic and social position to other migrants; many of them have to study German as a foreign language since they speak no German and have little or no cultural connections with Germany.

There appears to be evidence that, since 1987, resentment against the large number of repatriates has been increasing. Whilst initially these 'ethnic Germans' received a warm welcome due to their perceived traditional virtues — hard-working, focused, reliable — more recently signs proclaiming "No Russians" have been seen in shops and pubs near half-way houses for these immigrants. Germany's official Aliens Policy has thus been aiming at restrictions on the numbers of new entrants, using the argument that a further influx would have negative social and economic consequences. However, the treatment of these immigrants provides an example of the dogmatic view of the Germans concerning Germanness and citizenship. Since the time of Bismarck, the Germans have conceived of themselves in ethnic terms, even though there is no scientific evidence that the German people are any more ethnically homogeneous than their neighbours.

Political refugees and asylum seekers

The comparatively liberal policy of political asylum in Germany has also contributed to the size of its 'foreign' population. Statistics show that for many years the number of political refugees and asylum seekers had been fairly low but that there have been dramatic increases over the last 10 years, prompting policy debates and changes. Thus, from 1953 until the end of 1968, only 70,425 persons applied for political asylum, while roughly another 116,000 did so in the decade to 1978. From 1979 onwards there was a significant increase with 107,818 persons recorded in 1980. After decreases during the 1980s, the figures have gone up dramatically since 1988: in 1992 there were 438,000 applicants, of whom 57% came from Yugoslavia, Romania and Bulgaria.

In the current economic situation, i.e. in the extremely competitive German labour market, both German repatriates and migrant workers may need to draw heavily on the social welfare system. To an extent, some politicians argue that members of both groups may in fact have been attracted by a social welfare system which enables individuals to survive on unemployment benefit. It has to be pointed out that Germany can probably not maintain high immigration levels and adequate social security payments for long if dependence on state welfare becomes more common among both Germans and migrants.

The Turkish community

As the largest single group of immigrants in Germany, the Turks clearly require particular attention. Around 30,000 people from Turkey continue to arrive each year. The recent increase in the Turkish population in Germany is due to family reunion and 'family formation', i.e. a Turkish person resident in Germany marries a partner from Turkey who is then, after a waiting period, allowed to migrate to Germany. Official attempts to reduce the Turkish population by recourse to re-migration incentives have not been successful and there is evidence that the overwhelming majority of Turks in Germany do not wish to return to Turkey.

After 1980 the number of self-employed Turkish people increased significantly, and with it the creation of new jobs in many different sectors of the economy. Many of these jobs have been taken by Germans and there is a significant share of businesses with international trade involvement. Many Turks have also started to buy their own homes. The growing economic prosperity of the Turkish community as a whole has many positive economic effects: a substantial rate of saving is matched by growing expenditure on consumer durables, and the manifold direct and indirect tax contributions of the community are a major economic factor. More Turkish youth are now entering universities, yet there are also continuing problems of access to the labour market. However, a significant number of doctors, dentists, lawyers and of other professions are Turkish. The real picture of the Turkish contribution to the social, cultural and economic life of German society is certainly more complex. However, due to the restrictive German immigration policies on citizenship it is impossible for Turks to hold dual nationality. Both the German Nationality Act and the Aliens Act clearly state that naturalisation is generally only possible if the other, i.e. previous, nationality is lost or renounced. This position is contested in current German political debate; but the basis of German legislation on immigration remains the conventional view that idenity does not derive from commitment to an idea but from membership in a people which Conservative forces have repeatedly described as a 'community of destiny and ancestry'.

The rise of extreme right-wing and neo-Fascist ideologies and violence towards minorities

In the first half of the 1990s, the increasing readiness to commit, support and justify violent crimes against minority ethnic groups in Germany has reached alarming levels. The complexity of this problem makes it necessary to clarify the meaning of some key terms of the political discussion in the German context, to identify the significant elements of right-wing extremist ideologies, to summarise the growth of right-wing extremist parties and to link these aspects with the dramatic increase in violent attacks predominantly on migrant workers and asylum seekers.

Key terms: their meanings and legal implications

A variety of terms are used to identify, define and to analyse the growth of right-wing ideologies and parties in Germany. Up to about 1974 the term 'right-wing radicalism' was commonly used in the public, political and academic discourse to exclusively refer to all political ideologies and activities right of the German Conservative Party (CDU). From the mid 1970s onwards the increasing use of another term, 'right-wing extremism', indicates a more differentiated approach. Although this distinction might appear to be only a verbal or technical one, it is crucially significant with respect to the German legislation: political ideologies and groups classified as **radical** are usually tolerated in the political system, whereas those ideologies and groups defined as **extremist** may be prohibited by the state. In the past this has happened on numerous occasions[1].

Several social-scientific investigations in the field of right-wing extremism have been carried out since the late 1960s. The results of these studies vary a great deal. The well-known SINUS study (1981) came to the conclusion that about 8% of the population have a consistent right-wing extremist view of life.

The Allensbach study found 6.2% (*cf* Merten and Otto, 1993: pp. 19-26); and the regular EMNID investigations (1989 and 1991) (*cf* Schneider-Haase, 1992: pp. 72-80) showed rates between 13-15% of extreme right-wing opinions in the whole population, and nearly 7% radical right-wing ideas[2].

Right-wing extremism in the German political system

Voting behaviour can be taken as a fundamental indicator for the success of political concepts and parties. Over the last few years many right-wing parties have been remarkably successful in nearly all Western European countries. In Germany, the combined results of all the Far Right parties have amounted to about 10% in a number of elections. However, there has been a significant decline in popularity over 1994-1995. The highest rate for a single party was reached by the neo-Fascist *Die Republikaner* in 1992 which gained 10.9% of the votes and, thus, 15 seats in the Länder-parliament of Baden-Württemberg, in the south of Germany. The same day, 93,000 people (6.3% of the electorate) in Schleswig-Holstein, the northernmost Land in Germany, voted for another extreme right-wing party, the *Deutsche Volksunion* (DVU). Both these Länder are in West Germany and they do not suffer from extremely high rates of unemployment, low wages, housing problems or any of those characteristics so often referred to as possible accounts for the growth of popularity of extreme right-wing political parties. *Die Republikaner* also had the political support of about two million German voters during the last elections for the European Parliament and were allocated six seats in Strasbourg.

However, it must be taken into consideration that a high percentage of these votes are from so-called 'protest voters'. These are defined as voters who disagree both with governmental policies as well as those of the established opposition parties. Apart from these protest voters, the 'true' supporters of extreme right-wing parties in Germany is estimated to be about 7%. Obviously, this varies and depends on the region as well as on the kind and importance of elections. Furthermore, several right-wing extremist political parties have to share these votes. The biggest parties, currently, are *Die Republikaner*, the National Democratic Party of Germany (NPD) and the German National Union (DVU). Some parties have been prohibited by the Constitutional Court (*Bundesverfass-ungsgericht*) or by the Home Office, e.g. the Free German Labour Party (FAP) in September 1993, the National Front (NF) in November 1992, and the German Alternative (DA) in December 1992[3].

More important is that these small parties have forced the Conservative Party (CDU) to pick up on many of the themes, e.g. focusing on immigra-tion policies, security, crime rates, etc. which were initially raised by the right-wing extremist parties, and to move further to the right in order to regain lost votes.

Although the emergence and increasing popularity of right-wing parties is not necessarily an exclusively German phenomenon, there are two remarkable differences to other European countries. Firstly, whilst Jörg Haider in Austria, Jean Marie Le Pen in France and Silvio Berlusconi in Italy do not only attract right-wing extremist voters but also integrate the more moderate right-wing forces to a certain extent, there is no such figure in Germany. Secondly, in Germany these parties are dominated by young people. Whilst in the past German youth has often tended to employ Nazi symbols and elements in order to be provocative, there is a now general tendency for young people to get actively involved in the German right-wing scene. In order to facilitate and absorb this interest many right-wing groups refrain from highly structured organisations and prefer loosely structured and theme-orientated forms of collaboration which are obviously more attractive for young people. At the same time, these groups are able to undermine and evade the increasingly strict governmental prohibitions concerning the formation of political organisations[4].

Criminal offences with a right-wing extremist background

In recent years there has been a dramatic increase in violent incidents with a xenophobic or racist background. The current statistics produced by the office responsible for defending the constitution (*Bundesamt für Verfassungsschutz*) show that the rates have risen by more than 2,000% since 1985[5]. An enormous increase can be observed after the so-called 'reunification' of the two German states in 1989/90. However, these data need to be considered very critically because the extent and the intensity of obvious or latent xenophobic and racist violence can hardly be registered precisely. There are three major reasons for this. Firstly, in the former German Democratic Republic, the government pre-scribed the ideology of 'international socialism' and 'international solidarity'. Therefore xenophobia and racism did — by definition — not exist. Racially motivated criminal offences were generally not recorded as such. Secondly, before 1989 racism, xenophobia and anti-Semitism were excluded from the public discourse in the Federal Republic of Germany. Even today, the pub-lication of statistics (see Figure 1) showing racially motivated criminal offences raises public discussions about Germany's international image.

Thirdly, data on this violence have been gathered by a variety of institutions and agencies and they are at serious variance with each other. However, as a general trend, all the data reveal an escalation of right-wing violence after the 'reunification' of the two Germanies, until 1992 when the state started to respond

Figure 1: Criminal offences with proved or assumed right-wing motives
(source: Bundesamt für Verfassungsschutz)

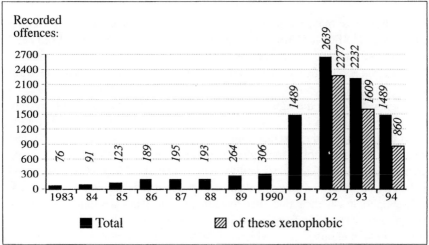

to this development after the neo-Nazi atrocity in Mölln in which three Turkish people were killed in an arson attack. The worldwide media coverage of this tragedy started to seriously damage Germany's international reputation, and consequently the state responded in a repressive way. Raids, arrests and banning of some neo-Nazi organisations dominated the aftermath of the Mölln atrocity.

However, the fact remains that the German state remained relatively inactive for almost two years, when in 1992 the government surrendered to racist and xenophobic terror in Hoyerswerda, Rostock-Lichtenhagen, Wismar and Quedlinburg and evacuated refugees and asylum seekers — leaving so-called 'foreign-free' cities.

After 1992 the number of violent attacks remained at a fairly high level over the next years but did not increase further. Most recently, a slight decline can be observed. At the same time, one primary 'target' of militant right-wing extremist attention, the issue of political asylum, has lost its significance for the following two reasons. Firstly, the number of political refugees seeking asylum in Germany is declining after the change of the German constitution. Secondly, a clear majority of the public objected to the violence against migrants and minority ethnic groups. Thus potential delinquents, who saw themselves acting on behalf of and in agreement with the 'silent' majority, realised that what they had perceived as their backing was in fact mythical.

Explaining the revival of racist and xenophobic ideologies and violence

Although the vast majority of migrants have settled in West Germany, according to the Federal Office for Crime (*Bundeskriminalamt*) one in four attacks in 1992 occurred in East Germany which clearly displays a higher intensity of violence. Nevertheless about 75% of racist and xenophobic violence occurs in the West. Consequently, any attempts to explain this phenomenon require a differentiated approach, recognising the significant differences in the development and structure of the two German societies prior to and post 1989 and their implications for the individuals living in these states. The media and many politicians tend to reject the notion that these violent incidents have socio-structural causes, whilst drawing attention to male working class youths with low levels of formal education and broken homes. But there is general agreement among social scientists that racist and xenophobic violence motivated by extreme right-wing ideologies should not be understood as arising from individual personality traits, but rather as a social and political phenomenon — which means that its magnitude is determined by and can be influenced by social and political factors.

Heitmeyer (1993a; 1993b) has shown that extreme right-wing ideologies are generally based on concepts of inequality, non-equivalence and unequal treatment of human beings. The firm belief in inequality can be seen in nationalistic exaggerations, racial discrimination, the distinction between life-worthy and unworthy creatures, 'natural' hierarchies based on socio-biological evidence, social-darwinistic beliefs in the concept of the 'survival of the fittest', a totalitarian comprehension of normality including a devaluation of 'being different', and a strong emphasis on homogeneity and cultural distinction. Equally obvious is the concept of inequality in the lifestyles of individuals and groups which emphasises the social, economic, cultural, political and legal exclusion of others. In addition, extreme right-wing ideologies display a high acceptance of violence which can be observed at different levels, ranging from the conviction that the existence of violence as a part of normal life is inevitable, to the actual use of violence. At the same time and as part of the lifestyle, rational discussions are generally rejected, whilst authoritarian para-military structures are adopted. Consequently, democratic procedures to solve social and political problems are rejected and their value generally denied.

However, the emergence of this ideology, combined with violent attacks on minorities in East and West Germany, has different causes. Generally, explanations focusing on the disproportionately high levels of violence in the East identify the following factors as key contributors:

- the social deprivation and disintegration after 1989 which led to various forms of polarisation and boundary-setting instead of the emergence of pluralist structures.
- a collective state of dissatisfaction and normlessness due to the disjunction between the definition of success in terms of material wealth and power and the reality of increasing unemployment, poverty and material failure and of blocked access to business opportunities.
- the perceived superiority of West Germans which has been hindering the development towards more self-confidence, and consequently requires the identification and definition of others as inferior.

In addition, it has to be recognised that a critical analysis of 20th century German history did not take place in the GDR and that the authoritarian socialisation did not prepare people for life in an individualised society.

Explanations concerning the situation in West Germany tend to focus on adolescents who perceive themselves as powerless, isolated and uncertain about how to influence their future lives in an increasingly individualised society where traditionally homogenous social environments have helped to provide social, cultural and political orientation. Uncertainties, feelings of powerlessness and experiences of isolation can cause 'natural' characteristics, such as skin colour, 'race' and nationality, to gain in importance as a means of distinction and nationalist feelings can substitute for the missing sense of belonging.

Football, racism and xenophobia in Germany

When the German *Bundesliga* commenced for the first time in August 1963 there were five foreign nationals playing for First Division teams. At the start of the 1992/93 season almost every professional team had signed up at least five 'foreigners'. However, this increase was accompanied by a dramatic rise of verbal xenophobic and racist attacks from the terraces. There is no doubt that the steadily increasing influx of 'foreign' players in the 1980s and 1990s has enhanced the quality of German soccer since these players have brought new ideas, fresh impulses and a cosmopolitan dimension to football in Germany. When the Cold War ended and African teams showed their potential as future soccer powers, German managers were quick to react and recruited dozens of players from Eastern Europe and the ex-Soviet Union and from Africa — a continent until then a no-go area for football talent spotters. Whilst the former group had hardly any problems to settle in Germany, the black Africans had to face a fairly cold and hostile welcome, often accompanied by verbal outbreaks of racist slurs, and were frequently treated as modern slaves by club officials and managers.

These introductory remarks have hinted at the complexity of the specific problem of football in Germany, which we address more precisely in the following sections. Anthony Yeboah, the outstanding black African striker playing for Frankfurt until 1994, was the focus of many controversies concerning racism in German soccer. Consequently, he features prominently in this chapter.

The historical context: football and 'Germanness'

Historically, racism, xenophobia and the most vicious nationalisms have arisen in those societies least confident of themselves, or in those most divided. Nationalism is never so intense as among people whose national identity has been cast into doubt, has not yet been fully developed or is challenged by a group within. The German Empire, as the political ancestor of the Federal Republic of Germany, was only founded in 1871 and, thus, this nationstate is one of the youngest in Europe. As a consequence, a significant number of political and cultural debates have, in the past, focused upon the issue of national identity and Germanness. Even the introduction of football was accompanied by such a debate.

The socio-historical development of football in Germany has been outlined by several writers (Hopf, 1979; Lindner and Breuer, 1983). According to Hopf (1979, pp. 54-80), at the end of the last century the introduction of football instead of Rugby, the other well known game among early sport enthusiasts in Germany, can be attributed to three causes, of which the following one is extremely relevant for an understanding of the roots of nationalism surrounding soccer in Germany. Of political importance was that soccer could be declared to be 'German football' while Rugby was considered to be 'English football'. Since Koch, the German equivalent to Thomas Arnold, was aware of the resentments the introduction of an English game would provoke, he tried to provide evidence that football also had a long tradition in Continental Europe and that it was already played in 'Germany' in the Middle Ages. He did this in order to gain approval from the members of the Gymnastics Movement (*Turnbewegung*), whose power and influence, however, was at that point in time gradually declining.

This consideration clearly shows that the introduction of football in Germany was accompanied by some heated debates about sport and 'Germanness'. In the second half of the 19th century the entire concept of competitive (English) sport was disapproved by the Germans, i.e. by the Gymnastics movement, because such sport was labelled decadent, un-German, trivial (i.e. lacking metaphysical aspects) and, most important, because it was essentially English. Publications like '*Fusslümmelei*' (1898), literally translated football hooliganism, ridiculed this 'English fashion' and denounced football as the 'English disease'. Obviously, this stands in sharp contrast to the modern perception and the popularity of this sport which is seen as the most German of all games and the ultimate embodiment of the German soul and character; in short: the incorporation of 'Germanness' — an important aspect which needs to be kept in mind when we look into racism, xenophobia and nationalism in more detail. Although most recently some work has been concerned with football and the issues of identity and nationalism (Merkel, 1994), football writing in Germany is certainly not in general as extensive as, for example, in the United Kingdom. This is caused by a number of factors: it is considered too trivial as an academic topic, too celebratory of reactionary values and too dominated by pseudo-systematic analysis of journalists. But most important for insiders: full of myths which have to be unveiled before a constructive discussion can commence. One of these myths (that football is originally German) has already been mentioned. Another one concerns social relations in football: it is supposed to bring different cultures together, to unite people of different ethnic origins and to integrate minorities. Public statements particularly in the print media, such as "Sport and Church help to find new home" (*Frankfurter Allgemeine Zeitung*, May 24,1994), "Sport creates links because it speaks all languages" *(Deutscher Sportbund*, May 19, 1994), etc., clearly indicate the apparently most important function of modern sport — the integration of people. Of course, football can fulfil this function, but the dark side of this shiny coin displays a different picture: ethnocentrism, chauvinism, nationalism, xenophobia and racism.

Racism, xenophobia and nationalism in German soccer

After winning the World Cup in 1990, it was a shock to many that two years later in the final of the European Championships in Sweden almost the same team lost to Denmark — a team which was only admitted since there was no Yugoslavia left to represent this fragmented state. The next blow was the defeat by Bulgaria in one of the quarter finals of the World Cup in 1994 in the USA. Despite these two disappointing defeats, some Germans certainly took comfort in the fact that almost half of the Bulgarian and Danish players belonged to German *Bundesliga* clubs.

Although the increasing internationalisation of national football leagues is usually characterised as one of the key developments in the 1980s, the German *Bundesliga* has never been a purely German affair. Since its inauguration in 1963 there have always been foreign players involved in the game. During the 1993/94 season the German Football Association (DFB) registered 208 foreign players who played for either First or Second Division teams, from 43 countries ranging from Albania to Zaire. The largest group came from ex-Yugoslavia (23 players) followed by Croatia (17), Denmark (13), Russia (11), Poland (11) and

Ghana (10). Players from Eastern Europe, the ex-Soviet Union and from Africa comprised the majority of foreigners. Whilst the latter's mobility increased due to the remarkable performances of African teams at the World Cup in Italy in 1990, the former two groups in particular benefited from the upheavals in many Eastern European countries and the ex-Soviet Union.

Despite Germany's large 'foreign' communities there are very few 'black' people. However, among the foreign players in the *Bundesliga* they are no longer a minority. On the other hand, the Turkish community is most evident in everyday life, but there are hardly any Turkish players in the *Bundesliga* despite soccer's popularity among the Turks. The few Turkish players who had been with German First Division clubs in the 1970s and 1980s were very often the first to be addressed by the abusive chants of their own supporters if things went wrong.

Whilst there are more than 50 black Africans playing in France's First Division, there are about 20 in the German *Bundesliga*. Most of them came to Germany after the impressive performances of African teams during the 1990 World Cup in Italy. However "the circumstances which accompanied this migration had much in common with the slave trade of colonial times" (*Spiegel*, Jan. 5, 1992). Extremely popular for Western European clubs have been the young and talented players of Ghana's U17-team. Three months after this team became World Champions more than half of the players had left the country and signed up with Western European clubs. German club managers ("we simply had to have some of those players" [*Spiegel*, Jan. 5, 1992]) are excited for two reasons. Firstly, they compensate for the lack of talented native offspring and, secondly, they are expected to make a big profit for the club when they are sold on. In addition, the politics of 'integration' of the German Football Association support this 'slave trade' due to an extremely arbitrary policy: once these Africans have played for 3 years in a youth team and for 2 years in a professional team they become 'Football-Germans' and thus do not incriminate the limited contingency of foreign players per team. The consequence: the younger the African players the more lucrative the business. For Western agents this means that the Africa-Cup and other top tournaments and matches have to be attended to get a fair share of the big catch.

Whilst Danish, Swiss, Russians and Americans have hardly ever been the targets of racist or xenophobic chants (at least, as long as they are white), being Colombian, Brazilian, French, Nigerian or from Ghana and Morocco *and* black makes a huge difference and can become a real problem, as the persistence and pervasiveness of racist chants and symbols in German football grounds clearly shows. Whether the different forms of racism are instrumental (to support one's own team and to weaken the opponent's spirit) and/or manifestations of racist ideologies is difficult to establish. At this stage it is more important to describe the key features of racism in German football. The following examples illustrate the diversity of overtly racist behaviour both from players and spectators:

- Cologne's sweeper Paul Steiner was accused of a racist outburst in October 1989 during a match against Wattenscheid. Souleyman Sane, the black African striker of Wattenscheid, reported that Steiner shouted at him, "You fucking nigger, piss off. What do you want in Germany?" (Weber-Klüver, 1993: p. 54)
- "It has become part of the weekend-by-weekend normality in the football grounds to hear sounds such as 'Uuuuh Uuuuh, Uuuuh' imitating the sound of the jungle. Subsequently, bananas are thrown at the black stars Anthony Yeboah and Sammy Sane". (Weise, 1994)
- "Yeboah experienced how quickly a 'black monkey' or 'black rat' could turn into a 'black pearl'". (Weber-Klüver, 1993, p.51)
- "Ojokojo Torunanigha from Gabun playing for Chemnitz was insulted by the fans through chants such as 'nigger out'". (Weber-Klüver 1993, p.27).

Evidence suggests that these examples are far from uncommon in German football grounds, which means that there are sinister and disturbing racist and xenophobic elements, combined with extremely arrogant attitudes, present in contemporary German football culture. However, this is not restricted to players and spectators but includes managers and coaches, as the following examples demonstrate:

- At the end of the 1993/94 season Anthony Yeboah was not available to play for his team in Frankfurt as he was playing for the national team of Ghana in the Africa Cup. Uli Hoeneß, general manager of Bayern Munich, was offended by Yeboah's priorities, as for him this Cup was simply a 'jungle championship'. (Scherzer, 1994)
- African players are very popular among German managers and coaches because of their "skilfulness, dynamics, speed and power — the black antelopes, as they are often called, have however, limited intellectual capacity". (Weise, 1994)
- "[Abedi] Pele ..., at 27, still hopes to reach Italy. He is still slightly bitter about his struggle for recognition in Europe. Munich released him after a trial match, Dieter Hoeneß' testimonial against Liverpool. 'We made the English look like schoolboys' he said, 'Mathäus, Lerby and me, but they let me go because I was black'." (Barclay, 1992)

Racist and xenophobic chants and other forms of abuse are perceived by the majority of soccer players, coaches, administrators etc., not to be a big problem.

Julio Cesar and Ruud Gullit constitute the exception. Whilst the latter was said not to have signed up for Bayern Munich because of his awareness of the extreme nationalistic attitudes of Bavarian fans, Julio Cesar has agreed an opt-out clause in his contract with Borussia Dortmund in the event of racist problems. However, in the same way that football officials in the 1980s denied any responsibility for hooliganism, in the 1990s they are happy to repeatedly point out that racist abuses of players are single incidents which do not have anything to do with the sport. Other players have also down-played the issue: "I don't have any problems with the colour of my skin here in Germany. There will always be some crazy people shouting 'nigger' but that doesn't affect me" (Anthony Yeboah: quoted in Martin, 1994).

Heitmeyer and Peter (1988) concluded as the result of an empirical research project that despite a fairly common subcultural style, three different groups of football fans can be distinguished according to both their motivation to come to the ground and their norms and values: those who are attracted by the sport (*Fußballzentrierte Fans*); those who regard the game as one among many interchangeable leisure activities (*Konsumorientierte Fans*); and those who come for the excitement, the action on the terraces, the adventure (*Erlebnisorientierte Fans*) (pp. 56–63). It is the latter group in particular which displays authoritarian and nationalist attitudes as well as a fairly high degree of acceptance of violence. Although to a lesser extent, the football-orientated fans show the same configuration. They, too, share authoritarian and nationalistic values and perceive violence as acceptable. Heitmeyer and Peter also show that despite the high affinity to authoritarian and nationalist attitudes these fans are not prepared to join political organisations and parties but, rather, prefer fan clubs or informal cliques (1988: pp. 82 -89).

However, ethnographic studies have shown that there are exceptions, such as the *Borussenfront*, a group of Borussia Dortmund fans who formed a paramilitary association with close contacts to the NPD and FAP. It emerged at the beginning of the 1980s and disappeared in the second half of that decade. Xenophobic chants as well as violent attacks on Turkish businesses in a residential working class area of Dortmund drew the attention of both the media and researchers to the *Borussenfront* — which, in turn, blurred the boundaries between myth and reality. But there is no doubt that the leader of this group was also a leading member of the FAP. Generally however, the aim of integrating football fans into the rigid structures of right-wing parties turned out to be unworkable since it contradicted the fan ethos of drinking and fighting (Weber-Klüver, 1993: pp. 38-9).

There is plenty of anecdotal evidence that football grounds have been used as a public forum for 'broadcasting' of political messages. Banners protesting the closure of mines or steel companies (particularly at matches in the Ruhr area) as well as chants supporting anarchists and squatters in St. Pauli's stadium in Hamburg have become common features of soccer matches. In the late 1980s the impact of right-wing groups and parties was considerable. Although the attempts to recruit new members for the FAP, e.g. in Dortmund, were in the main unsuccessful (according to the street and social workers we interviewed), the visibility of Nazi-symbols and terminology in German football grounds was considerable. The war-flag of the Third Reich (*Reichskriegsflagge*), swastikas and SS-symbols, as well as chants referring to the concentration camps, their gas chambers or addressing the referee as a "Jewish swine" (*Judensau*) clearly demonstrate the influence of right-wing and fascist ideas. Due to the German law which explicitly forbids the use of symbols specific to the Nationalist Socialist era (1933-45), many of the signs are slightly modified in order to avoid prosecution by the law enforcement agencies. It is not the racism and xenophobia which are the targets for legal action but the use of specific Nazi symbols.

The use of international football matches, particularly against European neighbour countries, as a forum for the expression of extremely patriotic and nationalistic ideologies has, too, increased since the beginning of the 1980s. Almost all matches against the Netherlands, Belgium, Luxembourg and France were accompanied by massive riots and the public display of right-wing and neo-Nazi attitudes. Chants such as *"Deutschland den Deutschen!"* ("Germany for the Germans!"), giving Nazi-salutes and symbolic maps (drawn or sewn on jackets, identifying Germany with its borders of 1933) have caused some serious concerns. The German flag has always been part of the standard equipment of German fans attending matches of the national squad. In 1988 the German Football Association introduced a new shirt for the players which is dominated by the three colours (black, red and gold) of the German flag. Already in 1984 — after a public outcry about the muteness of the team during the playing of the German anthem — the then new manager, Franz Beckenbauer, had ordered his men to learn the lyrics and to sing the anthem passionately during the opening ceremony of international matches.

It is particularly in the context of international matches that nationalist, racist and xenophobic attitudes are most openly displayed. Weeks before a match against Turkey in 1983, the same flyer was distributed in a number of German football grounds, accusing Turkish migrants of stealing German jobs and flooding the country, and threatening the Turkish population openly with violence.

Consequently, the police planned to be present with more than 5,000 officers; and the unions, the political parties of the German Left and other organisations used this opportunity to demonstrate their solidarity with the Turkish population. However, on the night of the match, the Berlin stadium, with a capacity of about 70,000 people, was only half full. Considering the popularity of football among Turkish migrants and the size of the Turkish community in Berlin (about 120,000 people) the absence of Turkish supporters clearly indicated fear. The potential presence of the German and English Far Right in Berlin also led to the cancellation of the match between Germany and England in 1994 which was scheduled to take place on Hitler's birthday.

These examples clearly demonstrate the widespread racism and xenophobia in German football and links to nationalist attitudes, as well as the complexity of these problems whose existence has yet to be acknowledged by the relevant institutions in order to be combated successfully.

Separatism in German football

The absence of Turkish players in Germany's professional leagues has already been mentioned. There are two obvious reasons for this situation. Firstly, the few Turkish players who in the past had been signed up by professional teams were frequently subjected to racist and xenophobic abuse. Since they played at a time when 'foreign' players were not as common as they are nowadays all the abuse was directed at them, and thus the frequency and intensity was extremely high. Due to the popularity of professional football and leagues in Turkey these successful players usually took the first chance to transfer 'home'. Secondly, because of the size and length of stay of the Turkish community in Germany there exists a network of exclusively Turkish clubs which are very popular among Turkish migrants, attracting large audiences and having financial backing from Turkish businesses. It is the latter which has caused some intense debates about cultural identity and ethnic differences in Germany.

For members of the 'first generation' of migrant workers in particular, these clubs provide an opportunity to relax from the social pressures and to mix with members of the same ethnic background and to avoid isolation. Another significant social and cultural function of these clubs is their ability both to provide members and supporters with a distinct identity and to represent their community publicly. Sporting success can significantly contribute to a general process of de-stigmatisation, particularly if the represented group is usually considered to be inferior, but proves in the sporting context to be (at least) an equal opponent.

One fundamental question is whether these forms of self-organisation increase the cultural as well as individual isolation and, thus, are counter productive in terms of the integration process. However, there is a sense that this model increases the self-confidence and self-awareness of the minorities concerned and, thus, promotes interaction with, as well as participation in, the culture of the majority ethnic group and prevents these people from losing their original identity.

Resisting racism and xenophobia and fostering integration in German sport

Whilst the previous section identified the complexity and magnitude of racism and xenophobia in German soccer, this section sets out to analyse strategies and campaigns to combat the problems mentioned above, as well as to identify some of the key features of the common belief that sport, particularly team sports, is an ideal instrument to promote the integration of minorities.

Subsequent to the incidents in Mölln, the Germans organised massive candle-lit demonstrations, torch light vigils and other symbolic actions which involved hundreds of thousands of people across Germany, but also demonstrated a highly fragmented and improvised response which can also be observed in the area of sport and leisure.

Strategies, campaigns and ad hoc activities

There is no doubt that in an ideal world — with full employment and equitable education systems and without various social problems — racism and xenophobia would be less likely to occur than under the current conditions. Therefore a fundamental task for all states should be to provide young people with a future they can look forward to. However, such a long-term project needs to be accompanied by short-term measures in order to, at least, reduce racism and xenophobia and, in turn, to foster the integration of minority ethnic groups. In 1995, the Council of Europe took an active interest in racism and xenophobia and developed, initiated and organised a number of events and activities as part of a wider campaign. "Bridges for Friendship", international youth camps, seminars and discussions, music festivals, etc. were all part of the "All Different — All Equal" campaign. Whilst many of these measures were European-wide, all participating countries were expected to develop their own national campaigns and events. In Germany this happened in conjunction with the Home Office, and subsequently the campaign "*Fairständnis*" [merging the two terms *Fairness* and *Verständnis* (understanding)] was started, and a monument ("United Colours of Germany") was erected. Part of the wider supra-national approach is the campaign "No Chance For Hatred" of the German Sports Youth (*Deutsche Sportjugend*) which encourages and supports all clubs to develop and organise activities against racism, xenophobia and other forms of discrimination. However, whilst this campaign is exceptional in the German context as it is fairly systematic and structured, addresses the complexity of the problem(s) adequately and aims to cover all sports, the German sport organisations generally rely heavily on token gestures, individual initiatives and Public Relations associated measures as the following examples demonstrate[6].

Frankfurt:

"One of Germany's most popular rock bands, the Scorpions, played at a huge concert against right-wing violence in Frankfurt yesterday. ... About 150,000 people attended the first occasion that 28 of the top German rock groups performed for free without charging admission. The concert sponsored by several multinationals, who took out full-page advertisements in newspapers to demand a halt to attacks on immigrants.

The day was not confined to pop music: All 18 clubs in the football premier league took a stand against neo-Nazism on the terraces and several hundred thousand staged rallies against right-wing extremism. During the last games before their winter break, players in the *Bundesliga* took to the pitch wearing jerseys bearing the motto: "My friend is a foreigner" and foreign players showed their value by scoring the decisive goals. ...

At the home game against Hamburg, fans of Eintracht Frankfurt carried banners declaring that "Germany without foreigners is like a piano without black keys" as Anthony Yeboah, the *Bundesliga*'s joint top-scorer and Ghanaian striker, shot the home side into the lead after only nine minutes.

In Munich's Olympic Stadium children carrying the flags of the world's countries joined hands to march round the perimeter of the pitch at half-time as Bruno Labbadia, Bayern's Brazilian centre-forward, claimed the goal that earned the league-leaders a draw." (Gow, 1993)

Oberhof (Bavaria): Following the violent skinhead attack on an American athlete, the headline of one national paper read as follows:
"State prosecutor investigates against ... skinheads — Hansen talks of 'scandal' — Apologies to the athletes — Stricter prosecution demanded." (*Frankfurter Rundschau*, Nov. 2, 1993)

Frankfurt/Vienna:

"The Board of Directors of Casino Salzburg formally apologised to Anthony Yeboah, the Ghanaian striker playing for Frankfurt, for the recent chants during the match against Salzburg. Before the start of the second leg Yeboah will be given flowers. He has also been invited to a free skiing weekend in Saalbach, Austria." (*Kölner Stadt-Anzeiger*, March 15, 1994)

Dortmund:
> "Disco Ban with consequences — Revolution of Sympathy for Brazil's Julio Cesar. ... Maio Elsner, manager of the disco 'Laufsteg', gave the very upset Julio Cesar a special VIP membership card as 'small compensation and a symbol indicating that not all discos are racist....'" (Loose, 1994)

This *ad hoc* and fragmented approach to combating discrimination and violence against minorities and right-wing violence can be adequately understood only if we recognise first that the majority of German sport associations, among them the German Football Association, fails and rejects, vehemently, to acknowledge the problem and, second, believes in and refers to the integrative qualities of sport.

Although the German Football Association approved and supported the initiative "My Friend is a Foreigner" and encourages fan-projects to include the fight against racism and xenophobia in their catalogue of tasks, the majority of measures taken by the German Football Association are concerned with Law and Order in German football grounds. Hence, when asked about the German Football Association's response to the increased racist and xenophobic abuses in German football grounds, officials of the German Football Association usually refer to the improved security in German stadia, the training of police and security services, the central police information service, entrance restrictions for potential trouble-makers, and so on.

If German sport was willing and prepared to tackle the problem of racism and xenophobia in a systematic and structured way, it is our opinion that established strategies and concepts of social work with young people could easily be adjusted and used.

Integration through sport and leisure

A more systematic approach can be identified when looking at concepts employing sport as a means of integration. According to the German Sports Association (DSB) sport is perceived to be of vital significance to foreigners and members of minority ethnic groups in Germany as:

(1) sport can help to decrease their social isolation and enhance their integration without the necessity of giving up their cultural distinctiveness and identity;

(2) sport provides an opportunity to overcome cultural and language barriers;

(3) sport is an ideal leisure activity providing both compensation from work and an innovative set of experiences.

In 1981 the DSB discussed the merits and demerits of three very distinctive models of membership and organisation of foreign athletes:

(1) the organisational integration of individuals in German sport clubs;
(2) the provision of ethnically homogeneous departments in German sports clubs;
(3) clubs exclusively for particular nationals or minority ethnic groups.

These concepts clearly reflect the wider discussion about the meaning of 'integration'. The most common interpretation of integration means that the integrating minority take on the culture of the majority, i.e. of the 'host nation', and gradually lose their own traditional culture. This concept is usually referred to as 'assimilative integration'. The concept of a 'pluralistic integration' recognises the need to keep certain cultural practices and to add new ones to them. In this case there is a strong likelihood that the majority ethnic group will also absorb some minority cultural practices into the dominant culture. This process is usually referred to as 'integrative integration'. The latter can clearly be observed in the relationship between the Danish minority and the German majority in the North of Germany.

These basic concepts can easily be assigned to the organisational models suggested by the German Sport Association: whilst the individual membership of 'foreigners' in German clubs supports an assimilative integration, the idea of 'foreign clubs' clearly relates to a pluralistic understanding of integration. Members of the 'second generation of migrant workers' tend to join German sport clubs and, thus, opt for assimilative forms of integration. However, the above-mentioned popularity of ethnically homogeneous sports clubs, particularly in urban areas, shows that sport does not overcome social and cultural differences but reinforces them.

However, the German Sport Association has never been in favour of this model and has repeatedly stressed that 'foreign' or 'ethnic' clubs are only an intermediate step on the way to full integration.

Conclusion

There are, to draw an almost simplistic but necessary distinction, two kinds of nation: immigrant and non-immigrant. Germany belongs, in fact, to the former, but asserts to be one of the latter and, thus, struggles to come to terms with its obligation towards immigrants — which is most evident in the anti-immigration backlashes and the growing number of violent attacks on migrants.

The Germans are a less homogenous people than some of their European neighbours, and they still conceive of themselves in ethnic terms. Although 'race' is one extremely potent element in the German national identity, in general, anti-migrant feelings and attitudes have less to do with 'race' than with cultural and religious differences, as well as with economic problems and concerns. Therefore the key concept in the wider German context which needs to be addressed is the relationship between xenophobia and 'Germanness'. Particularly after the so-called 'reunification' of the two German states, the Germans' fragile sense of identity has been challenged again and requires yet another new definition, crucial to the people's sense of identity and vulnerability, and decisive in securing the Germans' sense of themselves.

However, the situation is much more complex in the sporting context as there is evidence for widespread racism and xenophobia, particularly among football supporters whose behaviour cannot simply be explained as a reflection of developments in wider society, as it has also developed its own qualities and characteristics often directly or indirectly encouraged by managers, players and administrators. However, due to the complexity of these dynamics in the world of football, and also due to the limitations of this study, the fundamental question has yet remained unanswered: Is the racism and xenophobia in German football grounds instrumental and, thus, an exchangeable part of the repertoire of fan behaviour, or is it an expression of a deeply rooted commitment to (extreme) right-wing ideologies?

There is certainly no doubt that football in Germany has regularly been accompanied by nationalistic elements — which is not surprising, considering the potential and the reality of sport for the expression of such tendencies. However, football is the most popular spectator sport in Germany and for many the embodiment of 'Germanness' — a concept many Germans would struggle to define due to the relatively short and extremely varied history of this nationstate. It is this dilemma which appears to contribute significantly to various forms of boundary-setting and, thus, to a polarisation between 'us' and 'them'. Consequently, obvious and straightforward characteristics, such as skin colour, race or nationality, gain in importance as a means of distinction.

However, the most recent German history has clearly shown that the 'foreign' community in Germany also functions as a scapegoat, apparently being responsible for a number of social and economic problems as well as for the dilution of the purity of the German culture and 'race' which has led to a dramatic increase in violent attacks. The state has reacted slowly and with reluctance.

Almost the same applies to the world of sport. There is definitely an increase in racist and xenophobic manifestations; the majority are verbal and symbolic, a small number comprise physical attacks; and the majority of governing bodies hardly respond. If they do, they either stress the integrative functions of sport or they rely heavily on token gestures and on *ad hoc* measures. However, not all 'foreign' players are equal and, thus, subject to abuse. It is the few black (African) athletes in particular who have most frequently been the targets of racist insults, whilst white 'foreigners' appear to be more or less acceptable to the football audiences. Turks constitute an interesting exception; although subject to numerous and varied forms of everyday discrimination and hostility they do not constitute a problem in the football ground — simply because they are absent both as players and spectators. On the one hand, considering the size of the Turkish community in Germany and football's popularity particularly among the male Turks this is very surprising. On the other hand, Turkish football supporters have most systematically been targets for violent threats, and anecdotal evidence shows that the few Turkish players in Germany's premier division have regularly been subjected to blunt anti-Turkish abuse, even by the supporters of their own team. Consequently, it is less of a surprise that the Turkish community has founded its own — ethnically almost homogenous — semi-professional clubs from where the top players very often move into a professional career in Turkey. This development is, however, contested, particularly by the governing body of German sport since it does not comply to the normative understanding of integration in and through sport which contains a strong notion of assimilation.

Hardly any of the above-mentioned issues has ever been investigated thoroughly and completely. The few attempts which have been made in the past have remained fairly fragmented and isolated. In order to gain a fuller understanding of the complex dynamics of sport, with particular reference to racism and xenophobia on one side and the mechanisms of integration and exclusion on the other side, the following issues and themes should be followed up in more detail:

- Detailed quantitative and qualitative analysis of racist and xenophobic incidents in German football grounds;
- Ethnographic studies of terrace and club fan cultures with particular emphasis on the political attitudes of fans;
- Analysis of the policies of all institutions involved in football in terms of their stance on racism, xenophobia and nationalism and their approaches to combat these problems;
- Analysis of the media coverage of racism, xenophobia and nationalism as well as of the presentation of non-German football players;
- Analysis of the meaning of ethnic clubs with particular reference to the Turkish community in Germany.

Notes

[1] For more details see Der Beauftragte der Bundesregierung für die Belange der Ausländer (ed) (1994); Baratta (1994 -1995); Schneider (1993)

[2] Hüsers (1995) provides additional detailed information on this issue.

3   A concise overview of the develepmont of these extreme right-wing parties over the last years can be found in Schneider (1993).

4   See also Kowalsky (1993).

5   For the most detailed quantitative data on racist and xenophobic violence in Germany, see Bundesministerium des Innern (ed) (1993, 1994, 1995). The data referred to in this section derive predominantly from the 1994 Report (p.7 ff).

6   Another notable exception is BAFF (Association of Anti-Fascist Football Initiatives) which emerged in the late 1980s as a response to the presence of right-wing groups in German football grounds. Among other activities they actively campaigned for the cancellation of the 'friendly' against England on Hitler's birthday.

References

Baratta, M. von (ed) (1993 — 1996) *Der Fischer Weltalmanach*. Frankfurt am Main: Fischer.

Barclay, P. (1992) 'Mysteries of an African adventure', *The Observer*, 26 Jan.: p. 42.

Beauftragte der Bundesregierung für die Belange der Ausländer (ed) (1994) *Daten und Fakten zur Ausländersituation*. Bonn: Bonner Universitäts-Buchdruckerei.

Bundesministerium des Innern (ed) (1993, 1994, 1995) *Verfassungsschutzbericht 1992, 1993, 1994*. Bonn: Mirgel and Schneider.

Deutscher Sportbund (1994) Mit dem Sport gegen den Rassismus, press announcement, 17 May.

Frankfurter Allgemeine Zeitung (1994) 'Mit Sport und Kirche neue Heimat gefunden', 24 May.

Gow, D. (1992) 'One of Germany's most popular rock bands...', *The Guardian*, 14 Dec.: p. 8.

Heitmeyer, W. and Peter, J.-I. (1988) *Jugendliche Fußballfans. Soziale und politische Orientierungen, Gesellungsformen, Gewalt*. 2nd edition. Weinheim und Munich: Juventa.

Heitmeyer, W. *et al.* (1993a) *Die Bielefelder Rechtsextremismus-Studie. Erste Langzeituntersuchung zur politischen Sozialisation männlicher Jugendlicher*. 2nd edition. Weinheim und Munich: Juventa.

Heitmeyer, W. (1993b) 'Gesellschaftliche Desintegrationsprozesse als Ursachen von fremdenfeindlicher Gewalt und politischer Paralysierung', *Aus Politik und Zeitgeschichte*, No. 2-3 (8 January): pp. 3-13.

Hopf, W. (1979) *Fussball — Soziologie und Sozialgeschichte einer populären Sportart*. Bensheim: päd extra buchverlag.

Hüsers, F. (1995) 'Fremdenfeindlichkeit in Deutschland. Ergebnisse einer Repräsentativerhebung', *Aus Politik und Zeitgeschichte*, No. 48 (24 November): pp. 22-28.

Jarry, D. and Jarry, J. (1991) *Collins Dictionary of Sociology*. Glasgow: Harper Collins.

Kölner Stadt-Anzeiger (1994) 'Blumenstrauß für Yeboah', 15 March.

Kowalsky, W. (1993) 'Rechtsextremismus und Anti-Rechtsextremismus in der modernen Industriegesellschaft', *Aus Politik und Zeitgeschichte*, No. 2 (January): pp. 14-25.

Loose, H. W. (1994) 'Ein Disco-Verbot mit Folgen', *Die Welt*, 20 September.

Lindner, R. and Breuer, H.T. (1983) *"Sind doch nicht alles Beckenbauers"*. Frankfurt: Syndicat.

Martin, H.G. (1994) 'Ausländer rein! Ohne sie wäre die Fußball-Landschaft ärmer', *Neuß-Grevenbroicher Zeitung*, 15 October.

Merkel, U. (1994) 'Germany and the World Cup: Solid, reliable, often undramatic — but successful', in J. Sugden and A. Tomlinson (eds) *Hosts and Champions — Soccer Cultures, National Identities and the USA World Cup*. Aldershot: Arena/ Ashgate Publishing Ltd., pp. 93-118.

Merten, O. and Otto, H. U. (eds) (1993) *Rechtsradikale Gewalt im vereinigten Deutschland. Jugend im gesellschaftlichen Umbruch*. Bonn: Leske and Budrich.

Pilz, G. (1982) (ed) *Sport und körperliche Gewalt*. Reinbek: Rowohlt Verlag.

Planck, K. [1898] *Fusslümmelei — Über Strauchballspiel und englische Krankheit* (reprint). Münster: Lit-Verlag (1982).

Pramann, U. (1983) Fußballfans — *Betrachtungen einer Subkultur*. Hamburg: Stern-Bücher.

Scherzer, H. (1994) 'Ghana entscheidet die deutsche Meisterschaft', *Kölner Stadt-Anzeiger*, 14 March: p. 19.

Schneider, H. (1993) 'Jugendlicher Rechtsextremismus in Deutschland seit 1945: Organisationen und Dispositionen, Kontinuitäten und Diskontinuitäten', in Deutsches Jugendinstitut (ed) (1993) *Gewalt gegen Fremde. Rechtsradikale, Skinheads und Mitläufer*. Munich: Juventa.

Schneider-Haase, D. T. (1992) 'Verständnis für rechtsradikale Tendenzen?', *Umfrage und Analyse*, Vol. 14 (5/6): pp. 72-80.

SINUS (1981) *"Wir wollen wieder einen Führer haben...".* 5 Millionen Deutsche. Die *SINUS-Studie über rechtsextremistische Einstellungen bei den Deutschen*. Reinbek: Rowohlt.

Spiegel (1992) 'Gnadenlos ausgenommen', 5 January, pp. 142 -145.

Weber-Klüver, K. (1993) '"Neger Raus" gegen "Zeugen Yeboahs" — *Fußball* und Rassismus in Deutschland', in Verlag die Werkstatt (ed) *Fußball und Rassismus*. Göttingen: Verlag Die Werkstatt, pp. 27-72.

Weise, K. (1994) 'Fremdes Brot ist herbes Brot', *Junge Welt*, 19 September.

FOOTBALL, RACISM AND XENOPHOBIA IN HUNGARY: RACIST AND XENOPHOBIC BEHAVIOUR OF FOOTBALL SPECTATORS

Gyöngyi Szabó Földesi

Introduction

Since the rise of institutionalised and organised football, racist abuse of players has been common in Hungarian football stadia in all political regimes, including the early communist era when people's public behaviour was rigidly controlled. At that time, freedom of speech was limited in Hungary to such an extent that sometimes even impartial, casual remarks on ethnic and/or national minorities were interpreted as malign. Nevertheless, football fans' racial and xenophobic abuses were tolerated. In the years of 'hard' dictatorship of the socialist system, and also later during the 'soft' dictatorship, football matches were commonly considered by the state as vehicles for releasing social pressure. This policy was well known; even the football crowds knew that they were being manipulated, as the following chant — yelled about twenty years ago in support of the most popular Hungarian football team, whose supporters were perceived as sympathisers with racist ideologies — illustrates:

> Fradi has become, has become a champion,
> Because János Kádár* allowed it all.

Notwithstanding, there is very little systematic investigation into the forms and manners in which discrimination by spectators manifests itself. Discriminatory behaviour — like other deviant forms of behaviour such as violence, aggression, vandalism, etc. — was a taboo subject and, then, not on the research agenda. It could not be officially investigated and was not even reported by the media until the collapse of the socialist system.

The first attempt to study racist and xenophobic abuses and discrimination in Hungarian football stadia was made recently as a part of a wider project dealing with Hungarian football fans. The history, objectives and methods of this research project was outlined in previous publications (Földesi, 1994, 1995).

• Hungarian President 1956–58 and 1961–65; First Secretary of the Hungarian Socialist Workers Party (HSWP) 1957–1985; General Secretary of the HSWP 1985–1988.

Main social and demographic characteristics of Hungarian football fans, as well as their motivations to attend first league matches, were also presented earlier. In this chapter only the issue of racist and xenophobic abuse and discrimination by spectators in Hungarian football stadia will be discussed.

Methods

A group of 16 participant observers attended football matches in all first league stadia at least three times in the autumn of 1992 and three times in the spring of the 1993 season. Matches of football teams whose supporters were perceived by public opinion as 'racist' or as sympathetic to racism were visited a further five times, both at home and away. The task of the observers was to register all kinds of misbehaviour amongst spectators during football matches, with emphasis on racist behaviour — from offending gestures to verbal attacks and violent offences. In this chapter the latter are analysed. Observations were recorded both in and outside the stadia, but — in the absence of systematic empirical data on support- ers' conduct before and after matches — the latter was considered to be com- plementary information, and only data collected during matches were analysed. Altogether, records of 106 football matches were available for further analysis.

According to guidelines given to the participant observers, the circum- stances and the nature of discriminatory behaviour, the targets of racist and xenophobic abuses and the number of people involved in the individual incidents were to be recorded. Here it should be emphasised that this chapter does not intend to precisely quantify the frequency of racist and xenophobic incidents inside football grounds: it attempts rather to approach the problem qualitatively. However, attempts were made to describe the major differences in the extent of racist abuses and discrimination between football crowds in different stadia.

Manifestations of racism and xenophobia among spectators at football matches

Frequency

Discriminatory forms of behaviour were distinguished at three levels: individual, small group and large group. This distinction was made in part on the basis of the estimated number of persons involved in a given manifestation; in part on the basis of the number of people by whom certain manifestations could be perceived. The main criterion to distinguish between these levels was whether a discriminatory activity could be detected (1) close to relevant participants; (2) in the more remote vicinity; (3) all over the stadium.

The impossibility of recording all manifestations at a match cannot be denied. When summing up the frequency of manifestations of racism and xenophobia, discriminatory behaviours at the individual level were not included. Comparisons between football crowds in this respect comprised only racist abuses and discrimination committed by small and large groups. However, there remains the question of the significance of the more or less isolated discriminatory conduct of individual spectators. It is thought that although they must not be added to the frequency of discrimination at a match, they must not be neglected either. This is especially true for Hungary where there are many so-called 'quasi-spectators'. Their presence means a potential increase of spectators' violence in general; and their racist conduct could lead to further manifestations of racism and xenophobia in particular.

The seriousness of occasional racist remarks noticed by the observers must not be minimised, because — according to recorded cases — they were made in all stadia, at all matches, and everywhere by a great number of supporters of all ages and with (apparently) different social backgrounds. Nowadays, when the revival of racism in Hungary is doubted in certain political circles, such discouraging results should be reported in order to promote the recognition of a real problem.

The occurrence of racist behaviour by groups was also very high. Though the number of spectators involved in them and the significance of the events varied greatly, there was not a single stadium where researchers did not observe abusive incidents; they reported them not only from all stadia but from 72% of the attended matches. Moreover, the fact that 28% of all reports on football matches by observers did not mention any racist and xenophobic abuses does not mean that at those matches smaller incidents did not occur, but merely that they might have remained unnoticed by the researchers. *Mutatis mutandis*, the same applies to matches where discriminatory behaviour was reported. At these matches, obviously stadium-wide manifestations were in all probability registered. However, it is also very likely that observers walking around football stadia did not witness all abusive behaviours, e.g. by small groups.

About half of the registered cases of stadium-wide incidents were caused by large groups — initiated and stimulated by 'hard cores'. The rest were caused by smaller groups. It was almost impossible to classify the type of group in stadia where stands and terraces were rather empty, because abuses displayed by relatively smaller groups could be noticed stadium-wide. In crowded stadia, similar forms of behaviour might have been perceived only in the immediate area.

In the absence of reliable indicators, no attempts were made to measure the duration and the intensity of racist and xenophobic abuses. However, on the basis of the analysis of the observers' reports, some major tendencies can be identified. Above all, it can be stated that, with the exception of a few teams, the atmosphere in a football stadium is determined only to a small extent by the home spectators. It depends rather on whether or not supporters (to be more exact, the 'hard cores') of four or five teams from the capital, Budapest, are involved. Their presence at matches — whether as home or away spectators — dramatically increases the occurrence of racist incidents. Since they normally attend all home and all away matches of their teams in Budapest, the frequency of racist and xenophobic abuses is higher here, but when they follow their team to away matches — as they often do — the consequences are similar. In their absence, the climate in the stands and on the terraces proved to be far less tense, and far fewer abusive incidents were observed; and local police forces could much more easily control the situation, both in Budapest and outside the capital.

The ethnic and national composition of the football teams actually playing also appears to have a significant impact on crowd behaviour in this respect. According to our findings, the more heterogeneous a team was, the greater was the likelihood of observing racist and xenophobic abuse amongst spectators. The mere presence of players belonging to minority ethnic groups or to other nations was often sufficient to provoke certain spectators and these players' mistakes were immediately 'punished' by abusive spectator conduct.

Discriminatory interactions between players of different nationality and different ethnic backgrounds were rarely noticed. However, the events on the pitch influenced the frequency of racist and xenophobic abuses in the stands and on the terraces to a very great extent — the more boring a match, the more likely that discriminatory behaviours would occur; and when a team was playing very successfully, supporters of its rival tried to disrupt it by chanting racist abuses.

Due to the lack of both official statistics and surveys covering past decades, it is impossible to say whether the frequency found in this research indicates an increase or decrease in discriminatory behaviours. However, according to sport officials, representatives of the police, stadium attendants and older fans, there are good reasons to suggest that right after the political changes in Eastern Europe there was an increase in overt racism and xenophobia in Hungarian football stadia, although for the past two years it has remained constant.

Targets

Racist and xenophobic abuses were targeted at fans, either to certain groups of supporters or to spectators in general, and at players, coaches and referees, as well as club officials personally or in general.

In the first case, the particular targets of discrimination were Gypsies, Jews and homosexuals. Insults were directed most frequently at Gypsies: generally towards Tziganes (Hungarian Gypsies), but sometimes — with the intention of offending some groups even more heavily — towards Romanian Gypsies and towards Wallachian Gypsies.

Manifestations against Gypsies occurred more often when those teams playing were known to have Gypsies as their supporters. This usually led to a general disparaging of Gypsies, and not only of those groups who were actually in the ground. The occurrence of such cases was the highest at matches played in regions or in suburbs with large Gypsy communities. However, discriminatory behaviour against Gypsies was displayed even in situations in which Gypsies were not identifiable as spectators. In these cases, labelling of others as "Gypsies" was meant to vilify these players or spectators, and clearly shows the status of Gypsies in Hungarian society. In addition, the attribute "Gypsy" was used in a disparaging and derogatory way not only against football supporters, but also against the population in a certain town or in certain suburbs.

The outstanding position of Gypsies both as target groups and as sources for discriminatory labelling at football matches coincides with their position in Hungarian society at large. According to findings of research carried out in 1994 by the editor of REPLIKA* — with the backing of the Department of Ethnic and National Minorities at the Ministry of Education and Culture and with the assistance of Szonda Ipsos — the social perception of Gypsies is less favourable in today's Hungary. Comparing their acceptance by the Hungarian population with the acceptance of eleven other ethnic and national minorities, their level of acceptance was by far the lowest. Otherwise the term "Tzigane" or "Gypsy" has become so pejorative in the Hungarian language that for one or two years officially they have been called "Romany", in order to express their acceptance.

Although much less often than "Gypsy", the label "gay" was employed in a similar way. Regardless of the target person's sexual orientation, they were characterised as homosexuals with the aim of causing insult.

While Gypsy fans were abused in all football stadia and at almost all observed matches, Jewish spectators were the object of serious anti-Semitic abuse only in certain stadia and at particular matches. In the first league in Hungary there is one football team which is widely known for its traditional backing by the Jewish community. Its supporters have been the target of abuse

---

* REPLIKA ["reply"] is a series of books on social issues published by the Replika Club, and sponsored by the Soros Foundation.

for many decades because of this Jewish background. Although initially the supporters of its oldest rival team were chiefly responsible for such anti-Semitic behaviour, since then offensive behaviour has gradually become much more common. According to our findings, wherever this team played its supporters were insulted for being Jewish or for sympathising with the Jews, but there were huge differences between the intensity of anti-Jewish attitudes of the different football crowds. The highest intensity of anti-Semitic abuse could still be observed when the above-mentioned traditional rivals met, closely followed by the spectators of three or four other big clubs in Budapest. Although anti-Semitic chants and songs are common in all Hungarian football grounds, in more than half the stadia they are less frequent and less intense.

When individual players, coaches, club leaders and referees were the targets of abuse or ridicule, the racist and xenophobic elements were more personal, and the victims' race and/or nationality were more or less precisely addressed — except for referees who were called "Gypsy", "Jew", "paid Jewish agent", "gay", regardless of their actual ethnic and/or national background.

As for the players, the target groups for discrimination were wide-ranging. Beside Gypsies, Jews and homosexuals, 'black' people and people of foreign nationalities (Russian, Yugoslavian, Serbian, Romanian) were insulted. Despite the disintegration of the Soviet Union and Yugoslavia, the players from the successor countries of these two former states were addressed as "Russian" and "Yugoslav" respectively. Occasionally, they were referred to as "Serbs", but generally no differentiated distinctions were made.

When black players were subjected to abuse, their nationalities were never mentioned: insults referred above all to their skin colour. Foreign players, as a rule, were not abused in Hungarian football stadia without specifying their nationality or race. The word "foreigner" has no pejorative meaning in the Hungarian language such as it has in some other languages.

The targets of discriminatory behaviour were generally the players of the opponent team. However, it was not rare that supporters of certain teams vilified a player of their own club because of his nationality or race. In a subsequent football season one of the most popular black players in Hungary made the following reply to a journalist's question, "Are you often insulted?":

> What can I say? Of course, it happens. And not only by the supporters of the other side. And not only if my performance is poor. Often just the VASAS supporters pick on me even when the match has not started yet. I try not to pay attention to them and to concentrate on the match. (Szekeres, 1995: p. 15)

The nature of discrimination

The overwhelming majority of cases observed at matches consisted of verbal insults. For the most part, spectators bawled or chanted the name of a 'race' or a nationality either in attributive constructions or in bawdry. The adjectives used to describe specific aspects of certain 'races' and nationalities were in part global, in part very specific. Thus a number were addressed to all 'races' and nationalities such as dirty, foul, rat, louse, trash. Other expressions were used with the aim of describing stereotypical features of a particular 'race' or nation, for instance: 'smoky-faced' gypsies, 'black monkey', 'locomotive blond' gypsies, smelly Jews, sandalled Romanians, lazy Nigers. In some phrases, the intended insults could only be understood by those familiar with their ulterior or double meaning, for example: 'Give him bananas', 'Serbians go home to fire away', 'Russian go home', 'Go home to the jungle'.

According to our research, foul language prevailed in all football stadia attended by the observers. Cursing, blasphemy and swearing could be heard everywhere. To tell the truth, foul language has been a cultural problem for some years in Hungarian society. However, some participant observers were shocked by the fans' general bad language: "In whatever direction I went, I overheard foul language. 'Son of a bitch' and 'Shit' were used …[and]…'Fuck it" [extract from a report].

The bulk of discriminatory slogans and chanting contained obscenity, as the following examples (despite the problematic nature of such translations)show:

> *"Fuck your mother; Gypsies of Újpest"*
>
> *"Dirty Jews; Dirty Jews"*
>
> *"Gá gá·, gá; Fuck it eMTéKá"* *

Other racist and xenophobic chants contained threats and menaces and expressed hatred, such as:

> *"Get away from this field; Smoky-faced, trash gypsies"*
>
> *"Russians, clear off; Russians, get out"*
>
> *"You will perish; Dirty Jewish"*
>
> *"Dirty Jewish, dirty Jewish; Jewish agents, Jewish agents;*
> *To gas chamber, to gas chamber"*

The first two chants — in different versions — were reported from the majority of matches, the third and fourth ones were exceptions and were witnessed

---

*   MTK = Magyar Testgyakorlók Köre (Hungarian Gymnastics Club)

when the football team of Jewish background and its oldest, traditional rival team were playing.

On the other hand, it should be mentioned that chanting was also observed in the favour of one foreign player who was abused on other occasions on the basis of his nationality. However, when he was contemplating leaving Hungary, the fans' response was:

"Don't leave us Sergei: Don't leave us Sergei"

Verbal abuses were shouted, sung or chanted before, during and after matches. Home spectators, while waiting for the supporters of the other side, often 'warmed up' by shouting insults, and away supporters usually not only returned, but tried to surpass their insults.

During the matches, abusive chants normally started when Gypsy or foreign players were in possession of the ball, regardless of whether their actions succeeded or not. But of course if they failed, the crowd's resentment was doubled.

Spectators also vented their rage on Gypsy or foreign players (coaches, referees, club officials) when other players failed to hit or committed other errors, or quite simply when the level of a match was substandard, and spectators were bored and looking for a scapegoat.

The non-verbal forms of racism and xenophobia occurred much more rarely at first league football matches and were displayed by fewer spectators. These took the form of fascist salutes, producing the sounds of hissing or monkey hoots, waving banners with insulting words or symbols, wearing T-shirts displaying discriminatory texts or symbols, and of throwing bananas on the pitch.

Anti-Jewish symbols were used mainly by the hard core of a few football crowds and mostly when the team with Jewish background was playing against its oldest rival. Hostilities between these two teams have a fairly long history, in the course of which special symbols were adopted for affronting 'Jewish sympathiser' fans. In one of the very few studies on football fans' anti-Semitic conduct, when analysing the origin of the above mentioned rivalry and the impact on politics on anti-Semitism in Hungarian football stadia, the authors recall a peculiar custom: a group of supporters of the other side brings to the field a white goose whose neck is tied up with a blue ribbon, with a view to allude to the habitual activity of rural Jewish population in the 19th century and to mock the Jews, since their former attachment to goose-related business has been a laughing-stock for many decades in Hungary (Karády and Hadas, 1994).

The researchers of this project also observed such situations, but quite exceptionally and compared with the large number of verbal anti-Jewish abuses, they saw relatively little graffiti, banners, caps or T-shirts with anti-Semitic texts in the football stadia and in their vicinity. In all probability this is largely due to the fact that in 1993 a new law [Act on Changes in the Criminal Code] was issued in Hungary concerning the display of symbols of despotism —including above all the symbols of fascism and of those of communism, and it strictly prohibited wearing them or displaying them publicly.

Throwing bananas at black players and imitating monkey noises are relatively new phenomena in Hungary, since sports clubs gained the right to employ foreign players only a few years ago. Nevertheless, according to our research experiences, these customs have become common in football stadia; wherever black players were fielded, such actions were widely directed at them.

Reactions and responses

According to the reports of the participant observers, in several cases the supporters' discriminatory conduct was the concomitant of football hooliganism intended to induce disorder. When racist and xenophobic abuses were directed at identifiable groups, most of them returned the insults immediately and their hostilities often led to aggression, fighting or to vandalism. Abusive forms of behaviour were also observed on a much larger scale; they were displayed not only by 'hard-cores' and football hooligans, but by common spectators and by large audiences as well.

Racist and xenophobic manifestations which did not involve violence were sometimes blunt and rude, sometimes took more sophisticated forms; but all of them were unambiguously malign. Nevertheless, they seemed to be rated by the majority of supporters as harmless mockeries on the whole, and to be an integral element of the fans' subculture.

While certain groups of fans consistently appeared to seek revenge on the supporters of the other side, if not by assault and battery then in words, insults directed at players were usually not reciprocated. It looked as if forbearance had been a self-evidently obligatory reaction of the persons concerned. This was not because they were ready for tolerating anything, particularly not for humbling themselves; rather, the actual circumstances forced them to avoid counter-attack, and their coaches, sports leaders, team-mates — with good intention — tried to convince them to accept the situation. One outstanding Hungarian football player of Gypsy origin whose nickname was "the greatest Gypsy", related the following in the course of an interview:

> "When I was transferred to the Honvéd, the spectators' behaviour very much hurt my feelings; I was not able to make myself independent from the fans' remarks. I always followed their offending words, phrases with

keen attention. But no wonder, such shouting, like 'dirty gypsy', 'the greatest gypsy' would have brought down everybody. And then some leaders and team-mates had a long chat with me and made me understand that I should not mind abuses, because spectators cannot be replaced. Especially the Fradi football crowd was unbearable — they offended me at all matches, but finally I paid less and less attention to them, I concentrated on playing."

A black player from Africa, who had worked previously in other European countries and was now living in Hungary, expressed his opinion as follows:

"I was taught that I would not have any problems if I know my place... And humiliating as it is we must not ignore that my people have an inferior place in all white societies. Hungary is neither better, nor worse, than other countries."

It is regrettable that the football crowds' conduct justified the above mentioned player's views. By far the largest number of spectators sitting or standing near racist and xenophobic incidents did not intervene. Even apparently open-minded fans did not 'stick up' for the victims. At the matches attended, only two cases were registered when football fans stood up for the offended target groups. On one occasion a few spectators objected to the display of anti-Semitic symbols on banners waved in the stands and they called upon the organisers to clear them away. On another occasion, when some supporters of a certain football team were chanting slogans against the Gypsies, a fan of Gypsy origin in their vicinity protested against the racist remarks, arguing that he should be considered as equal, because he supports the same team. After a short discussion they agreed that belonging to a minority ethnic group is of secondary importance, the major issue is which team a fan supports.

Discriminatory actions in Hungarian football stadia remained unanswered not only by peaceful, unbiased fans, but for the most part also by club administrators responsible for the organisation of matches and for keeping public order in the grounds. On the evidence of reports from more than one hundred matches, it can be stated that only two kinds of measure were taken occasionally. First, by means of loudspeaker, crowds were requested to cheer in a more sportsmanlike manner. In several club leaders' opinion — backed up by our research experiences as well — such a formal demand is a double-edged weapon: once in a while it calms the public down, at other times it adds fuel to the flames and some groups of spectators break into racist chanting with renewed strength.

The other step against racism and xenophobia was that match organisers confiscated banners with offensive texts from certain groups of supporters. Such actions were noticed by the participant observers only twice, but sports club authorities who granted interviews said that it happens regularly, and when negotiating with the representatives of 'hard cores' they are warned not to use either discriminatory texts or symbols. From these interviews it also emerged that sports club leaders have a thorough knowledge of racist and xenophobic abuses at football matches but they try to minimise their significance; they usually pay attention to abusive behaviour if it is a part of football hooliganism — but even then they neglect its racist element, if it is possible. This is not because they consider it a negligible issue, and certainly not because they go along with it. While coping continuously and often hopelessly with disorder, their responsibilities press heavily upon them, and they believe that it is not in their power to do anything against racism and xenophobia of football fans at matches.

Similar attitudes were encountered in the National Football Federation and in the National Police-Office whose representative also agreed to be interviewed. Their openness demonstrates their new approach both to such investigations, the lack of which in the past has rendered their work in this field more difficult, and to the topic under investigation which has been a taboo subject for a long time. There is a close cooperation between the above mentioned bodies, with the objective of keeping order in football stadia and discouraging spectators from aggressive, violent actions. They have made huge efforts indeed to check football hooliganism and to gain control over the situation at matches. Notwithstanding, they still shrink from dealing with racist and xenophobic abuses in football stadia, reasoning that:

(1) Discriminatory behaviour is not a universal problem in Hungarian football stadia, it occurs just occasionally.

(2) Supporters displaying discriminatory conduct usually are not racist or nationalist; they only look for a pretext for insulting the other side; very often they even do not know the meaning of abuses they use.

(3) Racism and xenophobia are not merely a product of the world of Hungarian football; their patterns and reinforcement come partly from international football, partly from the entire Hungarian society.

(4) Football and police authorities are left alone in the battle against spectators' racist and xenophobic manifestations; the media do not cooperate with them.

(5) Increasing levels of aggression and violence in Hungarian football stadia put enormous burden on sports clubs and on police authorities; scarce financial means should be concentrated on violent events; racist and xenophobic chanting and actions are generally harmless in this respect.

(6) On the one hand, racist and xenophobic abuse at football matches cannot be sanctioned, because the individual person's misbehaviour cannot be identified within a crowd; and on the other hand, there are no laws enacted in Hungary in terms of which legal proceedings could be initiated against such perpetrators.

Conclusion

A critical evaluation of the above mentioned arguments provides a succinct summary of our research and allows us to draw some preliminary conclusions.

1.   Assessment of the seriousness of the problem depends heavily on the definition of 'discriminatory behaviour'. Since for several reasons there is a considerable reluctance to admit the presence of racism and xenophobia, officially only a few of the most severe abuses were in the past defined as discrimination.

The only official sources of relevant data are the records of the official observers of the Hungarian Football Federation at the matches. The form on which they are supposed to give their report has since 1991 contained a separate column for recording racist and xenophobic abuses. The inclusion of discriminatory insults in the report was a great step forward, and somehow it is understandable that only the major ones are recorded there. In 1993, at the 240 first league matches, the Football Federation entered 57 abuses on record. These data provide some rough orientation, but it is not at all sufficient to judge the real significance of the problem.

In addition, until recently no research concerning this issue has been carried out, but everyday experience disproves the assumption that the occurrence of racism and xenophobia at football matches in Hungary is insignificant. Regularly attending fans learn just the contrary in any football season. Besides, over the last years a few, but powerful, studies on Hungarian football were published, which intended to draw attention to the spectators' intolerance towards minority ethnic groups (Mihancsik, 1988; Karády and Hadas, 1994; Földesi, 1994). The findings summarised in this chapter also show that, whether officially recognised and admitted or not, discriminatory behaviour is a problem in Hungarian football culture.

2.   No doubt it would be an oversimplification to assume that each spectator involved in racist and xenophobic chanting is a committed racist or nationalist. It is quite probable in many cases that fans do not create disturbances because they intend to express racist and xenophobic feelings, but just the other way around: they engage in racist or xenophobic behaviours because they want to create a disturbance.

In all probability it is also true that many fans involved in racist and xenophobic incidents are not familiar with the relevant ideologies and/or with the underlying meaning of different symbols they employ. For instance, our researchers asked several supporters yelling anti-Semitic abuses why "goose" is associated with the Jews: the majority of them did not know. To furnish another example, participant observers reported the usage of the emblem of the former Soviet Naval Forces by the 'hard core' fans of a certain team. It was a puzzle to them why and how this emblem was chosen, and the members of the group themselves were also unable to explain.

More than ten years ago, two eminent scholars pointed out that the commitment to right-wing political ideologies of young football fans giving fascist salutes and chanting racist abuse must not be exaggerated. The meaning of their comments "...should be perhaps understood in their immediate and local context rather than read as some implicit political commentary" (Pratt and Salter, 1984: p. 217).

While fully accepting and supporting their view, which can easily be adapted to the present Hungarian situation, attention should be paid here to their inference as well, which was worded as follows:

> Nonetheless, the very fact that such comments can be made as a matter of course and indeed similar sentiments repeated in the stands where supposedly respectable people sit ... is, perhaps, reflective of an incipient racism that is deeply ingrained in British culture and society: and occasionally, as we have indicated, this can overtly manifest itself in British Movement/National Front activities. (Pratt and Salter, 1984: p. 217)

3.   Although Hungarian football has never been free from racial prejudices, there is a great deal of truth in the argument that patterns observed today both in international football and in Hungarian society contribute to a stimulation and to reinforcement of discriminatory conduct at football matches.

In international football, the origins of several customs which came into fashion in Hungarian football stadia over the last decade can be easily traced back to common practices in some Western European stadia one or two decades earlier. Otherwise Hungarian fans, especially members of certain 'hard cores', copy not only the 'bad habits' of foreign supporters but also their habits of impartial, indifferent nature. For instance, they often write English phrases and slogans inscriptions on walls, banners, pamphlets and T-shirts, without being proficient in this language. Notwithstanding, it is a thought-provoking phenomenon that while the customs of foreign fans 'cross' Hungarian frontiers promptly, information about anti-racist initiatives undertaken by foreign fans or sport organisations seems to stop at the border stations. Hungarian fans are not in the least familiar with them, and they have never initiated or joined such campaigns. As a matter of fact, there has never been any campaign of this kind in Hungary.

It can be rightly stated that events on the Hungarian football pitches essentially do not inspire discrimination. There is little aggression of a discriminatory nature by players or referees, and the football field itself is practically free from racist and xenophobic abuse. As a well-known Hungarian journalist and writer put it:

> Anger is diffusing to the stands not from the playing field. [It is] rooted in society. And the odd, alarming thing is, that while conflicts are declining in sports, they are becoming more tense in the stands. (Frenkl, 1995: p. 16)

Likewise in several other European countries, racism and xenophobia have been renewed in Hungary since the end of the 1980s. There is insufficient research to satisfactorily explain this process. It is probable that, in part, it is due to latent racism, suppressed in the communist era, now becoming overt. It is also likely that certain political, economic and social developments — such as increasing unemployment, seemingly unmanageable migration, declining standards of living, growing social inequality and disappointment with changes in the political and economic spheres — have in part promoted the spread of discriminatory ideologies and behaviours.

Sometimes the official responses to abuses committed by young people against Gypsy or Jewish Hungarian citizens and/or black people actually encourage other Hungarian citizens, including football supporters, to overtly express their racist and xenophobic feelings. It is the case that in recent years some sentences on persons who committed abuses against minority ethnic groups were passed as if the action had been 'simple' vandalism — with the effect of reducing the maximum time of imprisonment. That is, instead of enforcing Article 156 of the Code of Criminal Law on 'Crime against National, Popular, Racial and Religious Groups', article 271 on Vandalism was put into operation. Persons convicted under Article 156 can be imprisoned from two to eight years. Those convicted for 'vandalism' can be imprisoned only for two, or in case of crime committed by groups, for three years.

4. This investigation did not intend to study the role played by the media in the portrayal of racism and xenophobia in sport. Since in almost all interviews with sports authorities in the course of the research, complaints could be heard about sports journalists and reporters, a few selected issues of sports newspapers in 1993-1995 were analysed, along with coverage of a number of first league football matches by channels 1 and 2 on Hungarian television. However, the following thoughts are based more on speculation than on research results.

During the communist regime, when football spectators were, surprisingly, allowed to express their racist and nationalist feelings to a certain extent in the stadia, the media were strictly prohibited from informing the public about such incidents. Subsequently, since the disintegration and collapse of the socialist system, neither censorship nor other prohibitive measures exists to prevent sports journalists and reporters from presenting the real picture of the atmosphere at football matches. However, they usually ignore outbreaks of racism and xeno-phobia; they do not provide the sports consumers with accurate information; and they are far from fulfilling their educational role in this area. In the absence of empirical data, the reasons for this attitude cannot be clarified, but it looks as if discrimination by football fans is still considered a taboo subject in the media. Though a few articles discussing racist and xenophobic abuses in football have been published recently in newspapers, their authors still do pioneer work in this area.

Concerning this issue most sports journalists and reporters seem to share the football authorities' opinion. The latter reproach the media for, in sensitive situations, often taking the side of deviant supporters, and claim that for some journalists it is more important to ensure the circulation of their newspaper through writing about scandals, than to report the news in an objective way. Several sports leaders referred to a particular case when banners with death's-heads were confiscated from football fans by police authorities: on that occasion the print media accused the police of harassing 'harmless' spectators.

5. Since 1991, football and police authorities have discussed safety-related problems annually. The fact that they recognise the growing violence in Hungar-ian football stadia is a very positive sign and an indicator of their new approach. According to official statements published even in daily papers, aggression and vandalism have grown significantly over the last five years, and it has to be admitted that while the struggle against football hooliganism would require more

funding, both sports clubs and police forces have relatively little financial support for this task. Safety in football stadia is guaranteed partly by police forces, and partly by private security services who are paid by the sports clubs, but both sides are struggling with financial difficulties. A responsible police lieutenant-colonel formulated the problem as follows:

> Before the start of each football season the police experts tour every stadium and they realise that the sports clubs are generally poor. They are unable to plan and to rebuild sports facilities, no reconstruction can be realised. The police are in the same boat. We have got money only for solving the questions of the hour and not for developing, improving conditions. And — as the skilled experts of sports clubs say — you can keep order only if the public realise that the organisations and the police are well prepared. Since working forces at police stations are always being reduced, no sufficient numbers of policemen could be sent to football stadia. (Kósa, 1995: p. 23)

It is an absurd situation indeed that "criminals often have faster cars than the criminal investigators chasing them", as it was put in another interview. Nevertheless, racist and xenophobic abuses and discrimination by football fans must not be ignored due to shortage of money. When they are incidental to football hooliganism their nature could be and should be identified without any great supplementary outlay.

6.   Racist and xenophobic abuses and discrimination by football fans have never been sanctioned in Hungary. The argument that supporters displaying discriminatory behaviour cannot be identified might sound true. However, when several people throwing bananas or waving banners with offending texts could have been easily identified but were not, then the argument reveals itself as weak. Here, to set a few precedents — by identification and prosecution through law — surely would have an educational impact and would serve as a deterrent.

The awful, worrying thing is that at present there is no law in Hungary that would classify the most verbal racist and xenophobic insults as illegal. Some years ago there was a paragraph in the Code of the Criminal Law that could be enforced in such cases, but the Constitutional Court abolished it at the motion of members of the Hungarian Parliament who argued that this paragraph was anti-constitutional because it prevented citizens from asserting their rights to freedom of speech. Since then there has been a legal gap which it is to be hoped will be filled in the near future.

With full knowledge of this fact, it is not surprising that in Hungarian law there is a deficiency of legal regulations concerning the safety of football stadia as well as aggressive and violent behaviour of supporters. The European Convention on Spectator Violence and Misbehaviour at Sports Events and in Particular at Football Matches was ratified by the Republic of Hungary as early as in 1990, but it has not yet come into effect.

Hungarian sports and football authorities have regularly sent their representatives to the working party of this Standing Committee, and according both to their formal reports and their informal declarations they make good use of the documents produced by the Standing Committee. But even these papers cannot bridge the difficulties caused by the lack of legal regulation.

Recognising the significance of the above mentioned legal issues, it has to be said that although a 'law and order' approach is definitely needed under certain circumstances, it surely does not solve either the problem of football hooliganism in general, or the question of discrimination by spectators in particular. This has been pointed out by prominent researchers; for example:

> While the law and order approach to soccer hooliganism may prove useful in the short run because it is practical, possible and produces immediate results, the fact that it fails to address the underlying causes of the problem it seeks to solve must inevitably doom it to failure. (Melnick, 1986: p. 15)

> ...this 'law and order' approach has had relatively little effect on the football hooligans except to increase their solidarity, displace their activity away from grounds and make them better organised and more sophisticated at evading controls. (Dunning, 1990: p. 77)

It is most desirable that in Hungary the 'law and order' approach should be just one item in the catalogue of measures adopted in order to combat racism and xenophobia amongst football fans. It is suggested that more positive measures should be taken as well, such as raising the supporters' awareness of racism, increasing their tolerance of minority ethnic groups and increasing their feeling of responsibility for their club, for their community and also for people of different backgrounds. In Hungary, neither football authorities nor fans have ever initiated any anti-racist campaign, so the first educational measure could be the launching of such an initiative. It is to be wished that this time the initiative will be taken by the sports authorities.

References

Dunning, E. (1990) 'Sociological reflections on sport, violence and civilization', *International Review for the Sociology of Sport*, Vol. 25, No. 1: p. 80.

Földesi, S. G. (1994) *Helyzetkép a lelátóról*. Budapest: TF,

Földesi, S. G. (1995) 'Magyar NB 1-es labolanigó-merközések, nézöinek társadalmi összetetele és motivációi', *Szociológiai Szemle*, No. 3: pp. 73–94.

Frenkl, R. (1995) 'Az erőszak forrása', *Respublika*. No. 15: pp. 16-17.

Karády, V. and Hadas, M. (1994) 'Football et antisémitisme en Hongrie', *Actes de la reserche en sciences sociale*, No. 103: pp. 90-101.

Kósa, T. (1995) *Erőszak a lelátókon, Magyar Hírlap. Május 15.*

Melnick, J.M. (1986) 'The mythology of football hooliganism: A closer look at the British experience', *International Review for the Sociology of Sport*, Vol. 21, No. 1: pp. 3-19.

Mihancsik, Zs. (1988) *Hajrá MTK! Hungária körút*. Budapest: Háttér.

Pratt, J. and Salter, M. (1984) 'A fresh look at football hooliganism', *Leisure Studies*, Vol. 3, No, 2: pp. 201-220.

Szekeres, T. (1995) *Angyalföldi négersors, Vasárnap. Május 1*, Vol.1. No. 2: p. 15.

Index